THE PIRAT

Tales of the Sea-Ro

By the Same Author

[From *The Voyage of H.M.S. "Samarang."*

H.H. OMAR ALI SUFFEDIN, SULTAN OF BRUNEI.

THE PIRATE WIND
Tales of the Sea-Robbers of Malaya

by

OWEN RUTTER, F.R.G.S.

*With 18 illustrations
and 5 maps*

SINGAPORE OXFORD NEW YORK
OXFORD UNIVERSITY PRESS
1986

Oxford University Press

Oxford   New York   Toronto
Petaling Jaya   Singapore   Hong Kong   Tokyo
Delhi   Bombay   Calcutta   Madras   Karachi
Nairobi   Dar es Salaam   Cape Town
Melbourne   Auckland

and associates in
Beirut   Berlin   Ibadan   Nicosia

OXFORD is a trademark of Oxford University Press

Originally published by Hutchinson & Co. (Publishers), Ltd. 1930
First issued as an Oxford University Press paperback 1986
Reprinted by kind permission of Century Hutchinson Ltd.

ISBN 0 19 582691 4

Printed in Malaysia by Peter Chong Printers Sdn. Bhd.
Published by Oxford University Pte. Ltd.,
Unit 221, Ubi Avenue 4, Singapore 1440

AUTHOR'S NOTE

These chronicles have been collected from a variety of sources. Some, now published for the first time, have been traced in the archives of the Public Record Office, others have been pieced together from books long out of print. Since detailed documentation of the text would have entailed a host of footnotes, I have preferred to give my authorities for each narrative in an appendix, except where verbatim quotations have been made.

My thanks are due to the officials of the Public Record Office, without whose courtesy and expert knowledge my researches would have been more difficult; to the officials of the Records Department at the India Office, who allowed me to see documents in connection with the Balambangan settlement and gave me permission to reproduce Dalrymple's plan; and to the Librarian of the Royal Geographical Society and his assistants, whose kindness never fails the seeker after geographical or historical truth.

O. R.

CONTENTS

CHAPTER I

THE PIRATE WIND

CHAPTER II

THE ILLANUN PIRATES

CHAPTER III

THE BALANINI

CHAPTER IV

SLAVES

CHAPTER V

THE RAIDING OF BALAMBANGAN

CHAPTER VI

THE LOSS OF THE " SULTANA "

CHAPTER VII

THE PIRATES OF SARAWAK

CHAPTER VIII

THE ATTACK ON THE SEKRANG STRONGHOLDS

CHAPTER IX

THE PIRATES OF PEDIR, AND THE CASE OF THE NAMELESS MAN OF KENT

CHAPTER X

THE PIRATES OF JILOLO

CHAPTER XI

THE STRANGE CASE OF THE " PREMIER "

CHAPTER XII

THE SULTAN OF BRUNEI

CHAPTER XIII

THE DOWNFALL OF PANGERAN USOP

CONTENTS xiii

CHAPTER XIV

THE BATTLE OF MARUDU

PAGE

Admiral Cochrane's squadron in Marudu Bay—Serip
Usman's stronghold—The strength of the British
expedition—The advance held up by the boom—The flag
of truce—The action begins—Gallantry of the pirates—
The boom forced—The marines carry the first battery
—The capture and burning of the forts—Guns and
booty taken—The episode of the . wounded woman
—British casualties—Captain Talbot's leadership criticised—The ruins of the fort to-day—The magic pebbles   193

CHAPTER XV

THE MURDER OF RAJAH MUDA HASSIM

The Sultan gives Muda Hassim the title of Sultan Muda—
The evil influence of Haji Saman—The plot against
Muda Hassim and his brothers—Muda Hassim's house
attacked—His end—Pangeran Bedrudin's last stand—
Sends his ring to Rajah Brooke—Bedrudin's slave boy
brings news of the massacre to the Rajah   –   –   206

CHAPTER XVI

THE CAPTURE OF BRUNEI

Admiral Cochrane returns to Brunei—Sultan's preparations
for defence—His attempt at treachery—The attack on
Brunei—The batteries carried—Guns captured—
Sultan flees to the jungle—New Government established   213

CHAPTER XVII

HOW LABUAN BECAME BRITISH

Admiral Cochrane destroys pirate nest at Tempasuk—
Captain Rodney Mundy pursues Haji Saman—His
strongholds taken and burnt—Captain Mundy's
audience with the Sultan—Promises of good behaviour
—Captain Mundy instructed to take possession of
Labuan—A stormy audience—The treaty signed—
Hoisting of the flag   –   –   –   –   –   –   221

CHAPTER XXI

THE " LIZZIE WEBBER " SEES IT THROUGH

LIST OF ILLUSTRATIONS

LIST OF PLANS

The Pirate Wind

CHAPTER I

THE PIRATE WIND

The pirate fleets of Malaya—Attack on Dutch and Spanish shipping—The taking of the *Maria Frederika*—Pirates seize the
American vessels *Friendship* and *Eclipse* off the coast of Sumatra—United States frigate *Columbine* exacts retribution—The
terrible fate of Captain Ross of the *Regina*—Malay pirates
and buccaneers contrasted—Sir Charles Hedges' definition
of piracy—How piracy in the Eastern Seas began—European
responsibility—The Sultans of Sulu and Brunei implicated—
No efforts made by Great Britain to repress the power of the
pirate chiefs.

A CENTURY ago, and for more than half a century before
that, piracy was rife in the Malayan seas. From Manila
to Sumatra, from Malacca to Celebes, no trading ships
were safe from the sea-rovers, no coastal villages immune
from their attacks.

In those days the Archipelago was split up into
countless petty kingdoms, and each rajah was the commander-in-chief of a pirate fleet. These squadrons
could shelter in a thousand lonely bays; a thousand
rivers gave them hiding-places whence the swift war-
boats could dash out to seize a peaceful merchantman:
and, once sighted and marked down, scant chance had
any vessel against those ruthless warriors who, arrayed
in scarlet and coats of mail, came sweeping across the sea
brandishing their two-handed swords, and yelling
their war-cries as they leapt on deck in quest of slaves
and plunder.

Native craft and Chinese junks fell an easy prey to
these Vikings of the Eastern seas, but European ships,

and those of America, suffered too.   In the Philippines,
schooner after schooner was taken; brig after brig.
Every year something like 500 Spanish subjects were
sold into slavery, and betweer 'he years of 1778 and 1793
the Spanish Government spent a million and a half
pesos in attempts to stamp out the pirate settlements,
but in vain. The Dutch were forced to organise a
system of cruising gunboats, but with little better success,
for the pirates grew so bold that they did not hesitate to
attack these vessels, and on one occasion a pirate squadron engaged a Dutch gunboat in the Straits of Sunda,
and, having carried her, murdered every soul on board.

In 1806 a merchant ship, belonging to two Dutchmen
named Phefferkorn and Wensing, was attacked in the
Straits of Banca by a fleet of forty pirate prahus.   Seeing
no chance either of resistance or escape they allowed a
number of the pirates to board the vessel and then blew
her up.

In the following year the Dutch war cruiser *de Vrede*
(Lieut. C. Beckman) was attacked in the roads of Indra-
mayo by seven pirate boats, each of which carried 100
warriors.   For a while the crew fought the ship, then
broke, and, taking one of the boats, made for the shore.
Lieutenant Beckman and his second-in-command, named
Stokbroo, remained at their posts until the pirates
boarded, then flung themselves into the sea.   Beckman
was drowned, but Stokbroo was captured in the water.
The pirates stripped him, shaved his head, and later
gave him as a present to the Rajah of Lampong, who
in turn sold him to the Prince of Linga Island for thirty
Spanish dollars.   Here he remained in slavery until
the Chinese owner of a brig trading from Java, taking
compassion on him, bought him for $50 and landed
him at the Dutch settlement of Samarang, refusing any
recompense for his generous act.

On another occasion, thirty years later, when the
Dutch schooner, *Maria Frederika*, commanded by Captain Andrew Gregory, was lying becalmed off the coast

of Lombok, two pirate vessels approached on the pretence of obtaining a few supplies. The captain was
in his cabin sick, and one of the crew whom he had
recently punished encouraged the pirates to come aboard.
Immediately forty of them leapt on to the schooner's
deck, drove the crew below, seized the captain and the
mate, and took the vessel to Tunku, their stronghold
on the north-east coast of Borneo. There they buried
the white men up to their waists in sand. Then an
elderly chief, Rajah Muda, who was famous for his long
beard, walked up to Captain Gregory sword in hand,
and with one blow cleft his body from the shoulder
to the side, while his companions fell upon the mate
and cut him to pieces.

In February, 1831, while an American vessel, the
Friendship, was lying off Kuala Batu, on the west coast
of Sumatra, taking in a cargo of pepper, a native boat
came off from the village ostensibly to deliver part of
the cargo. While it was being got aboard, the Malays,
at a given signal, suddenly set upon the officers and
crew, killed every soul on board and then ransacked the
ship, carrying off goods and money to the value of
$8,000. The captain, who had been ashore with four
of his men, returned to find his ship a shambles. He
sought the aid of other American vessels that were trading along the coast. These assembled at Kuala Batu and
demanded the punishment of the robbers and the restitution of the property, but they could obtain no satisfaction, the chiefs denying all knowledge of the affair.
A year later retribution visited Kuala Batu in the shape
of the U.S. frigate *Potomac*, which assaulted the settlement, burnt the houses and killed some 300 of the
inhabitants. Little sympathy can be felt for them, for
there is no doubt that they were pirates one and all.

Seven years later this act of vengeance on the part
of the American Navy had been forgotten, for in August,
1838, on the same coast, the U.S. ship *Eclipse* (Captain
Wilkins) suffered a similar fate. While trading at a

village called Trabongan, twelve miles from the port of
Muka, she was visited by a party of twenty-four Malays,
who asked permission to come aboard. The captain was
down with fever in his cabin, but the second mate, having
no suspicion that the Malays were anything but peaceful
traders, allowed them on deck, but asked them to give
up their arms in accordance with the practice that was
observed on that coast. This they did without demur.
When the captain finally appeared on deck, however,
the headman of the party complained of the second mate's
lack of confidence in him and his companions, and asked
that their weapons might be given back as a mark of
good faith. Now Captain Wilkins had done business with
this man before and, trusting in his protestations of friendship, unwisely gave way and restored to each man his *kris*.

The second mate then began to weigh some pepper
the party had brought on board, and a few minutes later
heard Captain Wilkins, who was sitting near the binnacle,
cry out, " I am stabbed "; at the same moment he
himself was wounded in the loins, but saved himself
by leaping overboard. Several of the crew followed
him. Others ran up the rigging. An apprentice was
cut down by the captain's side. The pirates then began
to plunder the ship. Going below, they found the
cook in irons, and he offered to show them the where-
abouts of the opium and specie the ship was carrying
if they would spare his life. The pirates broke his
irons and with his assistance found four chests of opium
and eighteen casks containing in all 18,000 Spanish dollars.
With this booty they left the ship and took to their
prahu, the cook accompanying them.

While the pirates had been busy looting below, the
men who had jumped overboard had climbed up the
rigging, and when the Malays had left the ship the second
mate and four sailors took one of the boats and made
for the French barque *L'Aglae*, which was lying at a
neighbouring port. The carpenter and two other sailors
went ashore to join the chief mate and others of the crew

who were in the village buying pepper. The chief
mate then took command of the ship, but his efforts to
recover the booty that had been seized were unsuccessful
and he was forced to leave the coast with empty hands.

News of the outrage reached Commodore Read, of
the U.S. frigate *Columbine*, at Ceylon. He sailed immediately with his squadron for Sumatra and learnt that the
leader of the pirates was at Kuala Batu, living under
the protection of the local rajah. Arriving at Kuala
Batu, the Commodore demanded the surrender of the
man, together with the property in his possession. He
was met with evasion, and retaliated by bombarding the
town. Then he sailed for Muka, where he had learned
that five of the pirates were living. Being equally
unsuccessful in obtaining redress from the Rajah of
Muka, he landed a party of thirty officers and 300
men from his squadron and within the hour Muka was
blazing heaven-high and its inhabitants in flight. Thus
for the second time in seven years the pirates of
Sumatra were taught that American shipping could not
be molested with impunity.

In those years, however, the shipping of every nation
trading in the Eastern seas suffered at the pirates' hands,
and that of Great Britain not least. One instance will
suffice here, the peculiarly horrible case of the barque
Regina, owned and commanded by Captain James Ross.
A rumour appears to have got abroad that she was
carrying a large quantity of silver dollars, with the
result that a pirate fleet lay in wait for her. As soon as
she was sighted the pirates gave chase, overhauled her,
and carried her by weight of numbers. The captain
was taken prisoner and the pirates began to plunder the
ship, but without finding the money they believed to be
on board. Their chief then promised Captain Ross
his life if he would reveal the hiding-place of his treasure.
In vain did the unhappy man protest that the ship held
nothing but what the pirates had already found : and
this was the truth, for he had invested his money in

a cargo of rattans, rubber and other jungle produce. The pirates refused to believe him, however, and to make him speak they lashed his son to one of the ship's anchors and, when he still protested that he had no treasure, flung the anchor into the sea, drowning the boy before his father's eyes. This having no effect, they began to torture Captain Ross himself, cutting off his fingers joint by joint, and then inflicted other mutilations upon him. He was finally left a bleeding but breathing mass upon his quarter-deck, and the pirates, after killing the other officers and taking the native crew for slaves, set fire to the barque and sailed away.

◇ ◇

These are some isolated examples of the lengths to which the pirates of the Malayan seas would go. Compared with them the buccaneers of the Spanish Main were gentle and amiable creatures. Moreover, the Malay pirate led a far less hazardous existence than the buccaneer. At any moment the buccaneer might be hunted by ships of war, while the Malays could rove their seas unchecked. It is true that spasmodic reprisals were taken against them, but such punishment had no lasting effect; the great cruising fleets of the Illanuns and Balanini seldom suffered, and hundreds of ships were taken with impunity. Unlike the buccaneers, these pirates knew no anxieties as to supplies or markets, for they had but to land on the coast, or penetrate a short distance up a river, to find a village they could rob and men and women whom they could carry off as slaves, while for their captives and plunder they found a ready market in the towns of the petty Malay kingdoms, whose rulers neither dared nor cared to thwart them; then at the end of the cruise they could repair to their strongholds, secure from attack, and there they would divide the spoils of the season, pass their days in cock-fighting and their nights in opium-smoking—and plan fresh raids.

So that while the buccaneer was an outlaw, with

the hand of every nation against him, the Malay pirate chief was a prince who might range where he listed, taking what he would. Rulers would placate him and even come to do his bidding, and the seas over which he roved became a sort of Tom Tiddler's ground which traders crossed at their peril and, so far from picking up other men's gold and silver, frequently lost their own.

Although the sea-robbers of Malaya had different methods from those of the Spanish Main, they were none the less pirates, both in the popular and in the strictly legal sense of the term. Sir Charles Hedges, Judge of the High Court of Admiralty, thus defined piracy at Common Law in his charge to the Grand Jury on October 13, 1696:

"Now piracy is only a sea term for robbery, piracy being a robbery committed within the jurisdiction of the Admiralty. If any man be assaulted within that jurisdiction, and his ship or goods violently taken away without legal authority, this is robbery and piracy." Later in the same charge the jurisdiction was declared to extend . . . "to the most remote parts of the world; so that if any person whatsoever, native or foreigner, Christian of Infidel, Turk or Pagan, with whose country we have no war . . . shall be robbed or spoiled in the Narrow Seas, the Mediterranean, Atlantic, Southern or any other seas . . . either on this or the other side of the line, it is piracy within the limits of your enquiry and the cognizance of this court." [1]

◇   ◇

While it is clear, therefore, that these Malays were pirates, and as such a menace to European trade, it is but fair to say that it was largely European intercourse with the East that made them so. It is true that the old Malay romances contain references to piratical cruises, yet there seems no doubt that piracy was not

---

[1] At the Trial of Joseph Dawson and others for Felony and Piracy. *XIII State Trials*, p. 454.

practised on a wholesale scale until the eighteenth
century. Dampier, who in 1686-7 lived for six months
among the Illanuns, in later years the most formidable
of all the Malay pirates, subsequently wrote a detailed
account of them and made no mention of any piratical
propensities, and described them as a peaceable people,
who bought such foreign commodities as they needed
with the products of their gold mines.

What was it, then, that caused these people and their
neighbours to revert from peace to piracy? The
answer is: the greed of the European powers who
traded in the Eastern seas. From time immemorial
outside commerce with the Archipelago had been in
the hands of the Chinese, whose junks would come
down in the north-east monsoon and return in the
south-west laden with precious cargoes of spices, rattans,
edible birds'-nests, camphor, sharks' fins and pearls.
Then came the Portuguese, and after them the Dutch,
who, bent on securing the trade for themselves alone,
created a system of monopolies, and by treaties with
the Malay rulers were able to command the produce at
their own rates and so undersell the Chinese. By
planting " factories," or trading stations, in the Archipelago, they diverted to Malacca or Batavia the trade which
for centuries had gone direct to China, so that in time
the junks could compete no longer and came no more.

One result of this change was that the Chinese immi-
grants—the forebears of those settlers to whom modern
Malaya owes so much of its prosperity to-day—returned
to their native shores, and no others came to take their
places. These Chinese, most of them skilled craftsmen
or zealous agriculturists, had been a source of revenue to
the rulers in whose territories they settled; nor were
those revenues increased by the coming of the traders
from the west, who took all and gave in return as little
as they could.

As time went on, what might be called the bread-
and-butter lines of trade—rattans, sago, wild rubber,

[From *Borneo and the Indian Archipelago.*

AN ILLANUN PIRATE.

beeswax and other jungle produce—came to be neglected owing to the expense of the double carriage, so that thousands of natives were bereft of their normal occupations, both in collecting the produce and in carrying it from port to port; while the precious spice trade was regulated with such jealousy that the Dutch would wantonly destroy quantities of cloves and nutmegs rather than allow them to fall into foreign hands. Not content with this, they poked their fingers into the internal affairs of the Malay Governments and fomented dissension for their own ends, until they destroyed the authority of the rulers and disorganised the commercial enterprise of their people.

It would not be fair to say that this demoralising policy was practised by the Dutch alone. Those were the days before nations had vision to see that trade breeds trade. Dutch, Portuguese, Spaniards and English all played the same game; but at that period the influence of the Dutch was paramount in the Archipelago and consequently they caused the greatest harm. The Malay potentates were driven to replenish their depleted coffers; their people sought new outlets for their frustrated energies. They were a proud people, accustomed to freedom; they resented most bitterly the injustice shown them and the restraints imposed by those whom they regarded as white barbarians. They were accustomed to the sea, and under the leadership of their princes they turned their ways to piracy and plunder. If one may regard that metamorphosis through their eyes, one may see, in the attacks on European shipping that followed, acts of retaliation against those interlopers from the West, until in course of time this guerilla warfare by sea developed for many into an habitual mode of life, more lucrative and certainly more exciting than their former ways of peace.

Piracy became looked upon as an honourable occupation, so that any chief who wished to improve his fortune could collect about him a handful of restless

followers and settle with them upon some secluded island
in the Archipelago ; thence he could sail out to attack
ships and villages. If he were successful he would gain
fresh adherents soon enough ; his settlement would
become a little town, strongly fortified and stockaded,
while his fleet would become large enough to be divided
into several squadrons.

At this period two of the oldest of the established
Malay kingdoms were Brunei, on the north-west coast
of Borneo, and Sulu, an island in the westernmost group
of the Philippines. The Sultans of both these States
claimed sovereignty over the neighbouring islands, and
over large expanses of the northern coasts of Borneo,
but, by the eighteenth century, their former power had
weakened, the splendour of their courts had passed away,
and their Governments had become weak and corrupt,
with scarcely nominal authority over their scattered
vassals. Brunei came to be both a participator in
piracy and its victim too, for while the Brunei nobles
would buy slaves from one set of pirates, the people,
whom the State had no strength to protect, were plundered and enslaved by another. It came to be a saying
among the Sulu pirates, " To catch fish is hard, but it is
easy to catch a Brunei," and these wretched folk suffered
so much at the pirates' hands that the easterly wind
which brought the cruising fleets from their strongholds
came to be known as the Pirate Wind.

Sulu became the very centre of piratical activity,
and the Sulu nobles, like those of Brunei, acted as re-
ceivers and trafficked not only in slaves but in the
plunder brought back by the cruising fleets. The
Sultans were usually too weak to oppose their chiefs,
even had they wished to do so, and they were unable to
resist the temptation of being able to buy European goods
for half their real value, and such slaves as they desired.

Like Brunei, the town of Sulu was built mainly on

piles above the water, running out in three lines to the
sea ; the piles of the outer houses were set in four fathoms
of water, so that large vessels could ride at anchor in the
main street. Bridges of interlaced bamboo several
hundred yards in length formed a means of communication between the houses, but the Sultan's palace
and the residence of his chiefs and ministers were built
on shore. On shore, too, were the batteries that commanded the main waterway of the town. Such was
the capital that became a pirate mart and a clearing town
for slaves.

Since two principal independent sovereigns in the
Archipelago were without power to control their
subjects, it is easy to understand the precarious condition into which native trade amongst the islands
lapsed. Trade with the Borneo ports and those of the
Sulu Archipelago became almost impossible even for
European ships, and merchantmen using the Palawan
passage to China, which took them close to the Borneo
coast, were often cut off by the lurking squadrons.

Yet no concerted or continued efforts were made to
suppress the evil. Isolated reprisals were of small avail,
for they were followed by long periods of inaction, and
the pirates, taking this inactivity for weakness, reappeared
in their old haunts. The British Government allowed
her ships to be captured, her flag to be insulted, her
sailors to be enslaved, tortured and killed without effective reprisals, which was a curious contrast to the one
nation without any settlement in the Archipelago—the
United States—which took prompt and energetic steps
to avenge any outrages inflicted on her shipping, and in
addition did her utmost to prevent such outrages
occurring by appointing a political agent to visit the
various native States to arrange for trade to be conducted
to the best advantage of her nationals, and by sending
her warships on frequent visits to the Malayan ports.

As late as 1836, George Windsor Earl, commenting on the frightful prevalence of piracy, spoke his mind as follows :

" The Malay pirates absolutely swarm in the neighbourhood of Singapore, the numerous islands in the vicinity, the intersecting channels of which are known only to themselves, affording them a snug retreat, whence they can pounce upon the defenceless native traders and drag them into their lairs to plunder them at their leisure. . . . The detrimental effect that this predatory warfare must produce on the commerce of Singapore is obvious, and there can be no doubt that thousands of the natives of the islands, who would otherwise visit the settlement for the disposal of the produce of their industry, are now deterred from so doing by a dread of encountering these remorseless wretches. In mercy, therefore, to the native traders who visit the settlement on the supposition that they will at least be free from violence when within sight of the British flag, some measures should be taken to put an end to the system. . . . Nothing but the most rigorous measures, even to the utter annihilation of those who may be caught in the act, will tend to check the evil ; for the pirates, having long been permitted to commit their murders and robberies with impunity, now consider themselves to be almost invincible, and therefore require some very severe lessons to bring them to their senses. The frightful acts, daily committed, however, will never be entirely suppressed until those Malay chiefs who encourage the pirates by affording them assistance and protection receive some substantial proof that such practices will not be permitted with impunity." [1]

When they might plunder native trade and European shipping with such impunity it was small wonder that the power of the pirate chiefs grew stronger and stronger like a rising wind.

---

[1] *The Eastern Seas*, p. 384 *et seq.*

CHAPTER II

THE ILLANUN PIRATES

The chief Illanun stronghold at Mindanau—Protections against attack—Chain of settlements along the coast of Borneo—Their war-boats—Piracy considered an honourable career—Their extensive cruising grounds—How Mr. Wyndham escaped from an Illanun squadron—The steamer *Diana* saves a Chinese junk—Trial of the pirates.

IN the Sulu Archipelago there were two main groups of pirates, the Illanuns and the Balanini. Like the other Malay peoples, they were Mohammedans. The Illanuns were called by the Spaniards *los Illanuns de la Laguna* because their chief stronghold was on the shores of a lagoon in the island of Mindanau. On the east of an immense bay a long finger of land separated the lagoon from the sea; it was fringed with mangrove trees, which, standing upon their roots seven or eight feet above the water at high tide, provided a maze of narrow channels that afforded concealment from pursuit. To secure themselves still further, the Illanuns were in the habit of constructing runnels of timber along which they could haul their boats swiftly into the lagoon.

"The method of constructing these escapes is very simple," wrote Sir Edward Belcher. "Strong mangrove trees are driven at opposite angles, obliquely, into the mud, and their upper ends securely lashed to the growing, standing mangrove trees, forming a V-shaped bed at an angle of 120 degrees. These trees, being stripped of their bark, are kept very smooth, and when wet spontaneously exude a kind of mucilage which renders them very slippery. The outer entrance of this angular bed is carried into deep water, and at so gradual an inclination that the original impetus given by the oars forces them at once high and dry, and by the ropes then attached they are drawn instantly by their allies into the interior at a rate probably equal to that at which they were impelled by oars." [1]

So that, although the pirates might be hotly chased, they would suddenly disappear into one of these escapes, and when their pursuers reached the opening they would be met by a fire of round shot and grape from batteries concealed within the mangrove.

As a further precaution the whole line of the bay was guarded by tiny watch-houses built high up in the trees, and on an alarm being given the boats would be hauled into safety. Inside the lagoon they had extensive buildings, but also used old vessels as houses, in which they kept their wives, families and treasures. These mobile dwellings could be shifted to any part of the lagoon when danger threatened.

In addition to their main strongholds in the lagoon, they had a chain of settlements along the coast of Borneo, from Koti and Tunku on the east to Marudu in the north and thence as far west as Ambong and Tempasuk. With the Illanuns were associated the Bajaus, a tribe of sea-gipsies who lived entirely afloat, with their wives and families, their boats being their caravans and their high road the sea.

The Illanuns were the fiercest and most powerful pirates of the Eastern seas. They never hesitated to attack European ships, and, while they might give quarter to a native crew, to white men they showed no mercy, owing, it is said, to the former treatment they had received at the hands of the Spaniards.

Their cruising boats were built sharp in the prow and wide in the beam; some of them would exceed ninety feet in length and sixty tons burden. They were furnished with a double tier of oars, the largest carrying a hundred rowers, who sat cross-legged, about a foot

[1] *The Voyage of H.M.S. "Samarang,"* i, 264.

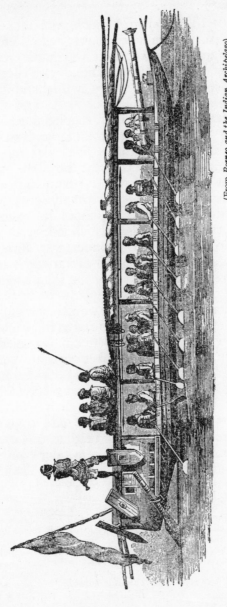

ILLANUN WAR-BOAT.

(From *Borneo and the Indian Archipelago*)

C

from the water line, on strong galleries built outside the bends. These rowers were slaves, who were not expected to fight unless the fleet was hard pressed. In place of masts these boats were fitted with sheers, which could be raised or let down very swiftly, and upon these was hoisted a huge mat sail.[1]

The captain of each prahu occupied a cabin aft. A larger cabin took up three-fifths of the vessel's length and two-thirds of her beam. The sides might be of bamboo or palm-leaf, but in the bow the cabin was solidly built out to the whole beam with baulks of timber sufficiently strong to withstand a six-pound shot. Here a narrow embrasure admitted the muzzle of a long gun, usually of brass, which might be anything from a six to a twenty-four pounder, with another in the stern. Numerous swivels (*lela*) of varying calibre were mounted in solid uprights along the sides and the upper works.

In the main cabin lived the women and children and such prisoners as were not required at the oars. Above the cabin was a wooden platform occupied by the fighting-men, who might number anything from thirty to one hundred. Here they would stand when going into action, regardless of danger and ready to board the vessel they were attacking. On such occasions they would array themselves in scarlet and coats of mail, with feathered head-dresses, and rather than use firearms they were accustomed to rely upon their own weapons, the spear and the *kris* and the great Illanun sword

---

[1] Sailors may be interested in the following technical description of the fitting of these sheers, from Belcher's *Voyage of the Samarang* i. 265 : " On the fore part of the fighting deck is a small pair of bitts, each bitt-head being placed about three feet on each side of the centre line ; through the heads of these bitts a piece runs, windlass-fashion, its outer ends being rounded, which pass through the lower ends of the sheers in holes, this arrangement completes a triangle, having this windlass base of six feet. The heads of the sheers are joined by a solid piece of wood, perforated as a sheave-hole for the halliards, by which the sail is hoisted ; a third spar is attached, which, taken aft as a prop, instantly turns this mast, upon its windlass motion, to its vertical, and almost, as by magic, we find the sail expanded or reduced instantaneously."

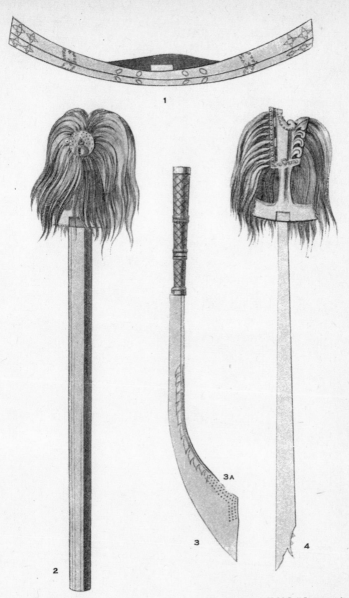

[From *The Voyage of H.M.S. "Samarang."*

1. Jilolo Shield
2. Scabbard of Illanun Kampilan
3. Illanun Beheading Sword
3a. Holes denoting number of victims
4. Illanun Tampilan

(*kampilan*), whose handle was long enough to be wielded with two hands. This weapon was brought into action with a sweeping, downward motion, either upon the skull or shoulder of the opponent, and its weight and the power behind the two hands that wielded it usually ensured death at a single blow. Once a *kampilan* had secured its first victim, the little " horn," which in the accompanying illustration may be seen projecting from the blunt side of the blade, might be removed and a brass stud inserted in the blade itself. I have in my collection a *kampilan* with no less than twenty-seven such studs.

◇   ◇

The Illanuns were accustomed to cruise in squadrons thirty or forty strong, although at times a fleet might number 200 vessels of different sizes. One chief, a man of high rank, would command the whole fleet ; each boat would have her own captain and many of the fighting-men under him would be his relatives. Most of these warriors were freemen, but their number might be made up of slaves, who had the right to plunder with certain reservations : prisoners, guns, money and the finest cloths and silks were divided amongst the chiefs and the freemen ; after they had been satisfied, the slaves might take what they could.

As time went by these chiefs came to look upon piracy as an hereditary career and the most honourable they could pursue, just as with us young men take pride in following their fathers in the Navy. Trade they despised, though it might have brought them greater profits : they loved plunder, but they loved slaves better, and they delighted in fighting for fighting's sake, deeming it the height of glory to be able to add to their fathers' swords more of the tiny brass studs, each one of which signified a foe slain in battle.

Their cruising grounds were not limited to the Sulu Archipelago, but they would range through the

whole of the Malayan seas, and a single cruise, lasting
sometimes as long as three years, might take them east
through the Philippines, round New Guinea, and then
along the coasts of Java and Sumatra as far as the Bay
of Bengal, and home by way of Penang and the Borneo
coast.

These cruises had a double objective : plunder and
slaves.   The plunder they found mostly in the ships they
boarded; slaves in the coastal villages they attacked.
They did not confine themselves to native vessels, but
approached square-rigged ships with caution, and learnt
to distinguish between merchantmen and warships by
the colour of their canvas.   When looting a ship they
were careful not to incommode themselves with anything but articles of value, such as gold, silver, arms,
ammunition and costly stuffs, and avoided taking objects
which might readily be identified as stolen property ;
so that if, as sometimes happened, a Spanish gunboat
overhauled one of their prahus it was difficult to obtain
definite proof that they were anything but the peaceful
traders they would then represent themselves to be.

❖   ❖

These pirates could be fearless in attack, and their
cunning matched their courage.   On one occasion at
least, however, they were themselves outwitted by a
ruse, as the following story will show.

An Englishman named Wyndham, who had served
as an officer under Lord Cochrane, was mate in a Spanish
brig that was trading in the Archipelago.   One morning,
when the vessel was near Wette, Wyndham heard the
man on look-out duty at the masthead sing out: " A
prahu in sight . . . two . . . three . . . four . . . I
cannot count them, sir ! "

Wyndham immediately went aloft with his glass
and made out no less then thirty-eight native boats.
He knew enough of those seas to be certain they were
Illanun pirates, and to be equally certain of their

intentions towards the brig. There was but a light breeze blowing, and there was no chance of running from them; nor was there any hope of fighting the ship, for most of the crew were sick. Wyndham called up the captain and they hit upon the idea of dressing up in some of Wyndham's old uniforms. Thus attired they walked up and down the poop and bore down upon the pirate squadron, which awaited their approach.

Sailing between the two largest of the boats (each the size of the brig herself) they observed that the guns had been carefully concealed by mats and that there were but a few men on the decks, though others could be seen peeping out from under the palm-leaf awnings.

As the brig drew abreast, Wyndham began to question them. They replied that they were traders. Letting them think that the brig was a warship, he then said that she was cruising in search of a pirate fleet. Those in the boats assured him that they had seen none, and asked permission to keep him company, for their own protection, as far as Macassar, the port for which they were bound. Wyndham answered that they might do so if they could keep up.

Shortly afterwards a breeze sprang up; the brig went ahead and by evening was clear of the fleet. During the night, however, the wind died away, leaving her becalmed. The hours that followed were anxious ones for all on board, since they could not tell whether the pirates would make up their minds to call the bluff and attack; but when daylight came, to their inexpressible relief they saw those peaceful traders pulling away from the ship as hard as they could, having decided that the brig was better left alone.

❖   ❖

It was seldom, however, that a quarry ever escaped an Illanun squadron; more seldom still that punishment overtook the pirates. Yet they did not always escape scot-free, and one of their severest lessons was given them by the Honourable East India Company's paddle steamer *Diana* in 1838.

On May 18 of that year the British sloop *Wolf* was lying in Trengganu roadstead, off the eastern coast of the Malay Peninsula, and soon after eight in the morning she sighted six large Illanun prahus standing towards a large Chinese junk which was in the offing. The operations of the prahus, as they closed on the junk, were visible from the masthead of the *Wolf*, and they were seen to begin the attack with a hot fire from their guns, which was vigorously answered from the junk. The *Wolf* immediately got under weigh, but had to work to windward, and unfortunately her own armed boats were absent, having been despatched on the preceeding day to the Redang Islands in search of some Illanuns who had lately killed and wounded a number of natives from Trengganu.

About midday, however, the *Diana* (Captain Congleton) was descried to the northward, and Captain Stanley of the *Wolf* promptly sent off to her his gig and jolly-boat, with two officers and a party of seamen and marines, with orders for Captain Congleton to proceed to the assistance of the junk.

It was not until after four o'clock that the *Diana*, with the party from the *Wolf*, came up with the pirates, who were then drawn up in line astern the junk, and fired upon the *Diana* as she approached. But now they had a different sort of enemy to deal with, and the steamer, stopping her paddles as she came opposite each prahu, and being able to get her guns to bear with terrible effect, poured in a destructive fire, stretching the pirates in masses on their decks. Even so the largest prahu maintained a fierce resistance, keeping up the contest until half-past six, when she was boarded in a sinking state. This vessel was fifty-six feet long and fifteen feet in beam; and she had to be cut adrift from the *Diana* and sank after the people on board her had been removed.

The other five boats, favoured with a breeze, hoisted

sail and edged away to the southward, with the *Diana*
in chase. As she was closing upon them the swift
darkness of the tropics descended and enabled them to
make their escape, but from the shattered and disabled
condition to which the steamer's fire had reduced them,
it seemed likely that they would be forced to abandon
several of their vessels, for scarcely any of them could
muster more than two or three oars a side and they
seemed to be bailing nothing but blood.

Thirty prisoners, eight of them desperately
wounded, were taken on board the captured prahu.
These men acknowledged to 360 men being on
board the six prahus—of whom ninety were killed
and 150 wounded. They openly confessed that they
were pirates, and said that they were commissioned
by the Sultan of Sulu to go and plunder on his
account. They acknowledged that they had taken,
during the three months of their cruise, three Malay
boats laden with rice, also one Chinese, a Siamese, and
three or four Malays who had been found on board the
captured prahu. Each of these men had about his neck
a twisted rattan collar by which he could be made fast
at night.

Eighteen of the pirates captured by the *Diana* were
brought to trial before the Recorder of Singapore, at a
special criminal session held on June 7, 1838. The
charge against them was that they had committed an
act of piracy near the Sambas River (western Borneo)
on the preceeding April 25. Four others were in hospital
too severely wounded to allow their being arraigned.

The witnesses against them were the Malays who had
been found on board the captured prahu.

Sabat, the first witness called, deposed that he resided
at Pontianak on the west coast of Borneo. About a
month previously he and eight others, being on a
trading voyage in a boat laden with coconuts, oil and
sago, had been captured off Tanjong Datu [1] by six

---

[1] The most westerly promontory of Sarawak.

large Illanun prahus, well manned and armed. He and three of his companions were put below in one of the prahus, bound hand and foot, and had rattan collars fastened round their necks. He was told that the other five persons taken with him, being *hajis*,[1] were released by the pirates and set on shore at Sirhassan Island. The pirates touched at several places on the east coast of the Malay Peninsula near Kelantan and Trengganu. The witness concluded by giving an account of the attack upon the junk and of the *Diana* coming to the rescue.

The next witness, Francisco Thomas, a Christian, stated that he was a native of the island of Luzon, and belonged to a place near Manila. He had seen the boat captured near Tanjong Datu, having been on board the pirate fleet for several months, during which time he had been compelled to work at the oars, being beaten if he refused to do so. His father, two brothers and himself had been taken by the pirates while fishing, the father having been shot. His brother Augustino confirmed this evidence, and a Chinese, who resided at Patani on the east coast of the Peninsula, gave evidence of having been captured by the pirates. Captain Congleton then described the engagement, and gave evidence as to the capture of the prahu.

The whole of the prisoners were found guilty, but sentence was postponed until the Court could make enquiry as to the truth of their statement that they had been sent out by the Sultan of Sulu. In his charge to the Grand Jury the Recorder, Sir W. Norris, with reference to this point, observed " Piracy, as such, cannot be committed by a nation; and should it appear that these men acted under the authority, express or implied, of their Sultan or Rajah I need scarcely say the case would be beyond the jurisdiction and powers of a

---

[1] Haji: one who has performed the pilgrimage to Mecca. The fact that a man was a *haji* gave him a holy flavour which was almost invariably respected by the Illanuns.

Court of Justice. An evil so serious and extensive could only be met by force of arms or the security of solemn treaties, the infraction of which might furnish justifiable ground of war."

On December 3, seventeen of the convicted pirates were brought up to receive sentence, the other man having died in gaol. The Recorder stated that although enquiries had been instituted by Government no evidence was forthcoming to show that the prisoners had been countenanced in their depredations by, or received support from, any recognised prince or State, in which case the latter would have been held responsible for their acts.[1] It only remained, therefore, to pass sentence, but in consideration of their long imprisonment since conviction, and the anxiety they must have experienced as to their probable fate, the Court did not exact the full penalty of the law. Thirteen were sentenced to be transported to Bombay for life; the other four, being young, were given transportation for seven years.

It must be presumed that these men were safely delivered to the authorities in Bombay, but such was the desperate character of these pirates that on one occasion at least they nearly succeeded in outwitting the ends of justice after receiving sentence. On September 15, 1839, the ship *Harriet Scott* left Penang for Bombay, having on board fourteen prisoners who had been convicted of piracy by the Court of Judicature and sentenced to transportation for life. When off Achin the pirates, who do not appear to have been properly secured, rushed the deck, killed the captain, and severely wounded the mate and several of the crew. For nearly five hours they kept possession of the deck, but some of the crew who had escaped the first onslaught fired on them from below, killing one man and mortally wounding three others. The remainder then lowered the quarter-boat and made

---

[1] Definite evidence of such support was, of course, almost impossible to obtain, but that does not necessarily mean that the prisoners' statements were not true.

their escape. They were afterwards picked up by a
native brig in sight of Penang and represented themselves
as having been shipwrecked, but the name of the *Harriet
Scott* and her captain being painted on the stern sheets,
their story was disbelieved, and they were carried to
Penang, where, being tried, they were sentenced to be
hanged.

CHAPTER III

THE BALANINI

The island of Balanini—Methods of attack—The victimisation of
Brunei—The *Sarah and Elizabeth* attacked by Balanini pirates
—The captain abandons the ship—The third mate's story of
his captivity.

THERE were times when pirate fleets from different
quarters would join forces and make common cause, and
it was rare for one set of pirates to attack another. The
Illanuns, however, had a bitter feud with the pirates
of Johore, in its day a kingdom almost as notorious
as Sulu for the piratical propensities of its inhabitants,
from the Sultan downwards. So deadly was this enmity
between the two that if their squadrons met at sea
either would leave a vessel it might be attacking in order
to engage its hereditary foe.

On the other hand, the Illanuns were closely associated with the Balanini pirates and often joined them in
their expeditions. These Balanini were second only to
the Illanuns in daring and ferocity, preferring self-destruc-
tion to capture, and derived their name from an island
in the Sulu Archipelago which they made their head-
quarters, though they had other settlements, notably
on the islands of Basilan, Binadan and Tawi Tawi, and
even at points on the island of Sulu itself. They were
principally Sulus, with a sprinkling of escaped criminals
from the Philippines and Dutch islands, captives of
many nationalities who infinitely preferred a life of
fighting and adventure to being sold as slaves, and
occasionally a renegade European.

The island of Balanini is within sight of Sulu, and
the coral reefs that surround it afforded its frequenters

as much security as the Illanuns found in their lagoon.
Like Mindanau, it is a lagoon island, and the narrow
entrance to the lagoon was staked so that only one vessel
could enter at a time. Even had an attacking gunboat
got through it would have been met by the fire of the
batteries within, which mounted over one hundred guns,
all laid upon the entrance to the lagoon.

In the heyday of their power the Balanini could
muster one hundred and fifty war-boats, often double-
banked, each capable of carrying thirty to fifty warriors; so
that, taking the average at fifty, they must have numbered
at least six thousand fighting-men. They seldom carried
large guns like the Illanuns, and their method of attack
differed from that of their neighbours, for each war-
boat would have attached to it a fast canoe capable of
holding from ten to fifteen men. The larger vessels
would hug the coast during the night and stand off just
before dawn, leaving the canoes to pull along the shore
and capture any fishermen or small trading craft they
might encounter. To enable them to get to close
quarters without arousing suspicion most of the pirates
would conceal themselves in the bottom of the canoe,
while two or three, disguised as natives of the country,
paddled towards the object of their attack. As they drew
alongside the boat those who were in concealment
would leap up with a kind of huge double-pronged fork,
with barbed ends, and with these instruments they would
yank the unsuspecting fishermen into the sea, when they
could be secured without difficulty. Disguised as
Chinese fishermen they carried off numbers of Chinese
from the mouths of the Pontianak and Sambas Rivers,
in southern and western Borneo, and their canoes they
often found useful for disposing of their loot. They
would even take them into Singapore harbour, the
war-boats remaining in hiding about the neighbouring
islands.

❖   ❖

The Balanini seldom made such long cruises as the Illanuns, usually returning within the year, while their favourite period was between May and October. Previous to quitting their main stronghold in the lagoon they buried their guns and valuable property, staked the entrance in such a way that no vessel unpossessed of the secret could enter, and left the settlement to the care of the old men, the cripples and the women.

If not of such long duration, their cruises were carried almost as far afield. They would frequently make the circuit of Borneo, often going as far to the south as Celebes. The islands which are strung out on the fringe of the South China Sea between Borneo and the Malay Peninsula were favourite lurking grounds from which they could sweep out on the passing merchantmen bound for China or Singapore. The chosen field of their operations, however, was Brunei itself. Every year a squadron of six or eight Balanini prahus would take up its station off the island of Labuan, whence it could blockade the town and cut off the trade descending or entering the river, and each season scores of Bruneis were carried off as slaves.

❖   ❖

The following account of how the Balanini pirates captured a British merchant ship sufficiently illustrates their methods of attacking larger vessels.

On May 19, 1843, an English whaler, the *Sarah and Elizabeth* (Captain Bellinghurst), anchored in a bay near Kupang in the island of Timor. Two boats, with the second and third mates and fourteen men, were sent for wood and water. For some reason the captain allowed them to take axes only and refused them fire-arms. It was a mistake of judgment for which all on board were to pay dearly, for they had scarcely started to cut the wood when five large Balanini prahus, followed by some smaller ones, appeared at the entrance to the bay. The sight of the ship's boats drawn up on the beach was too great a temptation for them to resist and they promptly landed some of their men to capture the ship's party with the object of holding the Europeans to ransom— for the Balanini, unlike the Illanuns, did not wantonly put white prisoners to death, preferring to make capital out of them.

On landing they first met the second mate, John Adams, who defended himself with his axe as best he could until knocked over by a billet of wood. The pirates bound him fast and also captured the third mate, Ebeneezer Edwards, and an apprentice named Thomas Gale. The sailors meanwhile escaped into the jungle that fringed the shore.

Those in the *Sarah and Elizabeth* had seen all this from the deck. The Balanini prahus began to close in upon them and the captain got out the muskets, but no cartridges could be found. Panic then seems to have possessed them (as well it might), and they put off in the two remaining boats and pulled away, leaving the brig to her fate. It is said that the captain abandoned his ship in such a hurry that he left his watch behind. (It afterwards found its way into the possession of the Prime Minister of Sulu.) He did not even wait to rescue his dog, which was the only living thing the pirates found when they swarmed aboard.

The ship's boats succeeded in picking up seven of the wooding party from the shore—what happened to the others there is no knowing—and then pulled out to sea and were picked up the same day by another whaler. Two other whaling vessels being in company, boats were sent from all towards the *Sarah and Elizabeth*, which lay about sixteen miles distant, but she was observed to be on fire, and as the boats neared her she blew up.

The captain of the *Sarah and Elizabeth* and the survivors of the crew were subsequently landed at Kupang. Edwards, the third mate, who had been taken aboard one of the prahus, made his escape, and by the assistance of some native fishermen reached

Menado, in Celebes, on July 10, having been six weeks
in the hands of the pirates. His account of his captivity
is worth recording in detail since it gives an intimate
and first-hand description of the activities of these
pirates while on a cruise.

" After having tied our arms and feet," he stated at
the inquiry, " the pirates carried us in their prahus towards
the vessel. They made us go on board, untying us.
The vessel had been abandoned by the captain and the
rest of the crew. They asked for opium, rice and money,
but we told them that there were none of these articles
on board. The pirates broke open everything, plundering the vessel, and carrying away whatever was of use
to them, such as powder, muskets, sails, etc., and placed
the plunder in the only ship's boat which was
left.

" After having again bound us, they set fire to the
ship, and rowed away along the coast to Timor. They
then proceeded towards Celebes, making several excursions in the three boats belonging to the *Sarah and
Elizabeth*, and taking in fresh water at the different islands
they touched at on their route. After a voyage of
forty-eight days they arrived at Buton. One of the
prahus parted company at Buton. On quitting Buton
they were chased by three large boats, which appeared
to be pirates, but they did not overtake them. The
pirates remained some days at Buton fishing, and made
a descent upon the coast, from whence they returned
with some prisoners as well as pieces of bambu filled
with gold dust.

" The prahu in which I was, mounted four guns, had
some muskets, with a crew of thirty-six men and eight
prisoners. There were amongst the pirates nine persons
who appeared to exercise some authority, and who
passed their time in smoking opium, without taking
any part in the navigation. I was transferred from one
prahu to another, but I did not suffer any bad treatment
at their hands, although I was indisposed to work.

Our only food was a little rice and water, very insufficient
to satisfy our hunger.

"As far as I could understand, these pirates came
from Balagningui. They repaired their prahus upon a
sandbank near the entrance to the bay of Gorontalo.
The last place where the pirates stopped was the small
island of Banka, at a short distance from Gorontalo,
where they engaged in fishing. Here I managed to
make my escape in one of the boats belonging to the
Sarah and Elizabeth."

Edwards did not know what had become of Adams
and Gale, who had been captured with him, but they
were in fact carried to Sulu (possibly in the prahu which
parted from the others at Buton) where they had the
good fortune to be ransomed by Mr. Wyndham, the
Englishman referred to in the previous chapter, who had
by this time settled as a trader in that pirate haunt.

CHAPTER IV

SLAVES

How slaves were captured and disposed of—Slave markets in the Archipelago—Two classes of slaves—Their rights—Prices paid—The story of the pirate chief who fell in love with a slave girl.

FOR a pirate squadron slaves were more lucrative than loot, and easier to dispose of. Such of a captured vessel's crew as remained alive would provide the pirates with slaves, but easier sources were the thickly-populated coasts of the Philippines. Here they would land, attack a village, and carry off the women and elder children. The woolly-haired Papuans were highly prized, hence their frequent visits to New Guinea; while in 1834 an island in the Straits of Rhio, opposite Singapore, had its entire community either killed or carried off by an Illanun fleet.

Once a full cargo of slaves had been secured in one quarter the pirates would sail away to dispose of it in another. Thus the Papuans might be sold to a rajah in Achin, and slaves taken in the south of Borneo would find a ready market in Brunei; while the island of Sarangani, off the coast of Mindanau, was a recognised centre of the slave traffic, traders coming from all parts to barter for them. Many of the Spanish and Philippino slaves were sold in this way and resold in Borneo, while the young women, if particularly good-looking, were saved for the Batavia market. The Chinese settlers in the Archipelago were always eager buyers of women slaves, since the laws of their country forbade female emigration.

For the proper understanding of what slavery meant

in the Archipelago at this period it must be remembered that the captives taken by the pirates were of two kinds —the natives of the country, and the subjects of civilised nations, both Europeans and Asiatics, who were often the crews of plundered ships. The latter undoubtedly suffered more than the former, both while they remained captives in the boats and afterwards, when they had been sold as slaves or retained by the pirates themselves to work in their settlements ashore.

While still in the war-boats neither class had an agreeable time. On being taken, a group of prisoners would be shared up among their captors at once. Any who were too sick or too badly wounded to pull an oar would be thrown overboard. The remainder would be fastened in pairs by means of rattan halters, and would be beaten with a flat piece of bamboo on the elbows and knees and on the muscles of the arms and legs so that they could not use their limbs to swim or run away. If one did succeed in escaping overboard the pirates would secure him by means of a three-pronged spear with a long handle. After the captives had been broken in, they would be put to the sweeps and made to row in gangs, one of their fellow-prisoners being set over them, armed with a rattan to keep them at work. If he showed himself too considerate he would be " krissed " and thrown overboard, and another would take his place. The cruises might last for months, and the wretched prisoners would be forced to work in relays night and day. To keep them awake the pirates would put pepper in their eyes or cut them with their knives and rub pepper into the wounds.

Once the fleet returned to its base, if the prisoners had not been sold at a port of call on the way, two things might happen to them : they might be kept by their owner to work ashore or might be taken to one of the principal slave-marts of the Archipelago—such as Sulu, Marudu or Achin—and sold.

A slave who remained with a pirate master might

accompany him on subsequent cruises, when he would
have to work at the oars, but was not expected to fight,
and he had certain rights. He could, for example, have a
share in the plunder after the freemen had taken what
they wanted.

If he was sold in open market it was, of course, a
matter of luck what sort of master he found, and here the
prisoners who had been sailors fared the worst, for they
were unused to the labour they were expected to perform,
while the native of the country, although reft away from
his village and his people, was at least used to a life
of manual toil on the land. He became a servant or
labourer rather than a slave in popular conception, while
a girl, if sufficiently attractive, would go into some
well-to-do man's harem.

A very active slave trade appears at this time to
have been openly carried on by the Achinese on the west
coast of Sumatra, the slaves being obtained from Pulo
Nias and other islands off that coast. A correspondent
of the *Singapore Free Press*, writing in 1847, spoke from
personal knowledge of the extent to which the traffic
was prosecuted :

'The island of Nias in particular, the largest and most
populous of those laying in a line opposite to that coast,
is the devoted land on which this curse has fallen. Board
any of the numerous small prahus to be found in the
direct route from that island to the N.W. coast, and you
will not fail to find undeniable proof of it, generally
young girls and boys, either kidnapped by the dealers
themselves or purchased there, chiefly from the numerous petty rajahs who divide the island among them, and
who obtain them by similar means ; but perhaps more
frequently by the operation of their own laws, which
permit the pledging of the body of the debtor to his
creditor. Land on the opposite coast of Sumatra, at any
of the numerous settlements, and you will find these

unhappy victims exposed for sale in their shops like any other merchandise. I happened last year to see four young women, newly imported, exposed for sale in the manner above mentioned; companions in misery, they had huddled themselves into the back part of the shop, and from native modesty, or absorbed in grief, their faces were turned from the light of day. On an intending purchaser making his inquiries, they fearfully and for a moment turned their faces, which, though almost entirely screened by their long and loose dishevelled hair, I could see were pale and swollen even to disfiguration by the un-heeded tears they so copiously shed, while their savage owner answered these inquiries with the same indifference as he answered those of another customer who was at the moment treating for a piece of Achinese cloth."

On the Borneo coast, and probably elsewhere in the Archipelago, slaves were divided into two classes—those who were slaves in a strict sense and those whose servitude was of a light description. The latter were children of a slave-mother by a freeman *other than her master*. These slaves were known as *anak mas*. If a female, a child so born would be the slave of her mother's master, but could not be sold by him; if a boy, he would be free for all intents and purposes. He could not be sold and if he did not care to remain with his mother's master he could move about and earn his own living, though he might have to share his earnings with him—custom on this point varied in different districts. In case of actual need, however, the master could call upon him for his services.

If an *anak mas* girl married a freeman she became automatically free herself, but the bridegroom would be expected to pay the master a bride-price (*berian*) of two *pikul* [1] of brass gun—in value about $20 or £3,

---

[1] 1 Pikul = 133 lbs.

which was the equivalent of purchase. If she married a slave she remained an *anak mas*. But such cases were rare, since the slave man was rarely in a position to pay the bride-price.

If an ordinary slave woman had a child by her owner, she and the child became free and she might remain on in the establishment as a wife.

On the whole, it is probable that these slaves did not suffer much actual hardship or ill-treatment : indeed, if a slave were notoriously ill-treated or insufficiently fed, and escaped, public opinion would condone the offence. If a slave were ill-treated by a freeman, his master could claim compensation from the aggressor. On the other hand, a master was entitled to beat his slaves with a rattan for laziness or attempted escape, and an incorrigible slave would be compulsorily converted to Mohammedanism and circumcised.

The ordinary method of buying slaves was payment in so many *pikul* of brass cannon. As a rough guide to selling prices the following approximate values may be quoted :

A boy, about two *pikul* (about £6)

A man, about three *pikul*.

A girl, three to four *pikul*.

A young woman, three to five *pikul*, according to looks and accomplishments.

A person past middle age, about half a *pikul*.

A young couple, seven to eight *pikul*.

An old couple about five *pikul*.

There was no difference in dress between slaves and freemen, nor in the arms which all carried. And the mere fact that the slaves were allowed to wear arms is fairly conclusive proof that they were not unduly oppressed. As a rule they became, as it were, one of their master's family, sharing the food of the household and being supplied with tobacco and betel-nut. They assisted in domestic duties and agricultural labour, fishing and trading ; but there was no such institution as the slave-gang working under task-masters. That was the institution of the white slave-master. Their real hardship was being carried far from their own people and their own land.

❖   ❖

Slave women were often highly prized by their masters—and sought after by others—as the following story will show. A celebrated Malay pirate—I will call him Daud—fell in love with one of the slave girls of a rajah who dwelt on the Sarawak River. He offered to buy her from her master, but was refused. To money offers he added entreaties, but in vain. The rajah was obdurate. She must have been a very alluring little girl, and doubtless the attraction she had for this young warrior, who had captured many slaves in his time, enhanced her beauty in the rajah's eyes. But every Malay in love is a Lochinvar, and Daud, unable to get his way by private treaty, waited for her one night and carried her off to a retreat he had made in the jungle.

It was not long before the rajah discovered the couple's hiding-place, and he sent a messenger to say that if Daud would present himself at the court on a certain day he should have justice done.

Daud did not lack courage. He promised to appear, believing that the reputation he had made for himself in the pirate world would be sufficient to awe his judges, and trusting that once the trouble had blown over he would be able to take his bride away without further concealment.

On the day appointed, therefore, he appeared before the rajah, accompanied by his brother. As they entered the audience hall, proud and defiant, each laid his hands on the handle of his *kris*. The rajah's council discussed the case at length, and finally gave judgment that if on a certain day Daud would produce a specified weight of brass cannon the girl should be his and both should go unmolested. The amount was enormous even for a wealthy young pirate, but Daud agreed to the terms and he and his brother were allowed to depart.

When the day of payment arrived Daud, true to his word, appeared again before the council. This time he came alone, for his brother had been called away on a piratical cruise. Daud told the council that he had done his best to find the amount required, but he had not succeeded. What he had collected he had brought; and he asked for more time in which to find the remainder.

The council consulted for a while and then announced that since he had not brought the stipulated amount of brass he must leave his *kris* as a pledge. Daud's eyes clouded as he heard these words. His *kris* was the most precious thing he had—the long wavy blade was exquisitely damascened, the hilt inlaid with gold and precious stones. It had belonged to his ancestors—had been a famous weapon when it came down to him, and he had added to its fame. For a while he hesitated. Then love conquered. He could not bear to lose the girl, and there seemed no other way.

Slowly, even sorrowfully, he unfastened the cord about his waist and then, bending down, laid his precious weapon upon the brass cannon that had been set upon the floor. But with his *kris* he laid aside his prudence, his watchful care against treachery that—in such as he—nothing but passion could have dulled. For as he straightened himself he stood before the council unarmed. That was the moment for which the rajah had been waiting. There was a sudden signal, and before Daud could bend down again to clutch his *kris* he was seized from behind and held; then he was forced to his knees and his arms were lifted until they came in line with his shoulders. In another moment one of the rajah's men had plunged his own wavy blade down into the hollow between Daud's collar-bone and neck—down to the heart that had beaten so wildly for the little slave girl.

CHAPTER V

THE RAIDING OF BALAMBANGAN

The Sultan of Sulu cedes Balambangan to the Honourable East
India Company—Correspondence between the Company and
Lord Weymouth relating to the occupation of the island—
John Herbert appointed Chief of the new colony—His instruc-
tions—Mismanagement and delays—The foundation of the
settlement—Sulu jealousy—Datu Tating's plot—The raid—
Immense booty taken—A treasure hunt on Balambangan—
Unsuccessful attempts to re-establish the settlement.

ON the fringe of the China sea, a few miles from the
most northerly point of Borneo, known as Simpang
Mengaiau, or the parting of the Pirate Ways, lies the
island of Balambangan. It is twelve miles long and is
so flat that as one approaches through its maze of coral
reefs it seems to rise from the sea like a gigantic crocodile.[1]
Its only inhabitants are a few fisherfolk and nowadays
it is visited by Europeans scarcely once in ten years.
Long ago it was to have been the centre of British trade
in the Eastern Seas. To-day it is the grave of an adventure that was wrecked by Malayan pirates.

In 1762 a British fleet under Sir William Draper
captured Manila from the Spaniards, and finding Alimudin, the Sultan of the Sulu Archipelago, a prisoner in
their hands, restored him to his throne and possessions.
As a mark of gratitude the Sultan ceded to the Honourable East India Company part of the northern coast of

---

[1] I take the etymology of the name to be from the Malay *belum bangan*—" not
yet risen."   Mr. E. P. Gueritz tells me that it was so named in distinction from
its neighbour Mulaiangin—" the beginning of the wind." Coming down
between Banggi and Balambangan the state of the wind, whether S.W. or N.E.,
would be *belum bangan* until Mulaiangin opened up.

Borneo, of which he was the nominal sovereign, together with the island of Balambangan.

For some time no advantage was taken of this cession.
But in those days the Company had no outpost in the
Far East, and Mr. Alexander Dalrymple, one of its officers
who had been instrumental in obtaining the cession,
repeatedly urged its occupation. It was less than a
thousand miles from China, and on the direct route of
the Chinese junks in their annual passage to Brunei.
It was equidistant from Japan, Korea, Bengal and New
Holland. It had two good harbours, from which trade
could be expected with Borneo and Sulu. Moreover,
the island itself was well provided with fresh water and
timber.

Dalrymple's proposals found favour with the Court
of Directors of the East India Company, for they wished
to extend their trade, and it was the policy of the time
to establish distant trading outposts on small islands
that lay close to a populous mainland. An island settlement was considered more healthy than one on the
continent, and more secure from aggression. It was
calculated to attract trade from all quarters and (in
theory) could be economically maintained. This was
the doctrine that in after years called into being the
settlements at Labuan, Penang and Singapore. It had
varying results, for while Penang and Singapore thrived,
Labuan and Balambangan failed, the truth being that
the commercial prosperity of such ports depends upon
their proximity to the main trading routes, and the
Borneo settlements were sufficiently remote to be denied
the prosperity predicted by those responsible for their
inception.

At the time, however, the Court of Directors, made
optimistic by Dalrymple's enthusiastic reports, saw in
Balambangan a clearing-house for eastern trade that
would come to rival Batavia and Malacca, and sent orders to
Bombay that an armed vessel should be prepared to
take possession of the island " in the name of the King

of Great Britain and the East India Company." Profound secrecy was recommended lest another State
should learn of their design.

This action is an example of the arrogant power
to which the East India Company had attained at this
time. Before directing its officers to take possession
of any territory in the name of the King, the Court's
proper course would have been first to have laid its
proposals before His Majesty's Government, but it
was not until after these orders had been transmitted to
Bombay that the Court of Directors thought fit to make
the following representation to the Secretary of State
for Foreign Affairs :

To Rt. Hon'ble Lord Viscount Weymouth.

My Lord,
*The Court of Directors of the East India Company
having given orders for Possession to be taken of the small
uninhabited Island of Balambangan, in order to open a trade
in the Eastern Seas within the limits of the Company's Charter ;
the Objects they have had principally in view in this Undertaking are to direct the Chinese trade into this Channel, by
procuring a Resort of Chinese to settle at Balambangan, and
engaging the Chinese junks to visit and dispose of their cargoes
there.*

*To extend the sale of the manufactures of Great Britain
to Cochin China and the Northern Provinces of China, and
receive from thence many of those Commodities which can now
only be obtained from Canton at very high Prices.*

*To open a market for the consumption of the manufactures
of Bengal by adding to the Ballance of Trade in favour of Bengal
to encrease the circulating Specie in the Bengal Provinces.*

*And finally to extend the Company's Trade with the
unfrequented parts of Asia.*

*And as the said Court flatter themselves that in their
motives, as above represented, for their Extension of the
Company's Commerce, it would appear they have been induced*

by such as will tend not only to the advantage of the Company's Trade, but also to the National Benefit, they therefore humbly entreat your Lordship to make such a favourable Representation on this subject to His Majesty, as that His Majesty may be graciously pleased to grant the Company His Royal Protection and Support in this undertaking.

We are,
With great Respect
My Lord,
Your Lordship's most Obedient and most Humble Servants,
The Court of Directors of the United East India Company.

East India House,
The 28th October, 1768.

Considering that the Court had first instructed its officers to take possession of the island in the King's name, and had then calmly informed His Majesty's Minister that it had done so, Lord Weymouth's reply began with surprising moderation, for he informed the Court that His Majesty was " pleased highly to approve of the Company's attention to the extension of their trade," and expressed his readiness to " promote every commercial object which should appear advantageous to their interests by a continuation of that protection of which they had so much experienced the happy effects."

The sting, however, was to follow, for even a monarch whose position was as insecure as George III.'s during the early portion of his reign could not pass over the Court's effrontery without rebuke, little as he could afford to quarrel with so powerful an influence. The letter continued :

As the Plan is not sufficiently opened for His Majesty's Servants to form a first Judgment on its Utility, so His

*Majesty trusts entirely to your Knowledge of your own Affairs,
for what it may produce in a Commercial View ; but considering it in a political Light, I must not conceal from you,
that His Majesty is extremely surprized to find the East
India Company desire his Protection with regard to a measure
upon which he has never been consulted, and to hear for the
first time that they have ordered their servants to take possession
of an Island, without the least information of any other Right,
upon which that measure is founded except that of Utility, nor
any account by which His Majesty might judge whether it can
interfere with the subsisting Treaties with other States, or
give umbrage to those Powers, with which he is on terms of
Amity and Friendship. If, therefore, you are apprehensive,
that any Objections may be made from any European Power to
the measure which you have now communicated, or that it can
be considered as an infringement of the Rights of any Power in
India, it will be highly proper that you transmit to me, without
delay, for His Majesty's information, the Orders you have
given upon this occasion, with such description of the Island
and such information's relating to it, as induced you to take
possession of it, with the Dates of all Papers and Consultations
relating to this matter, that His Majesty may be enabled to
judge whether it may be proper for him to grant to the Company
upon this occasion, that Support and Protection, which he has
always given, and will always continue to give, to their just and
reasonable Requests.*[1]

The Court justified their intentions by laying before
Lord Weymouth copies of the grants from the Sultan
of Sulu, together with a statement by Dalrymple.
Spain could make no claims upon the island, since it was
beyond the limits prescribed for her trade and navigation
by the treaties of Westphalia and Utrecht. Holland had
never made any pretensions to Sulu or Balambangan ;
and, moreover, the Court relied upon their Charter, by
which they were entitled to form settlements anywhere

[1] The originals of these letters are in the India Office Records.

in India (which then had a far wider application than it has to-day) with the consent of the natives, and to occupy any uninhabited place for the extension of their trade.

There is no doubt that the Company's claims to occupy Balambangan were perfectly legitimate, although the secrecy they enjoined in their first instructions to Bombay seems to show that they anticipated opposition from Spain at least. The King, however, accepted their contentions, and ordered Sir John Lindsay, the naval Commander-in-Chief in the East Indies, to assist and protect the Company in founding the proposed settlement; and for a time preparations were energetically pushed forward.

❖   ❖

Everything pointed to Alexander Dalrymple as the man most fitted to lead the expedition. He had personally examined the island, and the scheme for the settlement had been his. He was known to have more experience of the trading possibilities in those waters than any other Englishman. He was respected by the Sulus, and had acquired the friendship of Sultan Ali-mudin, with whom he had exchanged ceremonial vows of brotherhood, each party having drawn blood from the other, mingled it in a goblet and quaffed a draught. Since the good offices of the Sultan were essential for the well-being of the settlement, Dalrymple was obviously the man to govern it.

Dalrymple would certainly have been the first Governor of Balambangan had it not been for his own exorbitant demands. He wanted to command the expedition, to be appointed captain of the ship, and to have the choice of the crew. He was to have absolute control of the settlement, and power to appoint his own officers. He demanded a commission of four per cent on all cargoes bought and sold at Balambangan. At the expiration of three years he was to be paid £8,000 for his services, and this was to be guaranteed to him should the expedition fail.

The Court of Directors agreed to the commission, and offered him £1,000 a year as salary. They insisted on appointing the officers and on providing for a governing Council, in which Dalrymple was to have a casting vote. Instead of the grant of £8,000 in event of the expedition being abandoned they reserved the right to fix a suitable sum.

These terms were reasonable enough, but Dalrymple stubbornly held out for his own demands, with the result that, after a protracted and unseemly wrangle, he was finally dismissed the Company's service, and John Herbert was appointed Chief of the expedition and directed to proceed to Balambangan in the Company's ship *Britannia*, which was to be despatched from London to India under the command of Captain James Swithin.

This final decision to occupy Balambangan was to be of immense importance in the history of the British Empire, for not only did it mark a new era in the progress of the Company, but actually laid the foundations upon which British trade east of India was eventually built up. It is interesting to notice, therefore, the directions despatched for the guidance of the Chief of the first British colony in the Far East.

The essence of these directions were that the settlement was to be independent of India itself. The Chief (whose salary was to be £600 per annum), with his two assistants, were to form the governing Council, assisted in civil affairs by two factors and two writers. The *Britannia* was to take with her from India a combined force of European and Indian soldiers, and on arrival at Balambangan the ship was to be used as a floating factory and warehouse until suitable buildings, protected by a stockade, could be built. A Bombay cruiser was to act as a guardship under the command of the Chief and Council, who were expressly ordered to be most vigilant against treachery or surprise by the Malays.

Trade was to be carried on chiefly by barter, and Captain Swithin was directed to touch at the Cape of Good Hope and there procure sheep for breeding purposes and also a supply of vines, plants and seeds of all descriptions that might be propogated and cultivated on the island. Cattle were to be imported from the neighbouring island of Banggi, and from the mainland, where rice could also be procured.

Mr. Herbert was instructed to make contracts with the neighbouring native princes whereby opium, piece goods and other articles from Bengal might be exchanged for pepper, spices and such commodities, and to encourage the Chinese and the Malays to settle on the island and to trade. It was stipulated that Balambangan should be a free port and that all traders were to be exempt both from customs duties and fees for entry or clearance : the principle to which Singapore owes much of its prosperity to-day.

Beyond this, matters relating to trade and local administration and questions concerning the general policy of the settlement, or disputes with other European Powers, were left to the decision of the Chief and Council.

Vested, then, with this almost despotic authority, John Herbert set out for Balambangan. If ever a man had high opportunities it was he. He had the power and resources of a mighty colonial organisation behind him ; before him lay an unexploited field of commerce and the chance of extending his country's prestige and political influence in lands where her flag was unknown, and among peoples to whom she was but a name. Had he been worthy of the trust placed in him he might to-day have been honoured with James Brooke and

Stamford Raffles as one of the builders of the empire in the Eastern seas. As it was, it would seem that the Court of Directors could scarcely have found a man less fitted for that great enterprise with which they had entrusted him, so lacking was he in all the attributes which make for successful administration and command, and if he had talent he did but use it to defraud and swindle the Company he served.

From the first his dilatoriness appears almost beyond belief, and for different reasons—not unconnected with his private trading interests—it took him two and a half years to reach Balambangan, instead of eight months, by which time his activities had involved the Company in expenses and losses amounting to over £200,000. The Company never knew details of most of these disbursements, for Herbert would draw bills of exchange "for sundry purchases" to the amount, in two instances, of nearly £13,000 and while trading in the Dutch East Indies and Sulu he was in the habit of buying the Company's opium, allowing it a nominal profit, and selling on his own account at a much higher price—although private trade in opium had been expressly forbidden by the Court.

It was some time before the Court of Directors realised the true state of affairs, but finally the increasing evidence of Herbert's mismanagement and fraud caused them to express themselves in the following terms :

The extraordinary and unwarrantable Measures which you have adopted since we directed you to form a Settlement at Balambangan, appear so alarming to us that we sent Orders to Bengal overland to check effectually and without loss of time that extravagant Disposition which is manifested in your whole Conduct and to put a total stop to the dangerous Experiment you were making for carrying on the new Trade there. . . . We must notice in general the utter impropriety of your incurring a profusion of Expenses and entering into such extensive Plans of Commerce in an infant Settlement . . . we positively

*require you to confine your Expenses in future to the Line
prescribed by our Orders of 12 June, 1771.*

This censure was mild when applied to conduct that,
as events showed, deserved instant dismissal.   But
that did not greatly matter, since by the time their
despatch reached the East the fate of the new settlement
was sealed.

◇   ◇

The *Britannia* eventually cast anchor in the north-
west harbour of Balambangan on December 12, 1773.
In company with her was the *Success*, with provisions
from Madras and Bombay, and the *Devonshire*, laden with
treasure and stores from China.

To do Herbert justice, it appears that once he had
reached the island he set about the building of the
settlement with great energy.   Thanks to a plan made
by Alexander Dalrymple (dated 1788) and here reproduced by the courtesy of the Records Department of
the India Office, it is possible to see the exact positions
of the various buildings.   A low hill (the only rising
ground on the island) was selected as the centre of the
establishment : here were the Magazine, Secretary's
offices, the Barracks and the military officers' houses,
fortified towards the sea by a stockade and enclosed in
the rear by a belt of thick scrub and jungle.   A battery
of nine guns, mounted about sixty yards from the
beach, defended the stockade.   But a glance at the plan
will show that there was no battery in the rear.   Herbert
and his military advisers concentrated their defences
towards the sea, thinking, doubtless, that if the land side
required protection the wall of jungle was enough.
Time was to show their folly.

In spite of their elaborate preparations the little
colony showed few signs of prosperity during the first

year of its existence, for the Chinese junks upon whose trade Dalrymple had counted seemed to avoid the island, nor did settlers come readily. Herbert, however, sent messengers and ships in all directions to encourage trade and succeeded in obtaining from the Sultan of Brunei the exclusive right in the valuable pepper trade in return for a promise of the Company's protection from the Sulu, Illanun and Balanini pirates who habitually committed depredations against his subjects and carried them off as slaves. Some time later a factory was established outside the town of Brunei and a brisk trade in pepper began to develop.

But if Herbert showed zeal in extending the trade of Balambangan it was for his own ends rather than for those of the Company whose interests he had been engaged to serve. Huge expenses were shown, but no income, although large quantities of stores had been sent from India for sale. As an example, in July, 1774, 360 bales of broadcloth and 309 bales of piece goods, to the value of £34,000, were received from Bombay, yet not one penny for the sale of these cargoes was entered in any book, and Herbert continued to draw bills against the Company for enormous sums, until finally the patience of the long-suffering Court gave out. A new Chief and Council were appointed, and Herbert and his associates were ordered to return home to justify their administration.

Before these orders could reach Bombay, Balambangan was in ruins and the Company's last hope of saving anything from Herbert's clutches was gone.

❖   ❖

By the time the settlement at Balambangan had come into existence Sultan Israel had succeeded Alimudin on the throne of Sulu. Israel inclined to an alliance with Spain, and began to view the increasing power of his English neighbours at Balambangan with jealousy and suspicion. The fact that he was deeply in their debt probably did much to increase his resentment, and

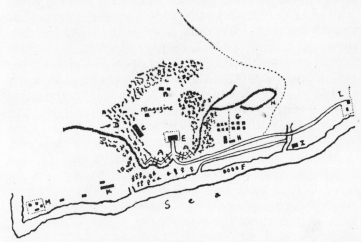

PLAN OF
THE SETTLEMENT OF BALAMBANGAN

After Alex. Dalrymple's sketch from a MS. at East India House

A   The Stockade, mounting 9 guns (60 yds. distant from beach).
B   Military Officers' Houses (200 yds. from the guns).
C   The Sepoy Barracks.
D   Thick scrub, where raiders hid and broke through.
    Secretary's Offices.
F   Sulu boats hauled up on beach.
G   Houses of Bugis troops.
H   House of Mr. Cole (2nd in Council) and one of Company's
    godowns.
I   Large godown.
K   Houses of Chinese.
L   Chief's House. From L to M, the House on the Point, was
    about 2 miles.
N   Road leading to houses behind the stockade.
O   Point where raiders from the boats entered the palisade.

the treatment his subjects received did not tend to create better feeling, for while Herbert had invited the Sulus to settle on Balambangan he would punish them severely if they misbehaved, treating even the chiefs

with contumely and placing their heads in the stocks.
Nor can one doubt that the vast stores of merchandise
and gold on the island excited the cupidity of his courtiers and chieftains, and of the pirates who swarmed in
the Archipelago. It would have been strange had not
these sea-rovers looked longingly upon that little
British settlement, so isolated, so open to attack, yet so
rich in booty for those who were bold enough to seize it.

One of the Sulu chiefs who came to Balambangan was
Datu Tating, a first cousin of the Sultan. He had
presented himself to the Governor as a carpenter, and
was given contracts to erect some buildings that were
required. There cannot be much doubt that Tating's
object in going to Balambangan was to spy out the
land, and his close relationship to the Sultan makes it
probable that Israel was at least conversant with his
plans, if he did not formulate them. But with a Malay,
plotting and direct action are two very different things,
and even though he had secured large advances, and was
heavily in debt to the Company, Tating might never have
got beyond scheming for the expulsion of the English
had he not been incensed by hearing his ruler contemp-
tuously referred to as " a sweet potato root " and had
his own feelings not been outraged by being himself
placed in the stocks.

No human being in the world is more sensitive to
insult than a Malay noble, or more ruthless in avenging
a slur. Had Tating had no political feelings against
the English, had he never received any covert instructions from the Sultan, the incident of the stocks would
have been enough to spur him from dreams to deeds.
He left the island and joined his cousin Dacula on the
neighbouring island of Banggi, and the two collected a
band of some 300 Sulus and Illanuns, to whom the booty
on Balambangan was sufficient inducement for a raid.

Tating had carefully studied the defences of the
settlement, and it had not taken him long to discover
their weak point. He saw that to attack from the sea

A SULU CHIEF.

would be madness : but the rear of the fort was open—
not only open, indeed, but fringed by that belt of scrub
which would afford admirable cover for an attacking
force. Accordingly, he began to dribble his men over
to Balambangan in small boats by night, landing them
on the far side of the island and ordering them to lie
concealed in the jungle until all was ready for the raid.

Tating had chosen his time well. The original
garrison had amounted to 400 European and native
troops, but the unhealthy climate of the island had by
March, 1775, reduced it to little over 100; and most of
the ships, with the exception of two brigs, were away
on commercial expeditions.

For some time there had been sinister rumours of an
impending Sulu attack. Even so, it was considered un-
necessary to post more than a look-out by day, though
a guard was on duty at night ; and in spite of the rumours
it never occurred to the garrison that the attack, if it did
come, could be delivered from anywhere but the sea.

March 4 was the Governor's birthday. It pleased
him to invite his officers to a fête, which lasted well into
the night. Tating had doubtless counted on the effects
of this entertainment when he planned his attack for
the following day.

At dawn next morning a gun in the stockade sounded
réveillé. The sentries began to march back to barracks.
A few moments later a pillar of smoke rose from a Sulu
boat that was hauled up on the beach. That was the
signal, and immediately, in three columns, the Sulus
rushed to the attack. A hundred men, led by Tating
himself, emerged from the jungle behind the barracks
(D on the plan), where they had lain hidden all night.
They surrounded and overpowered the sepoys in their
quarters before they could seize their arms. A second
party captured the guns on the stockade, turned them
on the Bugis troops, and dispersed them in a few minutes,
assisted by the third column from the boats, which
entered the stockade at the point O. The officers

rushed from their houses, but too late to rally their men. Panic ensued and in a few moments English, Indians and Bugis were streaming down to the beach in flight, leaving the fort and the booty in the Sulus' hands.

One can picture that scene : the pirates, arrayed in their scarlet coats and yelling their triumphant war-cries as they swarmed inside the stockade ; the troops, panic-stricken and demoralised by the suddenness of the onslaught, fleeing to the ships ; the indescribable confusion as the settlers joined the throng on the shore ; the victors' search for plunder ; the flames rising from the wooden buildings in the stockade.

Herbert, who always kept a small boat in readiness at the landing-stage by his house, seems to have wasted no time in escaping to the brig *Endeavour*. She and the *Phœnix* opened fire on the fort. Dacula returned it with the English guns and by a chance shot cut away the cable of the *Phœnix*. As luck would have it a stiff breeze was blowing off the sea, and she was driven ashore and seized by the pirates ; the crew and survivors from the settlement jumped overboard, and those who were not drowned were taken up by the *Endeavour*.

By this time the Chinese huts and the large store-house on the point (M) were blazing, and towards ten o'clock the establishment of Mr. Cole (Herbert's second-in-command) and the other storehouses were plundered and set on fire. But it was not until past midday that the Sulus turned their attention to the Chief's house, by which time Herbert and those with him were heading for the open sea.

In these matters it is easy enough to condemn, yet even when all allowances are made the conduct of the garrison does appear to have been craven. That they were overwhelmed by the suddenness of the attack is true, but only thirteen were killed and the officers made no attempt to organise a counter-attack, nor was an effort made to save anything from the Governor's house, which lay a mile from the fort and was not touched by the pirates for seven hours after the opening of the raid.

Not one book or paper was saved, not a single dollar or a bale of merchandise from the rich treasure that was on shore.   The pirates were left with 45 cannon, 20 tons of gunpowder, 22,000 rounds of shot, 250 muskets, as well as gold bars, 14,000 Spanish silver dollars and a vast quantity of muslins and other piece goods ; the total loss to the Company being estimated at nearly a million Spanish dollars or half a million sterling.

❖   ❖

Now there has always been a persistent legend in Borneo that the Sulus did not secure all the treasure that was left on Balambangan, and that, although eventually taken by surprise, the officers, fearing an attack from the sea, had buried some of the gold and silver in a well, and had had no time to unearth it before they fled. That is the story.   It was talked of when the British North Borneo Company took over the country a century later.   It is still talked of to-day.   I have heard it from the lips of many natives.   Before the war, when I was in charge of the district of Marudu, on the mainland opposite Balambangan, many times did I discuss it over whiskies-and-sodas with my friends.   We used to make plans for going in search of it, but never did.   The East is like that.

When I returned to Borneo after the war, intent upon collecting material for a book, my wife and I settled on a coconut estate, and from our house could see Balambangan.   Although we knew that at least one expedition had tried to find the treasure without success, we determined that instead of talking about it we would go and try our luck.

So one morning a small expedition set out, consisting of my wife, the Resident of Kudat, and myself, in the Government launch.   The Resident was visiting the islands on duty. He was sceptical about the treasure, but he took us as passengers, though he grinned when he saw that I was in earnest and had come equipped, not with picks and shovels, but with the native implement known as a *changkul*—a sort of aggravated hoe—and as good a weapon to dig for treasure with as any other.

A local chief had volunteered to accompany us as guide. He led us up a hill through the jungle to the ruins of the fort and the magazine. Only a shallow pit and a brick wall remained, but the communication trench that had connected the fort with the coast was plain to see. There were remains of redoubts and blockhouses; and we were elated to find an old well, choked up with sand. We got our *changkuls* to work and dug. Our followers dug with us. At first we were optimistic, but the finding of half a dozen more wells rather damped our ardour. We dug on, while the Resident smoked cigars and still looked sceptical. I should love to be able to say that he let his cigar go out in his excitement as we drew forth first a bar of gold and then an iron box of Spanish dollars. But the truth is that all we brought away from Balambangan were a few fragments of broken bricks and some pieces of Chinese pottery to remind us of that great adventure which started with such high hopes in the midst of the pirate seas.

Now one needs to be an optimist to go treasure-seeking, and at the time of my visit to Balambangan (and even after it) I really did believe there might be something in the story of the treasure in the well. After all, there had been an immense amount of specie on the island, the garrison had been forced to flee in haste, and it was not unreasonable to suppose that some of the officers might have had time to sling some gold bars down a well before they left. Indeed, since they had been warned that a raid was pending, they might even have secreted the treasure before ever the attack was made.

Further research into the history of the Balambangan settlement, however, has convinced me that the treasure is nothing but a myth. For the plain fact is that the colony was resurrected years later, and it seems probable that if anything had been hidden it would have been unearthed by the successors of the first settlers.

Herbert and his associates reached Brunei shortly after the raid, where they found a convenient refuge in the English factory. By this time John Jesse, the Company's Agent at Brunei (he is interesting as the first Englishman to put foot in this part of Borneo), had won the confidence of the Sultan, who, on March 28, 1775, signed a treaty ceding the island of Labuan to the East India Company. On April 16 Herbert hoisted the Company's flag, and there the Company's officers who had been sent to supersede him found him when they reached the island on November 9, 1775.

Since their orders were to return to India if prevented from reaching the settlement at Balambangan, they withdrew the garrison at Labuan and closed down the factory at Brunei.

When the truth of Herbert's conduct became known in England orders were sent out to arrest him, but he eluded capture and it was not until six years later, when the involved investigations into his maladministration were ended, that he was allowed to return to India. That he owed much to the leniency of the Court of Directors there can be no doubt, for there are grounds for suspicion that he connived at the raid, or at least did nothing to prevent it, wishing for nothing better than the destruction of the books and documents that would have proved his duplicity and fraud.

No serious attempt ever seems to have been made to recover the immense booty that fell into Tating's hands. For over a quarter of a century Balambangan was forgotten. Then, in 1803, political considerations induced

Lord Wellesley, the Governor-General of India, to give instructions for the re-occupation of the island, considering it, besides its value as a trading base, a fit centre for naval operations against any European power, particularly the Dutch in the Moluccas and the Spaniards in the Philippines, and for the foundation of a colony which would in time increase the influence of Great Britain in the Far East. It is beyond the scope of this chronicle to follow the fortunes of this fresh establishment. It is enough to say that it did not prosper, and partly for this reason, but more on account of political events in Europe and the fresh outbreak of war between Great Britain and France, it was withdrawn in 1805, and although now part of the territory of the British North Borneo Company the island has remained untenanted ever since.

It is not uninteresting to speculate whether, had the little colony been given time to establish itself, it would ever have fulfilled the hopes of Alexander Dalrymple and later of Lord Wellesley. Knowing the island as I do, it seems to me that each enterprise was foredoomed to failure. Much of the island is in the clutches of the mangrove, low, swampy and unhealthy. The harbour is filled with coral patches. The water is brackish. The soil is so sandy and barren that neither grain nor vegetables nor fruit-trees will grow in it, as the settlers found to their cost. The neighbouring island of Banggi, with its high ground and fertile soil, is superior in all these respects, and why Dalrymple passed over Banggi in favour of Balambangan has always puzzled me. Moreover, the situation of either island was unlikely to attract the immense Chinese junk trade or to capture the eastern commerce that had been shared for over a century by the Spaniards, the Dutch and the Portuguese.

Sir James Brooke, who examined Balambangan forty years after the British had abandoned it, describes it as "a melancholy and ineligible spot," and that

description is as true to-day. Of all the islands that
fringe the coast of North Borneo, Balambangan is the
most desolate—and for the reasons I have given it is
difficult to allow it even the distinction of being a
possible treasure island.

At the same time, let me not be one to throw a
damper on romance. Some who read these lines may
be more optimistic than I. They may believe that
John Herbert himself hid the treasure, hoping to return.
They may picture him being hunted from corner to
corner of the East—as indeed he was—never able to
recover that hidden hoard of bar gold and Spanish silver
dollars. Even though the tale may have got abroad,
that does not prove (they may say) that the treasure was
ever found, and others may have delved for it as earnestly
yet as unsuccessfully as I.

It may be so. And if there be any treasure seekers
who feel the urge to go and dig on Balambangan they
may take ship to Singapore and thence to the tiny town-
ship of Kudat in North Borneo. In the Chinese shops
they will be able to buy implements for their purpose,
and (possibly) the Resident will accommodate them with
his launch. But lest they should find nothing but
disappointment upon that lonely isle I would counsel
them to think of the Malay proverb my friend the chief
quoted to me consolingly as we walked along the sandy
beach after our treasure hunt : " A man is a prince
upon his own sleeping-mat, while another may sit on a
golden cushion with an unquiet mind."

CHAPTER VI

THE LOSS OF THE " SULTANA "

How James Brooke became Rajah of Sarawak—The *Sultana* struck
    by lightning—Captain Page abandons her and reaches Brunei—
    The Sultan of Brunei holds Captain Page and his people to
    ransom—Rajah Brooke receives news of their plight—He
    succeeds in rescuing them—Lascar's statement concerning
    European woman captive—Captain Sir Edward Belcher's
    attempt to rescue her.

FOR over half a century after the raiding of Balambangan
the pirates ranged the Borneo seas unchecked. It was
left to a private adventurer to put a restraint upon their
activities : and the word " adventurer " is used here in
its true sense, and without that sinister implication it has
acquired.

For if ever there was a true adventurer it was James
Brooke. The story of how he came to found the State
of Sarawak is too well known to need recounting in any
detail here—although one may still meet people, ostensibly " well-informed," who are under the impression
that the present Rajah of Sarawak is what is known as a
gentleman of colour. It is enough to say that while
cruising in the China Sea as an officer of the East India
Company, James Brooke, still in his twenties, had seen
the Malay Islands lying neglected and almost unknown,
and had conceived, then and there, the project of redeem-
ing them from piracy and slavery, and of substituting
for the misrule and oppression of the chiefs a just and
benevolent administration under which the people
might be free to cultivate their lands without molestation
and to sail the seas in pursuit of peaceful trade.

    " The tender philanthropy of the present day," he

wrote, "which originates such multifarious schemes for
the amelioration of doubtful evils, and which shudders
at the prolongation of apprenticeship in the west, for a
single year, is blind to the existence of slavery in its
worst and most exaggerated form in the east.   Not a
single prospectus is spread abroad, not a single voice
upraised in Exeter Hall to relieve the darkness of
Paganism and the horrors of the slave trade! Whilst
the trumpet tongue of many an orator excites thousands
to the rational and charitable object of converting the
Jews and reclaiming gypsies ; whilst the admirable
exertions of missionary enterprise in the Austral climes
of the Pacific, have invested them with worldly power,
as well as religious influence, whilst the benevolent plans
of the New Zealand Association contemplates the
protection of the natives by acquisition of their territory,
whilst we admire this torrent of devotional and philo-
sophical exertion, we cannot help deploring that the
zeal and attention of the leaders of these charitable
crusades have never been directed to the countries
under consideration. These unhappy countries have
failed to rouse attention or excite commiseration, and as
they sink lower and lower they afford a striking proof
how civilisation may be crushed, and how the fairest
and richest lands under the sun may become degraded
and brutalised by a continuous course of oppression
and misrule. It is under these circumstances I have
considered that individual exertions may be usefully
applied to rouse the zeal of slumbering philanthropy,
and lead the way to an increased knowledge of the
Indian Archipelago." [1]

If James Brooke had ideals, he was no mere dreamer.
He did not waste time in encouraging others to test his
theories (as would-be reformers would have done), but
set out to put them into practice himself. To this end
he left the service of the East India Company and, after

---

[1] The Voyage of H.M.S. " Samarang," ii, 177-8.

having devoted a large part of his private fortune to his preparations, in August, 1839, arrived off the coast of Borneo in his own schooner, the *Royalist*, 142 tons, with a crew of twenty tried men.

He arrived at a time when the country was in a worse state of distraction than was usual, even in those troubled days. The people of the province of Sarawak had been driven to open insurrection by the exactions of the Brunei proconsul, and Rajah Muda Hassim, the Sultan of Brunei's uncle, had been sent to quell the outbreak. Muda Hassim, although very different from the typical Brunei prince of that period, nevertheless lacked the resolution required to combat a determined rebellion. Chance brought the *Royalist* up the Sarawak River : and to James Brooke it must have seemed that fortune was favouring him by giving him an opportunity of translating his ideas into action so soon after his arrival in the Eastern Seas. He offered the Rajah the services of his little force. The offer was accepted, and it was not long before the refractory chiefs were reduced to submission. Muda Hassim, unwilling to see his ally depart as he had come, proposed that Brooke should take over the government of the province. After some hesitation he accepted. The grant was ultimately confirmed by the Sultan of Brunei, and in this way James Brooke became the first white Rajah of Sarawak.

Although Sultan Omar Ali Suffedin was ostensibly his friend, Brooke was to find that his task of bringing peace to those troubled hills and unquiet seas was made more difficult by this half-imbecile ruler of Brunei, who, if he did not himself openly encourage piracy, did nothing to stop it, and was not averse to making profit from the crews of shipwrecked vessels (of whatever nationality) that might seek refuge along his coasts or even at his court, as the following narrative will show.

On January 3, 1841, the *Sultana* (Captain Page), a

fine ship of 700 tons, with a cargo of cotton, sighted a vessel stranded on the Bombay Shoal off the island of Palawan. This turned out to be the French frigate *Magicienne*, which had run aground and been abandoned —apparently in haste, since Captain Page found in her provisions, arms, and water in abundance.

The weather was bad, with gales and thunderstorms, and the following day the *Sultana* was struck by lightning, which fired the cotton in her hold. Scarcely had the cutter and the longboat been hoisted out when the flames burst out fore and aft with such fury that it was found impossible to save anything but some money and jewels, and the officers and crew had to leave the ship with nothing but the barest necessaries.

As they pulled away from the blazing ship, Captain Page gave orders to bear up for the wreck of the *Magicienne*, now thirty miles away to the south-west, with the intention of taking from her sufficient supplies to last them until they reached Singapore. But on making the wreck they found so great a wash of sea on the lee side of the reef that it was impossible to board her.

There was nothing for it but to attempt to reach Singapore with such provisions as they had. Before continuing the voyage, however, they landed on the island of Balambangan, where they procured a few shell-fish and some brackish water. Here they proposed to spend the night, but, seeing some native boats on the neighbouring island of Banggi, Captain Page considered it discreet to light large fires after sunset and then to put to sea under the cover of darkness, the cutter taking the longboat in tow.

The monsoon buffeted them so hard that the tow-rope parted in the night and the cutter lost the longboat, eventually making Labuan, by which time those in her were reduced to an allowance of half a biscuit and a cup of water a day. They had now no hope of reaching Singapore without putting in somewhere for supplies, and it was decided to seek help in Brunei, and

accordingly they made their way up the river to the
Sultan's palace.

The arrival of these unfortunates—among them were
three women, the captain's wife and two other
passengers—caused no little surprise in Brunei.   So
far from receiving them with that kindness and hospitality which is the due of the shipwrecked, the Sultan
gave them nothing better than a miserable shack to live
in and obliged them to deliver all their property into his
hands, saying that otherwise they might be plundered by
his people.

Thus they remained, week after week, prisoners in
all but name.   Little by little everything they had in the
world was taken from them—even the baby-linen which
Mrs. Page had ready for the child she was expecting.
Not content with seizing their possessions, the Sultan
demanded that they should sign bonds for considerable
sums ; and, when Captain Page refused, their meagre
food supplies were stopped, until, unable to hold out any
longer, they signed the bonds and were forced to submit
to the stipulation that until the money should be paid
they themselves must be detained.

In this way, then, His Highness of Brunei outraged
the sacred rites of hospitality and, instead of acquainting
Rajah Brooke with the situation of his fellow country-
men, demanded ransom from them like a brigand chief.

In due course news of their plight reached Rajah
Brooke at Kuching, his headquarters in Sarawak; but
not until July.   Even then he had no more than native
reports to go upon, but at once he despatched the
Royalist to Brunei with the object of ascertaining what
truth there was in the story and of obtaining the release
of Captain Page and his people if they were indeed
there.

A few days after the *Royalist* had sailed the following
letter was put into his hands :

Island Sirhassan, off Tan Datu, [1]

July 10th, 1841.

A boat leaves this to-morrow for Sarawak; perhaps this may fall into the hands of Mr. Brooke, or some of my country-men, which, should I not succeed in getting to Singapore, I trust will lose no time in letting the authorities know, so that steps may be taken for the release of the remaining thirty-six British subjects now at Borneo; which I fear nothing but one of H.M. ships will effect. The pirates are cruising in great force between Sambas and this, and have taken thirteen Borneo prahus, or more; they know that there are Europeans in the prahu, and have expressed a wish to take them. Our situation is not very enviable. The bearer of this has just escaped from them. I have been living ashore with Abduramon, a native of Pulo Pinang, who knows Mr. Brooke, and has been very kind to me. Trusting penmanship and paper will be excused,

I remain, etc., etc.,

G. H. W. Gill.

On the reverse was the following attestation, which threw more light on the circumstances:

I, G. H. Willoughby Gill, late chief officer of the ship Sultana, of Bombay, do hereby certify that the said ship was totally destroyed by lightning, thirty miles N.E. of the Bombay shoal, coast of Palawan, on the 4th of Jan. 1841. Part of the crew, forty-one in number, succeeded in reaching Borneo [2] on the 16th of January, in a state of starvation and misery not to be described; the remainder are reported to have landed on the coast of Borneo per longboat:—[3] Captain John Page; G.H.W. Gill, chief officer; Alexander Young, second officer; one gunner; five sea-sunnies; two carpenters, twenty-three natives

---

[1] Tan; abbreviation for Tanjong = Cape. Sirhassan is one of the Natuna Group.

[2] *i.e.*, Brunei, or "Borneo Proper."

[3] The persons mentioned in the ensuing list are those who reached Brunei in the cutter.

*and lascars ; two Nakodas.   Passengers :—Mrs. Page (of a
daughter, 31st of March) ; Mr. and Miss de Souza ; Mrs.
Anderson, servant, one Ayah ; in all forty-one souls.   The
Sultan has permitted myself, Mr and Miss de Souza, with
three servants, to proceed to Singapore in one of his prahus,
where I hope to succeed in procuring the release of the
remainder of my companions from their present very un-
comfortable situation.   I dare not say more.   Mr. de Souza
and myself left on the 24th of May, and put in here dismasted
on the 20th of June ; since then have been detained by a fleet
of piratical prahus, which arrived on the 25th, and left 9th July.
Should nothing prevent, we expect to be ready by the 15th ;
but am very doubtful of ever getting to Singapore, as I fear
they are on the look-out for us outside.*

I have quoted Mr. Gill's letter in full because it
seems to me more vivid than any paraphrase I could
write.   A novelist is often concerned with securing
verisimilitude and with rendering drama with economy
of words.   But what novelist, writing what purported
to be a letter from a man in Gill's situation, would have
thought of 'apologising for " penmanship and paper,"
and could any page of purple writing be so eloquent
in implication as those words—" of a daughter,
31st March "—when the writer refers to Mrs. Page ?

Rajah Brooke received this letter late at night, after
he had retired to rest.   He knew, none better, what
the prisoners must have suffered.   The expression
" I dare say no more," raised his worst suspicions as to
what they must be suffering still, while there seemed
little chance of the party at Sirhassan escaping the pirates.
Sleep was forgotten.   He rose from his bed and instantly
made preparations for the despatch of a boat to the
island, with instructions to treat with the pirates if
need be.

Before his boat reached Sirhassan, however, Mr.
Gill and his party had sailed, apparently without molestation, but the *Royalist* returned from Brunei with bad

news.   The captain reported that he had not been able
to obtain the release of the prisoners.   His boat had
been detained at a fort near the entrance of the Brunei
River; he had been denied any communication with
Captain Page.   A letter from Captain Page had been
seized from the native crew, and even provisions and
water had been refused.   He had, however, been given
a letter for Rajah Brooke from the Sultan, who maintained that the crew of the *Sultana* had entered into an
agreement with him and that the merchant and the mate
(de Souza and Gill) had gone to Singapore to fulfil it.
In plain English, to obtain the ransom.   The letter
added that Captain Page preferred to remain at Brunei
owing to his wife's condition, and for this reason His
Highness did not grant their release; moreover (he
concluded naïvely) having entered into the agreement
mentioned he did not wish to be cheated.

This ingenuous epistle did not deceive Rajah Brooke
for a moment.   He knew the ways of the Brunei Court
too well.   Indeed, he had feared that the *Royalist's*
attempt to rescue the captives might prove abortive,
backed with no authority but his own, and, therefore,
on receipt of Mr. Gill's communication, he had demanded
help from Singapore on their behalf, with the result
that a week after the *Royalist's* return the East India
Company's steamer *Diana* (Captain Congleton) entered
the Sarawak River and sailed for Brunei two days later.

Captain Congleton showed at once that he was
prepared to stand no nonsense.   He ran the *Diana* up
river to the town and pointed her guns on the royal
palace.   The sight of the "fire-ship" caused the Sultan no
little perturbation, and he decided to forego his "agreement" and gave up the prisoners with as good a grace
as he could command.   The *Diana* then returned to
Kuching and delivered Captain Page and his people
to the care of the Rajah, but for whose energetic action
they would have languished even longer in captivity.
Even as it was they had been in the Sultan's hands,

suffering untold hardships and indescribable humiliation, for over eight months.

◇   ◇

Mr. Gill, one may suppose, in the absence of any evidence to the contrary, reached Singapore in safety. Those who had left the *Sultana* in the longboat, however, fared even worse than Captain Page and his party, and their fate would have remained obscure for ever had it not been that four years after the loss of the ship two of them were saved through the agency of Rajah Brooke.

These two seamen, or lascars, were Mahomed and Bastian, natives of Bombay. Some light is thrown on their adventures by the depositions they made before Mr. T. Church, Resident Councillor of Singapore, after their release from captivity. When the tow-rope broke and they parted company with the cutter, they must have been blown out to sea, for Bastian stated that they did not reach the Borneo coast for twelve days after leaving the ship. Unluckily for them they landed at Marudu, a notorious pirate stronghold, and were promptly seized by Serip Usman, the chief, who treated them exactly as he would have treated slaves captured on a raiding expedition.

After a time Usman handed over Bastian, Mahomed, and José, the *Sultana's* drummer, to one of his lieutenants. They remained with this chief for two years and were then sold to Pangeran Usop, who combined the activities of Prime Minister of Brunei and slave-dealer with no little profit to himself. Mahomed was sold for half a *pikul* of iron; Bastian did not hear the price paid for José or himself.

They remained with Pangeran Usop for the best part of another two years. Then José succeeded in getting aboard a ship bound for Singapore, with the result that Bastian and Mahomed were more closely guarded than ever.

At last the East India Company's steamer *Phlegethon* appeared off Brunei and anchored close to the town. On board was Rajah Brooke, who, having heard rumours that two British subjects were being held as slaves, had come to make inquiries. Bastian succeeded in getting off to the steamer and making his plight and Mahomed's known to Rajah Brooke. It was well he did so, for each time a ship had called at Brunei, Usop had done his utmost to prevent his slaves having any communication with Europeans, and the Rajah would have found it almost impossible to secure any evidence had he not had it from Bastian's own lips.

Once he was sure of his facts, however, it did not take him long to secure these men's release. They accompanied him to Singapore and were restored to their native land.

What became of the other eighteen men who had landed in Marudu Bay in 1841 there is no knowing, for Bastian stated, " I cannot say whether any more of the crew of the late ship *Sultana* are still in Borneo."

It seems probable that some of these people may have reached Brunei in the ordinary course of the slave traffic, and been released at the same time as Captain Page. At all events this is what happened to at least one man, a lascar named Haji Hassan, who had been one of the longboat's party and had reached Brunei ten days before the *Diana* arrived.

Like Bastian and his companions, Hassan had been made a slave, but, according to his own deposition, had been treated very well. After spending six months in Marudu Bay he was sold to Brunei, and while on his way thither he had a curious experience, which is best related in his own words :

" About three days after leaving Maloodoo for Brunei we touched at a place called Amboon,[1] for water, where there is a good harbour. There were about forty

---

houses on the beach. I had previously heard when on board the boat, from the crew, that there was an European female residing at Amboon. The house was pointed out to me, which induced me to enter. It was raised on poles about six feet high, and situated in the centre of the village. On entering, I saw, seated on a mat, an European female. She was dressed in the Malay costume, there was a Malay woman seated near her, and five or six children were playing about the house. I remained about a minute; the European female did not attempt to leave or did she say a word; she looked at me for a moment, and then hung down her head. I am most positive she was an European female, and about forty years of age, fair, with blue eyes and light hair. We remained at Amboon two days, but I did not see the female save on the occasion just stated. I heard that about fifteen years since the female alluded to had been taken to Amboon, but whether a vessel had been wrecked or captured about the time I did not learn."

At the time no serious attention by the authorities seems to have been paid to this statement, but it had a curious sequel. Haji Hassan's deposition was published in the *Singapore Free Press* of September 30, 1841. It was copied by a Bombay paper and was read in London by a Mr. Cooper, whose sister, Mrs. Edward Presgrave, had been the wife of a former Resident Councillor at Singapore. Mr. Presgrave had died at Penang in 1830 and his widow had taken her passage to England in the *Guilford*, which, after sailing from Singapore, had never been heard of again. Hassan's description of the " European female " he had seen at Ambong exactly corresponded with that of Mrs. Presgrave, and it seemed to Mr. Cooper not impossible that this lady might turn out to be his unfortunate sister. He therefore wrote to her brother-in-law, Mr. R. Presgrave, who was then in Calcutta. Mr. Presgrave, in his turn, approached the Government of

India, and finally the facts were put before the Governor of the Straits Settlements.

For over two years no action appears to have been taken, but Mr. Bonham, the Governor of the Straits, assured Mr. Presgrave that the woman at Ambong could not have been his sister-in-law " consequent on the prevailing winds at the season of the year at which the *Guilford* left Singapore." This assertion was an easy way out of the matter, but it left entirely out of consideration the possibility of Mrs. Presgrave having been taken to Ambong by pirates. This possibility must have struck Colonel Butterworth, who succeeded Mr. Bonham as Governor, and his interest was strengthened by a communication from Rajah Brooke, who had had distinct and more recent information as to the presence of a European woman at Ambong.

The Governor approached Captain Sir Edward Belcher of H.M.S. *Samarang*, which was then in Eastern waters, and Sir Edward volunteered to make the necessary inquiries, intending at the same time to make a searching inquiry into the practices of the pirates on the northern coast of Borneo and into the slave-dealing that was then rife.

The steamer *Phlegethon* was detailed to accompany the *Samarang*, and the Governor sent the following pacific letter by Sir Edward to the redoubtable Serip Usman :

(TRANSLATION.)

From THE HONOURABLE COLONEL BUTTERWORTH, *Companion of the Most Honourable the Military Order of the Bath, Governor of Prince of Wales Island, Singapore and Malacca,* To THE RAJAH OF MALOODOO, *Coast of Borneo. Dated Singapore,* 4th *October,* 1844.

(After Compliments.)

It having been brought to my notice that an European female is residing in my friend's country, I have sent my steamer accompanied by a man-of-war under Captain Sir Edward Belcher, C.B., in the full assurance, that should such a person be at Amboon or Maloodoo, my friend will do me the favour to allow her to come to Singapore on my vessel.

Should any trading boats belonging to my friend wish to come to Singapore, I shall be happy to afford them every assistance in my power.

J. W. BUTTERWORTH,
Governor of Prince of Wales Island, Singapore and Malacca.

The *Samarang* left Singapore on October 6, 1844, and after visiting Kuching and Brunei reached Ambong Bay on November 4. On board was Rajah Muda Hassim, Rajah Brooke's friend, whose presence was considered advisable if the woman were to be released without friction.

The coast of Borneo is broken by many a lovely bay, but of them all none is lovelier than Ambong, its water blue as a cornflower save where the coral shows, a crescent of low hills breaking the level of the plain beyond, the hilly forests of Marudu in the distance, the jagged peaks of mighty Kinabalu, veined white with waterfalls, towering behind. Since the visit of the *Samarang* Ambong has scarcely changed. It is still free from the thumb-marks of civilisation. Year after year it lies lazy in the sunshine, like a resting bather whose limbs are spread to catch the sun : as fitting a place as any in the world for the end of a romantic quest, and it grieves me now that I may not stage such a scene on those shores that once, when I was District Officer of Tempasuk, were part of my domain. I can see it all so clearly : the captain of the British man-o'-war waiting there upon the sandy beach in the blazing sunshine, a guard of marines behind him, the ship at anchor in the bay. From the hills a little procession wends its way towards him in single file ; in the van are a dozen warriors in coats of mail, spears in their hands; a drummer follows them, and then comes Rajah Muda Hassim in a headcloth of many colours, a jacket of emerald green and tight red trousers, a golden hilted *kris* at his side. Behind him marches an attendant carrying on high a yellow umbrella, the insignia of his royal rank. And then, sheltered by another umbrella, comes that English lady whose blue eyes long years of captivity have failed to dim. Sir Edward advances towards her. He salutes and then holds out his hand in greeting. She takes it in silence, for her rapture at the prospect of being restored to her friends and her native land at last is so overwhelming that she is scarce able to frame her thanks in words. . . .

Yes, it would have made a good story. And I feel it might have been like that—had the lady been there. But she was not, and since this is a truthful chronicle I must set down Sir Edward's rather bald report :

" A very slight examination of the place, and of the neighbouring people, the Bajows and Dusons, satisfied me that we should not find the female, of whom we were in quest, at Ambong. In the first place, it did not contain a single house in which she could have been concealed from the view or knowledge of the neighbouring people ; in the second, there were not four of these huts habitable, or inhabited, and they belonged to parties who resort here solely for the purpose of making salt ; finally, had such a person been in the possession of any of the higher powers, they were, evidently, too eager to find cause of complaint against those whom they term their oppressors, and would instantly have given the desired information. The place, moreover, was too insignificant to contain such a rarity as an European woman without their knowledge, and they informed us that the Sultan of Tampassook alone could possess her, if she existed at all."

So to Tempasuk the *Samarang* went, and anchored off the mouth of the river. The Sultan appeared and entered the captain's barge. It was intimated to him that if he could produce the object of the *Samarang's*

quest as much as $200 would be paid for her—nearly
ten times the value of the ordinary female slave.   The
Sultan, however, declared there was not a word of truth
in the story.   Had a white woman been held in
captivity at any point on the coast between Brunei and
Marudu, he must have known of it, and he protested
that not even so much as a rumour of such a thing had
ever come to his ears.

Sir Edward accepted his word.   In his opinion,
Haji Hassan had probably mistaken a Malay woman for a
European.   He suggested that possibly she had been one
of the wives of Serip Usman, who had married into the
Sulu royal family, the ladies of which were known to be
remarkably fair.   " It would require no stretch of
imagination on the part of a Lascar," thought Sir
Edward, " to term one of that race European."

So there the quest ended.   Personally, I find it
difficult to believe that Haji Hassan's statement was so
entirely without foundation as Sir Edward came to
believe.   Hassan knew what a European woman looked
like, and the royal ladies of Sulu, though light of skin,
have the black hair and brown eyes of their race.
Hassan's story was circumstantial ; he had no con-
ceivable reason for inventing it, and there is the
corroborating information that was furnished to Rajah
Brooke.

The *Samarang* reached Ambong over three years
after Hassan believed he had seen the woman.   In that
time much might have happened to her.   Sir Edward
did not present the Governor's letter to the Prince of
Marudu, and it is not impossible that he might have
found her in that pirate stronghold, perhaps in the
harem of Serip Usman himself.

For these reasons I cannot help feeling that some
forgotten tragedy may have lain behind Haji Hassan's
story after all.   Whether I am right or wrong no one
now will ever know.   And perhaps, had Sir Edward
ever found that lady, the end of the quest might have

been very different from the one I have so romantically imagined. She might have come to meet him accompanied by a growing family. She might have told him roundly that she had never asked the British Navy to come and look for her; that she did very well where she was and that she preferred to remain the wife of a Malayan prince rather than end her days in an English country town. For women are curious creatures and before now have said stranger things than that.

CHAPTER VII

THE PIRATES OF SARAWAK

The Saribas and Sekrang—Their war-boats—Rajah Brooke's meeting with their fleet—His regulations to enforce law and order—The Saribas remain defiant—Captain Keppel visits Sarawak in H.M.S. *Dido* and is asked to proceed against them —Start of the expedition—Attack on the pirate forts at Padeh—Destruction of Paku and Rembas—The submission of the chiefs.

WHEN James Brooke accepted the rule of Sarawak, one of his objects was, as we have seen, to free the Borneo seas from the scourge of the pirates. But before he could turn his attention to the activities of the Illanuns and Balanini, and those independent settlements on the northern coast of Borneo, he had first to cope with two formidable sets of pirates on the borders of his own State.

These were the Saribas, who inhabited the country watered by the river of the same name, and the Sekrang (or Sakarran, as they are called in the old books), who dwelt on the left-hand branch of the Batang Lupar River and the tributaries of the Rejang.

The piratical strongholds these people, formed on the river banks, were composed of two distinct groups —the Malay settlers, who were Mohammedans, and the pagan aborigines, generally known as Sea-Dayaks. It is supposed that these Malays came from Johore some time towards the end of the seventeenth century. Sprung from a pirate stock, they carried their roving habits with them to the land of their adoption, and although their cruises were not so extensive as those of the Illanuns or Balanini, they nevertheless became a

menace to the fishing villages along the coast. Their
neighbours the Dayaks they did not plunder, partly
because these folk had little worth taking, but even more
because they were themselves a powerful and warlike
tribe, having been headhunters from time immemorial.

Instead of plundering them, therefore, the Malays
made alliance with the Dayaks, who were far more
numerous than themselves, and in course of time
gradually trained them to piracy. The Dayaks began
their apprenticeship as rowers in the Malay prahus,

DAYAK WAR-BOAT.

being rewarded for their services with the heads of the
slain, and receiving also such captives as were useless
to the Malays as slaves. Before long, however, the
Dayaks became themselves expert seamen, and learnt
to build a class of boat (*bangkong*) peculiarly suited to
their stealthy and rapid movements, for their method
was surprise rather than open attack.

These craft drew but a few inches of water and were
both lighter and faster than the Malay prahus, which
were built on lines almost identical with the Illanun
cruising vessels. They were over 100 feet long, by ten
in beam, with overhanging stem and stern, and they
could turn at full speed in their own length. They did

not mount big guns like the Malays, but sometimes had a few brass swivels. They were propelled by anything from sixty to eighty paddlers, and besides the Dayak fighting-men would usually carry a few Malays armed with muskets. They also had the advantage of being easily taken to pieces, for the planks were not fastened together with nails but laced together with rattan and caulked with macerated tree-bark, which swelled when wet. So that if the crew were hard pressed they could make for the shore, unlace their boat and carry the parts with them into the jungle, where they would hide until their pursuers had given up the chase and then issue forth and assemble their boat again.

In these vessels, equally serviceable in pursuit or in flight, the Dayaks could creep up without warning upon their unsuspecting victims in the dead of night and overwhelm them with a shower of spears before they could recover from their surprise. These *bangkong* would cruise in company with the Malays, forming a fleet that might be composed of more than 100 vessels, which would sweep the seas and devastate the shores of Borneo over a distance of 800 miles.

The Dayaks soon grew to learn their own power; and, accordingly, both in their internal government and on their piratical expeditions, their chiefs in time attained equal authority with the Malay chiefs. The plunder also, whether of vessel or village, was equally divided between Dayak and Malay, but the Dayaks never willingly spared their male captives, even for purposes of slavery, owing to their innate passion for collecting human heads. These pirates made the rivers as unsafe as the sea. In their neighbourhood no trading boat dared to go up or down stream alone. Mrs. McDougal, the wife of the first Bishop of Sarawak, in one of her letters to her son, cites the case of a boat which was found with nothing but three fingers in it: three fingers, and a bloody mark on the gunwale.

On their return from an expedition these allies

THE PIRATES OF SARAWAK

95

would separate to their own strongholds, the Dayaks occupying the upper reaches of the rivers (whence they could sally out to attack their hereditary foes in the hills during the intervals between their sea cruises), while the Malays lived in strongly fortified positions nearer the coast. The Dayaks relied on these forts to protect them from any force that might come against them up-stream, while they themselves formed a barrier between the Malays and any raiding party from the hills.

Soon after Mr. Brooke's arrival in Sarawak, and before he had formally taken over its government from Rajah Muda Hassim, a fleet of over 100 mixed Sekrang and Saribas vessels, with a force of something like 4,000 men, arrived off Kuching and asked permission of Rajah Muda Hassim to ascend the river and attack a tribe of their enemies who lived up-stream. Mr. Brooke described them as " a remarkably fine body of people, handsome, intelligent, powerful, well-made, beautifully-limbed, and clear-skinned." In their ears they wore a number of brass rings and had grotesque caps of various-coloured cloths (particularly red), some square, some peaked, and others " like a cocked hat worn athworth-ships" (to use Mr. Brooke's phrase). These head-dresses were ornamented with tufts of human hair from the heads of enemies they had slain, shreds of cloth, and sometimes feathers. Their own hair was cut close to follow the shape of the cap, so that when the cap was removed the owner was seen to be " bare of hair about the forehead and posterior part of the skull, that over the ears cut into points, and the rest of the hair showing a good crop of black bristles."

The commanders of this party were called by their own people Bulan (Moon) and Matahari (Sun), and Mr. Brooke found both them and their followers reserved and quiet in their manners. They stole nothing and traded for rice, beeswax and cotton.

Rajah Muda Hassim assured Mr. Brooke that he

would not allow this force to pass Kuching; but as Mr. Brooke was finishing a late dinner one evening he heard the whole pirate fleet sweeping up the river. He immediately sent to find out whether Muda Hassim had granted permission for this move. Muda Hassim protested that he had been ill and that his ministers were responsible, and, on Mr. Brooke's insisting, he sent a party to recall them. The pirates returned with a bad grace, but finally left the river without actually making any hostile demonstration.

"The poor Dayaks in the interior," said Mr. Brooke in his Journal, "as well as the Chinese, were in the greatest state of alarm, and thence I gained some credit amongst them for my interference on their behalf. The very idea of letting 2,500 wild devils loose in the interior of the country is horrible; for though they have one professed object, they combine many others with it, and being enemies of all the mountain tribes they cut them up as much as they can. What object, it may be inquired, can the Malays have in destroying their own country and people so wantonly? I must endeavour to explain to the best of my belief and knowledge. The Malays take part in these excursions, and thirty men joined the Sakarrans on the present occasion, and consequently they share in the plunder, and share largely. Probably Muda Hassim would have got twenty shares (women and children); and these twenty being reckoned at the low rate of twenty reals each, makes four hundred reals, besides other plunder, amounting to one or two hundred reals more.

Inferior Pangerans would, of course, partake likewise. Muda Hassim *must* have given his consent, must have been a participator in this atrocity, nobody being desperate enough to do such a thing without his orders." [1]

❖   ❖

---

[1] Keppel's *Expedition to Borneo of H.M.S. "Dido."* i, 228-9.

KUCHING IN 1844.

[From Borneo and the Indian Archipelago.

When Mr. Brooke finally took over the reins of government from Rajah Muda Hassim, his first act was to draw up certain regulations to enforce law and order in his new kingdom. To-day, when Sarawak is a thriving State, these first laws are an historical exhibit and a significant example of the first White Rajah's diplomacy, which sought to combine mildness and patience with justice and firmness, and so tend the growth of that unhappy land which for generations had been tormented by headhunting, slavery and piracy. These laws were but eight in number. They were printed in Malay, and promulgated on January 10, 1843, and were as follows :

James Brooke, esquire, governor (rajah) of the country of Sarawak, makes known to all men the following regulations :

1st. That murder, robbery, and other heinous crimes will be punished according to the ondong-ondong (*i.e.*, the written law of Borneo) ; and no person committing such offences will escape, if, after fair inquiry, he be proved guilty.

2d. In order to ensure the good of the country, all men, whether Malays, Chinese, or Dayaks, are permitted to trade or labour according to their pleasure, and to enjoy their gains.

3d. All roads will be open, that the inhabitants at large may seek profit both by sea and by land, and all boats coming from others are free to enter the river and depart, without let or hindrance.

4th. Trade, in all its branches, will be free, with the exception of antimony-ore, which the governor holds in his own hands, but which no person is forced to work, and which will be paid for at a proper price when obtained. The people are encouraged to trade and labour, and to enjoy the profits which are to be made by fair and honest dealing.

5th. It is ordered, that no person going amongst the Dyaks shall disturb them, or gain their goods under false pretences. It must be clearly explained to the different Dyak tribes, that the revenue will be collected by the three Datus, bearing the seal of the governor ; and (except this yearly demand from the government) they are to give nothing to any other person ; nor are they obliged to sell their goods except they please, and at their own prices.

6th. The governor will shortly inquire into the revenue, and fix it at a proper rate ; so that everyone may know certainly how much he has to contribute yearly to support the government.

G

7th.   It will be necessary, likewise, to settle the weights, measures, and money current in the country, and to introduce *doits*,[1]
that the poor may purchase food cheaply.

8th.   The governor issues these commands, and will enforce
obedience to them ; and whilst he gives all protection and assistance
to the persons who act rightly, he will not fail to punish those who
seek to disturb the public peace or commit crimes ; and he warns
all such persons to seek their safety, and find some other country
where they may be permitted to break the laws of God and man.

It was one thing to promulgate such regulations as
these, but another to enforce them among such wild
elements as the Saribas and the Sekrang, who continued
to pursue their piratical pursuits both on sea and up
their rivers.   Accounts were continually reaching Rajah
Brooke of fishing boats being taken or villages surprised.
Sometimes the pirates would wait until they knew the
men of the village were away, working in the rice clearings.
They would then creep up the river and fall suddenly
upon the defenceless women and children, taking the
heads of some (the old ones), making slaves of the rest,
and looting the houses.   Sometimes, having taken a
village, they would dress themselves in the clothes of the
slain and go to another settlement, where they would call
out to the women, "The Saribas are coming, open your
doors and we will defend you and your houses"; and
only too often the poor wretches fell into the trap.
If they attacked a village while the men were at home
they did so always at night.   These villages consisted
of one, or perhaps two communal houses, often three
hundred feet in length, raised on posts several feet above
the ground.   The pirates would pull stealthily up the
river and, landing under the cover of their shields, would
creep under the long house.   They would then set fire
to some dry wood and to a quantity of chillies brought
with them for the purpose, thus causing a suffocating
smoke which drove the inmates into a panic, and during

---

[1] Small money.

the confusion they would cut down the posts of the house, and, when it collapsed, would fall upon their prey.

◇ ◇

In May, 1843, Captain the Hon. Henry Keppel, of H.M.S. *Dido*, brought Rajah Brooke back to Sarawak from Singapore, where he had been on a visit. There could be no better illustration of the lack of knowledge of the Borneo coast, even amongst professional sailors, than the fact that before reaching it Captain Keppel sailed eighty miles inland, according to the latest Admiralty charts.

The *Dido* was the first square-rigged ship to enter the Sarawak River, and it must have been a surprise indeed for the inhabitants of Kuching to see her anchored in the centre of their town, her mast-heads towering above the highest trees, to watch 150 sailors running aloft to furl the sails, and to hear the music of the band and the reports of her thirty-two pounders as she fired a salute to Rajah Muda Hassim, who was still nominally ruler of Sarawak.

Captain Keppel paid a ceremonial visit to Muda Hassim on his arrival, and his account of the audience is worth quoting in his own words :

"The band, and the marines, as a guard, having landed, we (the officers) all assembled at Mr. Brooke's house, where, having made ourselves as formidable as we could, with swords and cocked hats, we marched in procession to the royal residence, his majesty having sent one of his brothers, who led me by the hand into his presence. The palace was a long, low shed built on piles, to which we ascended by a ladder. The audience-chamber was hung with red and yellow silk curtains, and round the back and one side of the platform occupied by the Rajah were ranged his ministers, warriors, and men-at-arms, bearing spears, swords, shields, and other warlike weapons. Opposite to them were drawn up our royal marines ; the contrast between the two body-guards

being very amusing.   Muda Hassim is a wretched-looking
little man.   Still there was a courteous and gentle manner
about him that prepossessed us in his favour and made
us feel that we were before an individual who had been
accustomed to command.   We took our seats in a semi-
circle, on chairs provided for the occasion, and smoked
cigars and drank tea.   His majesty chewed his sirih-
leaf and betel-nut, seated with one leg crossed under him,
and playing with his toes.   Very little is ever said during
these audiences, so we sat staring at one another for
half an hour with mutual astonishment; and, after the
usual compliments of wishing our friendship might last
as long as the moon, and my having offered him the *Dido*
and everything else that did not belong to me in exchange
for his house, we took our leave."

Although the rajah had seldom been known to go
beyond his own threshold, he returned Captain Keppel's
visit in state.

" For this ceremony," says Captain Keppel, " all the
boats, guns, tom-toms, flags, and population were put in
requisition; and the procession to the ship was a very
gorgeous and amusing spectacle.   We received him on
board with a royal salute.   He brought in his train a
whole tribe of natural brothers.   His guards and followers
were strange enough, and far too numerous to be admitted on the *Dido's* deck, so that as soon as a sufficient
number had scrambled on board the sentry had orders
to prevent any more from crowding in; but whether in
so doing the most important personages of the realm
were kept out we did not ascertain.   One fellow succeeded in obtaining a footing with a large yellow silk
canopy, a corner of which having run into the eye of one
of the midshipmen the bearer missed his footing, and
down came the whole concern—as I was informed, by
accident!   The party assembled in my cabin; and the
remarks were few, nor did they manifest great astonishment at anything.   In fact, a Malay never allows himself
to be taken by surprise.   I believe, however, the Rajah

did not think much of my veracity when I informed him that this was not the largest ship belonging to Her Britannic Majesty, and that she had several mounting upwards of 100 guns ; though he admitted that he had seen a grander sight than any of his ancestors.   There was much distress depicted in the royal countenance during his visit, which I afterwards ascertained was owing to his having been informed that he must not spit in my cabin.   On leaving the ship, whether the cherry-brandy he had taken made him forget the directions he had received, I do not know, but he squirted a mouthful of red betel-nut juice over the white deck, and then had the temerity to hold out his hand to the first lieutenant, who hastily applied to him the style (not royal) of ‘ a dirty beast,’ which not understanding, he smiled graciously, taking it as some compliment peculiar to the English.” [1]

❖   ❖

Rajah Brooke had sent repeated warnings to the Saribas and Sekrang in vain, and their depredations had become so serious that Muda Hassim addressed the following letter to Captain Keppel :

This friendly epistle, having its source in a pure mind, comes from Rajah Muda Hassim, next in succession to the royal throne of the Kingdom of Borneo, and who now holds his court at the trading city of Sarawak, to our friend Henry Keppel, head captain of the war-frigate belonging to Her Britannic Majesty, renowned throughout all countries—who is valiant and discreet, and endowed with a mild and gentle nature :

This is to inform our friend that there are certain great pirates of the people of Sarebus and Sakarran, in our neigh-bourhood, seizing goods and murdering people on the high seas. They have more than three hundred war-prahus, and extend

---

[1] *Expedition to Borneo of H.M.S. “ Dido,” ii, 12-15.*

their ravages even to Banjarmassim ; they are not subject to the Government of Bruni (Borneo) ; they take much plunder from vessels trading between Singapore and the good people of our country.

It would be a great service if our friend would adopt measures to put an end to these piratical outrages.

We can present nothing better to our friend than a kris, such as it is.

20th day of Rabial Akhir, 1257.

To this letter Captain Keppel sent the following reply :

Captain Keppel begs to acknowledge the receipt of the Rajah Muda Hassim's letter, representing that the Dyaks of Sarebus and Sakarran are the pirates who infest the coast of Borneo, and do material damage to the trade of Singapore.

Captain Keppel will take speedy measures to suppress these and all other pirates, and feels confident that Her Britannic Majesty will be glad to learn that the Rajah Muda Hassim is ready to co-operate in so laudable an undertaking.

Having conferred with Rajah Brooke, Captain Keppel determined to attack the pirates in their own strongholds, beginning with the Saribas, who were said to be the most strongly-fortified. The Rajah accepted Captain Keppel's invitation to accompany the expedition and agreed to supply a force of 300 natives.

By July 4 the preparations were complete and the *Dido* dropped down to the mouth of the Sarawak River.

On the morning of the 8th, the force entered the Saribas River. It consisted of the *Dido's* pinnace, gig and two cutters, and the *Jolly Bachelor*, a large native-built boat belonging to Rajah Brooke, which mounted a brass six-pounder ; also a large tope of 35 tons which carried the commissariat and ammunition. With these boats were eighty officers and men from the *Dido*. Besides this there were the boats of the Sarawak chiefs, and a

Dayak contingent of about 400 men. Of these there
were few who had not suffered at the hands of the

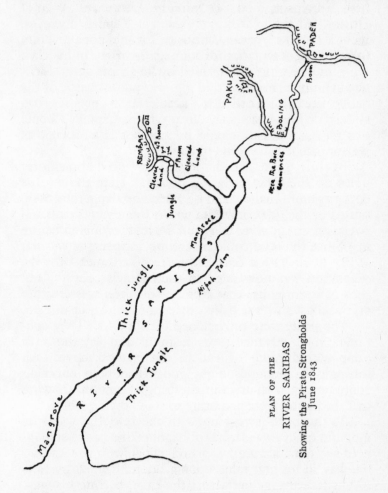

PLAN OF THE
RIVER SARIBAS

Showing the Pirate Strongholds
June 1843

Saribas, and had either their houses burnt, their relatives
murdered, or their wives and children sold into slavery,
while the novelty of the expedition was quite enough to
excite the British sailors, who had been cooped up for
weeks in a man-of-war.

The command of a man-of-war's boats, when despatched on a mission of this kind, is the perquisite of the
first lieutenant, and accordingly Lieutenant Wilmot
Horton led the expedition. Captain Keppel, however,
records that his " natural curiosity " would not allow him
to resist the temptation of joining the party in his own
gig ; and he was accompanied by Rajah Brooke. Lieutenant Gunnel, in the second gig, was put in charge of the
native fleet, with orders to keep it from pressing too
closely on the boats—an office which, Captain Keppel
observed in his narrative, " became less troublesome as
we approached the scene of danger."

By July 9 the expedition had advanced about forty
miles up the river as far as Boling. Here the Saribas
becomes more shallow and is subject to a dangerous bore,
caused by the tide coming in with a tremendous rush and
sweeping up the river in a great wave, carrying all before
it. Since the tope could ascend no further, she was left
at this point with a covering force of 150 men—for the
expedition was now fairly in the enemy's country, and
there were rumours that a pirate squadron was cruising
on the coast and was daily expected to return up-stream.

The boats were provisioned for six days. They continued their advance next morning and on the 11th
came within reach of Padeh, the first objective. All
through the previous night gongs had been booming
continuously, with intermittent firing of cannon, showing
that the pirates were preparing to stand their ground.

As the boats swept up with the tide, the war-cries
rang out on every side, but no sight of the pirate stronghold was obtained until Captain Keppel, who was leading
the way in his gig, came upon a boom, formed by tree-
trunks lashed together across the river, barring his way.
Seeing a small opening in this barrier, Captain Keppel
put the gig's head straight at it and sent her through.
Before him on the river bank was the stronghold of
Padeh, consisting of three formidable-looking forts,
which immediately opened fire. Luckily the guns were

ranged on the boom, through which the gig had passed so swiftly as to take the pirates by surprise, with the result that the shot flew harmlessly overhead.

But now Captain Keppel found himself cut off from his companions and being carried by the tide towards the enemy position. The pirates came charging down the bank to seize the gig, but Captain Keppel succeeded in getting her round and, while Rajah Brooke steered her, Captain Keppel and the coxswain kept up a fire on the embrasures in the forts to prevent the gun teams from reloading before the next boat, which was the pinnace, could get into action with her twelve-pound carronade.

In trying to negotiate the boom, however, she fell athwart, and while lying broadside on to the fire from the forts had three men wounded. But it was not long before the rattan lashings which secured the trees were hacked through and the *Dido's* first cutter joined the gig. The other boats followed and the pinnace opened a destructive fire on the forts.

The first to land were the crew of the *Dido's* cutter. Led by their commander, Mr. D'Aeth, they charged up the hill on which the nearest fort stood. This method of attack—the charge in the face of a direct fire—was completely foreign to the pirates' ideas of warfare. As they beheld that cheering line of British seamen dashing towards them with bayonets fixed, panic overwhelmed them, they abandoned their guns and fled into the jungle behind the position, and Captain Keppel records that " it was with the greatest difficulty that our leading men could get even a snap-shot at the rascals before they went."

The remaining positions were soon carried in the same manner. The guns were taken, the forts looted by the Dayaks and then burnt to the ground. It had been an easy victory, for the pirate force was reckoned at 6,000 Dayaks and 500 Malays.

❖   ❖

On the following morning, July 12, while Captain
Keppel and his officers were at breakfast in the *Jolly
Bachelor* (which was now the hospital), a clamour of
voices and beating of many drums was heard. The
British officers regarded one another in a wild surmise.
Could this be the pirate fleet of which they had heard
rumours, returning to attack them in the rear? A
moment later, as though in answer to the question, a
large prahu crowded with warriors came sweeping
round the bend of the river. As the startled officers
watched her, half a dozen others hove in sight. At once
there was a call to arms. Knives and forks clattered
down on plates. Muskets were seized. Orders shouted.
The *Jolly Bachelor's* six-pounder, loaded with grape and
cannister, was primed. Captain Keppel gave the order
to fire, but at that moment the priming blew off. Before
it could be replaced, the interpreter was shouting that
the newcomers were friends. It soon appeared that
they were Dayaks, 800 strong, from the river Linga,
under their leader, a half-bred Arab named Japar, come,
as they said, to give their assistance in the destruction of
the Saribas, with whom they had been at war for years.
They were in full war-dress, with short padded jackets,
and each carried a shield and a handful of spears.

Had it not been for that gust of wind nothing could
have saved the foremost prahu, and to avoid further
confusion each man was provided with a strip of white
calico, to be worn in his head-dress as a distinguishing
mark, and they were told to call out the watchword
Datu should they be challenged.

At Padeh the river divides into two branches. Both
were reconnoitred, and it was found that the left was
obstructed by trees. Since this seemed to have been the
line of the enemy's retreat the boats advanced up it in
the afternoon, accompanied by a native party of forty men

Lieutenant Horton took charge, accompanied by Rajah
Brooke.

Captain Keppel, who had remained at Padeh with the
main force, was just sitting down in the *Jolly Bachelor* to
a supper of ham and poached eggs when he heard the
sound of the pinnace's carronade. This was responded
to by a war-yell which seemed to come from every side.
His first thought was that his people were surrounded.
It was impossible to move so large a boat as the *Jolly
Bachelor* up the river, nor could the wounded be left
without protection. So, without a moment's delay, he
jumped into his gig, taking with him his bugler, John
Eager, and pulled up the river in the direction of the
firing.

After a two hours' pull through the rain and darkness
a sudden discharge of musketry showed him that he was
approaching the scene of action, but he still feared that
the boat party were surrounded and that he would have
to fight his way to reach them. His object in bringing
the bugler was to make it appear that strong reinforce-
ments were at hand, and now he ordered the boy to strike
up " Rory O'More," which was immediately responded
to by three rousing cheers. Then followed an ominous
silence—to Captain Keppel more dreadful than any war-
cry, for he felt convinced that the pirates must be between
him and his own men.

Against the sky, where the jungle had been cleared,
he could see the silhouettes of human figures. He hailed
them but received no answer. He hailed again. Still
there was no sound but the drum of the rain and the
gushing of the stream over its pebbly bed. At last he
fired, thinking the figures whose outline he could dimly
see must be those of the enemy. At once Lieutenant
Horton's voice replied: " We are here, sir ! " The
river had drowned Keppel's hail, and the boat party had
not hailed him, fearing to give away their position
to the enemy, who were in the jungle all round them.

Captain Keppel found they had taken up a strong

position on the right bank, where the current had made a little bay just big enough to hold the boats.   From the river bank the ground rose sheer to a cleared hill, and on the summit of this an officer and seven marines had been posted as a rearguard, with orders not to fire unless a target could be distinctly seen.

This position the party continued to hold throughout the night, beating back repeated attacks from the pirates, sustaining three casualties and killing many of the enemy.   One marine was dangerously wounded by a musket shot.   It was essential that he should be got back to medical attention, so a young officer named Jenkins gallantly volunteered for this service, and taking four men with the second gig got him down-stream to the *Jolly Bachelor*, and was back again before daylight.

Dawn found the pirates assembling in force up-stream.   When the tide began to rise, the boat party made preparations for a further advance.   This was more than the enemy had bargained for, since the boats were already close to the place to which the pirates had removed their families and such valuables as they had had time to collect before their flight.

Before a move could be made, a flag of truce was seen approaching.   Captain Keppel sent an unarmed Malay to meet it.   After some talk the party with the flag approached the boats.   They delivered their message that the Saribas would abide by any terms Captain Keppel might dictate.   Captain Keppel promised that hostilities should cease for two hours, and invited the chiefs to a conference at one o'clock.

At the appointed time the chiefs appeared.   They were clad in war-dress, but looked haggard and dejected. Rajah Brooke officiated as spokesman, explaining that the invasion of their country and the destruction of their forts and town were not for the purposes of pillage or gain, but as a punishment for their repeated and aggravated acts of piracy, that they had been fully warned for two years before that the British nation would no longer allow the native trade to be cut off and plundered, and the crews of the vessels cruelly put to death as they had been.

The chiefs were humble and submissive. They admitted that their lives were forfeited, and if death was to be their portion they were prepared, although, they explained, they were equally willing to live. They promised to refrain forever from piracy, and offered hostages for their good behaviour.

Rajah Brooke then explained how much more advantageous trade would be than piracy, and invited them to a further conference at Sarawak, where they might witness all the blessings resulting from the line of conduct he had advised them to follow. If, on the other hand, he heard of a single act of piracy being committed by them, he promised that their country would be again invaded and occupied, and their enemies, the whole tribe of Linga Dayaks, let loose upon them until they were rooted out and utterly destroyed.

The boats then returned to the still smoking ruins of Padeh, where the force was collected and, dropping downstream, reached Boling by midnight. But their work was not yet done. There still remained two other Saribas strongholds, Paku and Rembas, both of which were built on tributaries of the main river.

Accordingly, at daylight on July 14, the boats were provisioned for four days and started with the flood tide for Paku. It was almost dusk by the time they arrived before the forts, which were surrounded by two newly-built stockades. As at Padeh, the positions had been selected with sound judgment, but the attacking force surprised the defenders, who fled panic-stricken into the jungle on the first discharge without themselves having fired a shot. This was all to the good, for correction, not slaughter, was Brooke's object.

Once the forts were gained it was found that most of the valuables had been removed, but the place was alive with goats and fowls, and the catching of these afforded

the sailors great sport.   Some of the Dayak friendlies
succeeded in taking the heads of a few pirates.   Captain
Keppel mentions having seen one headless body into
which each passing Dayak " had thought proper to stick
a spear, so that it had all the appearance of a huge
porcupine."

The forts and the settlement were burnt that evening,
and soon after daylight on the following morning the
chiefs came in with a flag of truce, and during the conference that ensued proved as submissive as the people
of Padeh, offering their own lives, but begging that those
of their wives and children might be spared, for they
had never previously fought an enemy who showed
mercy to non-combatants, except to enslave them.   They
promised to abandon their piratical habits, and agreed to
attend the conference at Kuching, protesting that they
would be glad to have lasting peace.

The next point of attack was Rembas.   Although
there was a short overland route from Paku, the distance
by water was sixty miles, but the strong tides were of
great assistance to the boats, which brought up some
distance below the town on the evening of the 16th.
There was no moon, so that Captain Keppel deemed a
night attack inadvisable, particularly since he expected
the pirates would make a stronger stand, it being known
that Rembas contained a larger proportion of Malays
than either Padeh or Paku.

The expedition advanced early on the morning of
July 17, and soon encountered a succession of formidable
barriers, more troublesome to cut through than the
Padeh boom had been.   A mile below the town a force
of 700 of the Linga Dayaks were landed on the left bank,
with orders to creep through the jungle to the rear of the
forts and deliver their assault on hearing the first shot
fired from the boats.

Meanwhile the boats continued their work of nego-
tiating the booms, of which there were four. The last
was placed within point-blank range of the forts, but
Captain Keppel managed to haul his light gig over,
keeping close to the bank so that he remained out of
sight. Just as the first boat came up to the boom he
put the gig out into the stream and opened fire on the
stockade, which was full of warriors. His first volley
was answered by a war-cry from 700 throats in the rear
of the forts, which showed him that Serip Japar's men
were in position and advancing to the attack.

Even though the news of the destruction of Padeh
and Paku must have unnerved the Rembas garrison they
had been prepared to defend their stronghold. But
when they found the boats advancing up the river and
the Linga Dayaks assaulting them in the rear they threw
up the sponge and fled in all directions without waiting
to fire a shot, though every gun was loaded. So that
once again the sailors were baulked of a fight, though
Serip Japar and his men had some fierce hand-to-hand
encounters, lives being lost on both sides.

Rembas was found to be by far the most formidable
of the three pirate strongholds. Several large war-boats
were taken, one measuring ninety-two feet in length
with fourteen beam, and in addition to large supplies of
fruit, goats and poultry, the sailors were delighted to find
a number of bullocks, while the Dayaks took immense
booty in the shape of brass and gongs and other native
valuables.

The settlement was burnt, a flag of truce received, and
the Rembas chiefs promised to attend the peace conference at Kuching. The expedition had now accomplished what it had set out to do. The punishment
inflicted had been severe, but no gentler measures would
have been understood. A few heads were brought
away by the Dayak allies, but there had been no wanton
sacrifice of life, and Captain Keppel gave it as his belief
that not a woman or child had been hurt.

The destruction of these places, in so short a time and with so small a loss, created a tremendous impression throughout the country. Not only had the Saribas believed that their strongholds could never be taken, owing to the strength of their fortifications and their remoteness from the coast, but they had relied upon the bore as their main protection, imagining that none but their own light boats could negotiate it. As a matter of fact, the bore had never been known to be so quiet as during the days of the expedition, a phenomenon the Saribas Dayaks could explain only by saying that Rajah Brooke had charmed the river.

The native forces were now given permission to disperse to their homes, and the boats rejoined the *Dido* off the coast. Captain Keppel returned to Kuching with Rajah Brooke. As they ascended the river scores of boats, gorgeously dressed with flags, came down to escort them to the capital. The moment they entered the last reach every gun in the town burst out in a salute, and as they approached Rajah Muda Hassim's residence they were met by yells of triumph, the beating of drums, and the booming of gongs playing the chant that greets victorious warriors on their return.

CHAPTER VIII

THE ATTACK ON THE SEKRANG STRONGHOLDS

Serip Sahap and Serip Mular, leaders of the Sekrang—Renewed
    piratical activities—Captain Keppel prepares to attack them—
    The assault on their stronghold at Patusan—Booty captured
    —The fall of Undop—A night alarm—The death of Lieu-
    tenant Wade—An unexpected disaster—Flight of Sahap
    and Mular.

IMMEDIATELY after the Saribas expedition the *Dido* had
to return to the China coast, so that Captain Keppel was
prevented from attacking the Sekrang, those powerful
allies of the Saribas who had their strongholds up the
Batang Lupar River and were under the leadership of the
half-bred Arab brothers, Serip Sahap and Serip Mular.[1]

So far from being daunted by the punishment inflicted on the Saribas, Serip Sahap built himself a strongly
fortified position at Patusan, fifty miles up the Batang
Lupar, soon after the *Dido's* departure. Here he collected
5,000 of his followers, and then sent out small parties of
his fleet (which consisted of some 150 prahus) on piratical excursions. These cruising squadrons, in addition
to attacking trading and fishing boats, scoured the coast
in search of heads and plunder, so that not even a hut in
the jungle was safe from them.

On one occasion a detachment of three of these boats
came upon a poor hill-Dayak, who, with his wife and
children, had decided to make his rice-clearing nearer the
coast than was the custom of his tribe. For better
security he had built a hut in the branches of a tree on the
edge of the clearing. Even this precaution, however,

---

[1] Spelt Sahib and Muller in the old books. A Serip was nominally a descend-
ant of the Prophet.

did not avail him. The Sekrang discovered his hiding-
place, summoned him to descend, and when he hesitated
shot him dead. His body crashed to the ground, and
then the pirates, to save their ammunition, climbed the
tree and killed his wife ; after which they took the heads
of both their victims and returned in triumph to their
boats. The children, who had been playing in the jungle
when the Sekrang approached the tree, had hidden themselves, and were forced to watch the murder of their
parents. They themselves remained undiscovered, and
eventually made their way to Kuching, where they were
cared for by Rajah Brooke.

Fifteen miles above Serip Sahap's stronghold at
Patusan, on a tributary known as the Undop, was the
fortified settlement of Serip Mular, who also carried on
a system of organised piracy with the neighbouring
Dayaks and swore that he would defy any European
force that should be sent against him.

For months Rajah Brooke was powerless to act
against these two powerful chiefs and their followers,
but at length, in response to his earnest entreaties, the
Dido returned to Sarawak, accompanied by the East
India Company's steamer *Phlegethon*, which the Straits
Government had placed at Captain Keppel's disposal.

The two ships reached Kuching on August 1, 1844.
Once more visits of ceremony were paid, and Rajah Muda
Hassim presented to Captain Keppel a second letter, of
which the following is a translation :

*This comes from Pangeran Muda Hassim, Rajah of
Borneo, to our friend Captain Keppel, in command of
Her Britannic Majesty's ship.*

(After the usual compliments)

*We beg to let our friend Captain Keppel know that the
pirates of Sakarran, whom we mentioned last year, still continue
their piracies by sea and land ; and that many Malays, under
Seriff Sahib, who have been accustomed to send or to accompany*

the pirates and to share in their spoils, have gone to the Sakarran River, with a resolve of defending themselves rather than accede to our wishes that they should abandon piracy.

Last year Captain Belcher [1] told the Sultan and myself that it would be pleasing to the Queen of England that we should repress piracy; and we signed an agreement, at his request, in which we promised to do so, and we tell our friend of the piracies and evil actions of the Sakarran people, who have for many years past done so much mischief to trade, and make it dangerous for boats to sail along the coast; and this year many prahus, which wanted to sail to Singapore have been afraid. We inform our friend Captain Keppel of this, as we desire to end all the piracy, and to perform our agreement with the Queen of England.

Captain Keppel wasted no time, and by August 4 preparations for an expedition against the Sekrang were completed. The force consisted, as before, of the *Dido's* boats and the *Jolly Bachelor*, accompanied by the *Phlegethon's* four cutters, with a total complement of thirteen officers, 108 seamen and sixteen marines under the command of Lieutenant C. F. Wade, who was now the *Dido's* senior lieutenant, Mr. Horton, who had led the attack against the Saribas, having been promoted to the rank of Commander. Among the officers was a nephew of Rajah Brooke's, Mr. Charles Johnson, then a midshipman, who subsequently became the second white Rajah of Sarawak. Captain Keppel, with Rajah Brooke, accompanied the expedition in his gig.

In addition to the European force, 300 natives joined the expedition, led by Pangeran Bedrudin, who was Muda Hassim's brother and uncle of the Sultan of Brunei. The departure of a royal prince on a warlike expedition was an unusual event, and his departure from Kuching must have been impressive. His barge of state was decked with banners and silken canopies; all the chiefs attended, with an Arab priest at their head, and the barge pushed off to

[1] Of H.M.S. "*Samarang.*"

the reports of the cannon mingled with high-pitched invocations for the blessing of Allah.

The boats dropped down to the mouth of the river, where the *Phlegethon* took them in tow, and by nine-thirty the same evening the expedition anchored within the entrance of the Batang Lupar, which in its lower reaches is a magnificent stream from three to four miles wide. The first brush with the enemy had been the chase and capture of a small prahu which, under the pretence of trading, had come to spy out the strength of the expedition. Of the three men in her one had resisted capture and been killed; the other two stated that Serip Sahap was fully prepared for defence: all the women had been removed from his settlement at Patusan, and he and his followers were determined to fight to the last.

The expedition weighed at daylight on the following morning, August 7, and soon after eleven o'clock came in sight of Patusan, which was seen to be defended by four strong forts placed in the form of a crescent. The steamer anchored within musket range, and the boats of the *Dido* and the *Phlegethon* formed up alongside. Orders were given to pull inshore towards the centre fort and then to spread out and attack all four simultaneously.

As they advanced, the forts opened fire. The boat party replied without checking, and Lieutenant Wade in the *Dido's* pinnace was the first to break the line and pull directly in the face of the largest fort. His example was followed by the others, each boat commander pulling for the fort which seemed to him to offer the best chances of a fight. Captain Keppel stood watching his men going into action from the top of the *Phlegethon's* paddle-box.

The moment the boats grounded, the crews sprang out and charged up to their objectives with a cheer. The native force was not long in following them, dashing in under the fire from the forts and joining in the assault. But Serip Sahap and his followers, for all their fine words, did not wait to receive the attack, and, as the sailors entered the forts by the embrasures, the defenders fled by

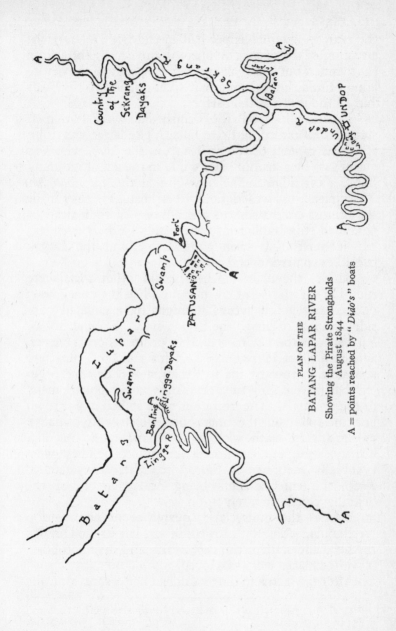

PLAN OF THE

BATANG LAPAR RIVER

Showing the Pirate Strongholds
August 1844

A = points reached by "*Dido's*" boats

the rear. Captain Keppel had intended to distract the attention of the enemy by opening fire on the forts from the steamer, but owing to the defective state of the detonating priming-tubes not a gun went off, and so the boats had all the glory to themselves.

The casualties on the British side were two men seriously wounded and one killed. The latter was John Ellis, the captain of the main-top in the *Dido*, who was cut in two by a cannon-shot while in the act of ramming home a cartridge in the bow-gun of the *Jolly Bachelor*. The pirates' loss was difficult to estimate, for they made the utmost endeavours to prevent any of their dead or wounded from falling into the hands of their enemies; but it must have been considerable, and the Dayak friendlies secured several heads.

Besides the main defences, eight other forts were found in the course of erection, and had the attack been delayed but a few weeks it might have entailed considerable loss of life to the British side. Even as it was, Patusan was the key to the other positions on the river, and each chief had contributed his share of guns and ammunition towards its fortification and defence. No less than fifty-six guns of various sizes were captured, many of them brass.[1] The iron guns were spiked and thrown into the river, but the brass ones, which were of native workmanship, each with its own name and peculiar history, were put on board the steamer. They were eventually auctioned in Singapore, where they fetched £900, the chief bidders being Malay agents of the Sekrang chiefs themselves.

Besides the guns, large quantities of ammunition were taken. The rest of the loot was left to the Dayaks, the forts and settlement were burnt, and over 200 boats of various sizes were destroyed.

After the men had dined and had had a short rest, the

---

[1] This is the figure given in Captain Keppel's despatch to Admiral Cochrane. In *The Expedition to Borneo of H.M.S. " Dido,"* ii, 90, Captain Keppel states that sixty-four brass guns alone were taken.

whole force was split up into two divisions and set off to attack a settlement two miles up a small stream, the entrance to which had been guarded by the forts. This settlement, which was where Serip Sahap had his own residence, was found to be abandoned, and here more loot was found, including two tons of gunpowder and a number of small barrels of powder, branded " Dartford," in exactly the same state as they had left the factory in England. Besides this the Serip's extensive wardrobe fell into the hands of the expedition, and Captain Keppel records that " it was ridiculous to see our Dayaks dressed out in all the finery and plunder of this noted pirate."

The expedition remained at Patusan for two days to complete the work of destruction, and then ascended the river to the point where it receives two tributaries, the Sekrang and the Undop. Twenty miles up the Undop was the stronghold of Serip Mular, the brother of Sahap; while on the Sekrang were the chief settlements of the Dayaks.

Captain Keppel decided to attack Undop first, leaving the steamer in the main stream. The boats' progress was slow, for the river was blocked by obstacles, and skirmishing parties of Malays and Dayaks were constantly encountered. The party brought up for the night close to the most formidable barrier met across the stream. This barrier was but a short distance from Mular's stronghold, whence sounds of shouting and confusion could be heard.

On the right bank, about fifty yards above the boom, a native house was discovered, and this Captain Keppel considered it advisable to occupy for the night with a volunteer force of fifty, to prevent the boats being surprised. Sentries were posted and the whole party was given " Tiga " as the watchword. Captain Keppel had with him his trusty John Eager, the sounding of whose bugle was to be the signal that the whole force was to come to the rescue of the outpost in the event of its being attacked.

Until midnight all was quiet. Then a blood-curdling yell broke the stillness. Immediately everyone was on his legs, questioning, shouting, groping for his arms. It was pitch dark. No one could see. No one could tell what had happened. To make matters worse the house was so crowded that the little garrison kept bumping into one another.

"It is impossible to describe the excitement and confusion of the succeeding ten minutes," wrote Captain Keppel. "One and all believed that we had been surrounded by the enemy and cut off from our main party. I had already thrust the muzzle of my pistol close to the heads of several natives, whom, in the confusion, I had mistaken for Sakarrans, and as each in his turn called out 'Tiga,' I withdrew my weapon to apply it to somebody else, until at last we found that we were all 'Tigas.' I had prevented Eager, more than once, from sounding the alarm which from the first he had not ceased to press me for permission to do. The Dyak yell had, however, succeeded in throwing the whole force afloat into a similar confusion, and, not hearing the signal, they concluded that they, and not we, were the party attacked. The real cause we afterwards ascertained to have arisen from the alarm of a Dyak, who dreamt, or imagined, that he felt a spear thrust upwards through the bamboo flooring of our building, and immediately gave his diabolical yell."[1]

By eight o'clock next morning, August 12, the last of the trees had been hacked away. The boats passed through, but only to find Mular's stronghold deserted by all save a few of his attendants, who were trying to

[1] *The Expedition to Borneo of H.M.S. "Dido,"* ii, 97-8.

remove the last of his personal effects. A large boat belonging to Mular was captured, and this Captain Keppel presented to Pangeran Bedrudin.

The settlement was looted and burnt, and then the expedition pushed on up-stream in pursuit of Mular and his followers. He was known to have fled to the Dayak settlement of Undop, but although this was only fifteen miles up the river it took the boats two days to reach it, owing to hundreds of large trees having been felled across the stream, so that it was not until the 14th that the lighter boats came within sight of the steep hill on the top of which the village stood. The river almost encircled this hill, and while searching for the best landing-place the Captain's gig came upon the large war-prahu of Serip Mular himself. His bodyguard did no more than fire their muskets and then flung themselves into the river, but a shout went up that Mular was escaping in a fast canoe. A noted Sarawak chief, Patinggi Ali, at once gave chase and Mular saved his life only by following his men's example and jumping into the water. He reached the jungle on the bank and escaped before he could be captured, but Patinggi proudly seized the boat. In the big prahu were two large and two small brass guns, and a variety of small arms, ammunition, provisions, colours, and personal property, including two pairs of handsome jars of English manufacture.

After this incident Captain Keppel pushed on up-stream in the gig, hoping to discover the landing-place which led to the village, but without success. He then put in to a grassy spot on the bank, intending to let the men have their breakfasts and to wait for the other boats. With him was Lieutenant Wade, who had begged for a place in the gig so that he might be in the van.

While breakfast was cooking they fancied they heard voices. Taking up their guns they crept into the jungle and had not gone far before they saw a crowd of boats concealed in a snug little inlet, the entrance to which had previously escaped their notice. The boats were filled with pirates, both Malays and Dayaks, and on shore at various points armed sentries had been placed.

Captain Keppel, who was in front, raised his hand as a sign that they should keep out of sight until the rest of the force had come up, for besides Mr. Wade he had with him only seven men. Mr. Wade, however, either did not see this signal, or disregarded it in his desire to fall upon the enemy, and he dashed forward, calling on the gig's crew to follow. The pirates were completely surprised by this attack, coming from the direction it did. "The confused noise and scrambling from the boats," says Captain Keppel, "I can only liken to that of a suddenly-roused flock of wild ducks," [1] and the pirates fled headlong to the village on the hill, turning, however, to fire as they ran.

The pursuers now paused to reload, but seeing the rest of the force approaching the landing-place Mr. Wade rushed on until he reached an open space of sixty yards at the base of the hill. This was devoid of cover and was exposed to the fire of the village. Captain Keppel caught up Mr. Wade and warned him that he must wait for his men before attempting to charge across. The words were scarcely uttered when this gallant but impetuous young officer fell dead at his captain's feet, having been hit by two musket shots. Captain Keppel remained with the body until the main force came up, and then led the men on and captured the Sekrang village without much opposition.

"I may here narrate a circumstance," wrote Captain Keppel, "from which one may judge of the natural kind-heartedness of my lamented friend. During the heat of the pursuit, although too anxious to advance to await the arrival of his men, he nevertheless found time to conceal in a place of security a poor terrified Malay girl whom he overtook, and who, by an imploring look, touched his heart. The village and the piratical boats

---

[1] *Op. cit.* p. 103.

destroyed, and the excitement over, we had time to reflect
on the loss we had sustained of one so generally beloved
as the leader of the expedition had been among us all.
Having laid the body in a canoe with the British union-
jack for a pall, we commenced our descent of the river
with very different spirits from those with which we had
ascended only a few hours before.   In the evening, with
our whole force assembled, we performed the last sad
ceremony of committing the body to the deep, with all
the honours that time and circumstance would allow.   I
read that beautiful, impressive service from a Prayer Book
—the only one, by the by, in the expedition—which he
himself had brought, as he said ' in case of accident.' " [1]

The Malay chiefs having been punished, Captain
Keppel prepared to attack the Sekrang Dayaks, whose
principal settlement was Karangan, thirty miles up the
Sekrang river from the junction where the *Phlegethon* lay,
and more than 100 miles from the sea.

On the 17th the same force, with the exception of two
of the steamer's cutters, which were left to get wood,
advanced up the Sekrang River.   On their way they
burnt a number of war-boats which they found concealed
in the creeks or hauled up in the long grass on the banks.
Occasional skirmishing took place with the light boats in
advance, but their progress was uninterrupted until the
19th, when the country, which had hitherto been highly
cultivated, assumed a more hilly and wilder appearance,
the river made more abrupt turnings and was narrower,
and the banks in many places were very steep, with large
overhanging trees.

While the sailors were at breakfast that morning some
of the native force under Patinggi Ali, accompanied by
Mr. Steward (an European trader at Kuching who had
volunteered to accompany the expedition), went ahead
to reconnoitre, with strict orders to fall back on the

---

[1] *Op. cit.* p. 105.

slightest appearance of meeting the enemy. Unfortunately, however, they advanced too boldly and fell
into an ambuscade at a sudden turn in the river between
two steep hills, where six war-prahus, with breastworks of
bamboo, holding about fifty men each, lay concealed.
Patinggi Ali had no sooner entered the pass with his
small boats than a large raft was launched from the bank
to cut off his retreat. Then the six war-prahus bore
down on him together, his small boats were upset and
many of the crews speared.

The first intimation Captain Keppel had of this
disaster was the sound of the shooting. He pushed on
up-stream, and his own account of what he saw when he
reached the scene of the engagement is worth quoting :

" About twenty boats were jammed together, forming
one confused mass ; some bottom up ; the bows or sterns
of others only visible; mixed up, pell-mell, with huge
rafts ; and amongst which were nearly all our advanced
little division. Headless trunks as well as heads without
bodies were lying about in all directions ; parties were
engaged hand to hand, spearing and krissing each other.
Others were striving to swim for their lives. Entangled
in the common *mêlée* were our advanced boats ; while on
both banks thousands of Dyaks were rushing down to
join in the slaughter, hurling their spears and stones on
the boats below. For a moment I was at a loss what steps
to take for rescuing our people from the embarrassed
position in which they were, as the whole mass (through
which there was no passage) were floating down the
stream, and the addition of fresh boats arriving only
increased the confusion. Fortunately, at this critical
moment one of the rafts, catching the stump of a tree,
broke this floating bridge, making a passage through
which (my gig being propelled by paddles instead of
oars) I was enabled to pass.

" It occurred to Mr. Brooke and myself simultaneously, that by advancing in the gig we should draw the
attention of the pirates towards us, so as to give time for

the other boats to clear themselves. This had the desired effect. The whole force on the shore turned as if to secure what they rashly conceived to be their prize.

" We now advanced mid-channel : spears and stones assailed us from both banks. My friend Brooke's gun would not go off, so, giving him the yoke-lines, he steered the boat, while I kept up a rapid fire. Mr. Allen, in the second gig, quickly coming up, opened upon them from a congreve-rocket tube such a destructive fire as caused them to retire panic-struck behind the temporary barriers where they had concealed themselves previous to the attack upon Patinggi Ali, and from whence they continued, for some twenty minutes, to hurl their spears and other missiles. Among the latter may be mentioned short lengths of bamboo, one end heavily loaded with stone, and thrown with great force and precision. The few fire-arms of which they were possessed were of but little use to them after the first discharge, the operation of reloading, in their inexperienced hands, requiring a longer time than the hurling of some twenty spears. The sumpitan[1] was likewise freely employed by these pirates. Although several of our men belonging to the pinnace were struck, no fatal results ensued from the dexterous and expeditious manner in which the wounded parts were excised by Mr. Beith, the assistant surgeon ; any poison that might remain being afterwards sucked out by one of the comrades of the wounded men.

" As our force increased, the pirates retreated from their position, and could not again muster courage to rally. Their loss must have been considerable. Ours might have been light had poor old Patinggi Ali attended to orders."[2]

As it was, the casualties amounted to thirty killed (including the gallant old chief, Patinggi Ali, and Mr. Steward), and fifty-six wounded. As for the pirates, all the prahus were either sunk or capsized and the slaughter must have been great for, as Captain Keppel stated in his

---

[1] Blowpipe.   [2] *Op. cit.*, pp. 111-13.

despatch to the Admiral, " with hundreds of pirates still fighting on the bottoms of the capsized boats, while thousands hurled spears and stones on us from the banks, it was useless to think of either giving or receiving quarter."

The survivors fled along the river banks, but the boats pressed them hard so that they might not have an opportunity to rally before reaching Karangan, which lay a few miles higher up. This proved effective, and Karangan was taken and destroyed without further opposition.

❖   ❖

The objects of the expedition being now accomplished, the boats rejoined the *Phlegethon* and the whole force returned to Kuching. They were scarcely back, however, when news came in that Serip Sahap had sought refuge with Serip Japar on the Linga River, and was again collecting followers. Both Captain Keppel and Rajah Brooke knew that if their work was to bear good fruit they must strike at once. That very day, therefore, the expedition set out again. This unlooked for promptitude of action so effectually deterred the Linga people and their neighbours from harbouring Sahap that he fled across the great mountain range that divides Sarawak from Dutch Borneo. He was never taken, but so close were the pursuing Dayaks on his tracks that he was forced to throw away his sword and left behind him one of his children, whom he had carried with him in his flight. What became of him there is nothing to show, but he never troubled Sarawak again. His brother, Mular, who had also fled far into the hills, was eventually pardoned and died at Sekrang. Serip Japar had undoubtedly been prepared to give him his protection, although it will be remembered that this same chief had taken part in the expedition against the Saribas, and Pangeran Bedrudin, acting as the Sultan of Brunei's representative, obliged him to resign all pretensions to the government of the province over which he had hitherto held sway.

CHAPTER IX

THE PIRATES OF PEDIR,
AND THE CASE OF THE NAMELESS MAN OF KENT

The brig *Futtal Khair* seized and plundered by the Rajah of Achin's brother—The owner and crew kept prisoners—They escape to Penang and seek redress from the Governor—The Master of the brig *Robert Spankie* murdered on the Pedir coast—The brig looted—The part played by Haji Abdullah, the nameless man of Kent—The Rajah of Murdu allows the crew to go free—Haji Abdullah sent in chains to Penang—His curious history—Commander Hastings leads a naval expedition against the pirates—The actions described—Rajah Brooke wounded—The end of Haji Abdullah.

In the middle of the nineteenth century Achin, in the extreme north of Sumatra, was an independent native State, split up into districts ruled by petty princes who, although under the nominal sovereignty of the Rajah, recked little of his authority and did not hesitate to enrich themselves by piracy when they saw the chance, so that although the Rajah of Achin had, as early as 1819, entered into a treaty with the British Government granting security of trade to British ships, for twenty-five years afterwards the coast of Northern Sumatra had an evil name. Not that the Rajah himself either broke the treaty or wilfully ignored it. He was powerless to control his vassals, that was all, and his ministers of State could do no more than warn British ships, when they put in to Achin, that it was dangerous to trade with the settlements up the neighbouring rivers or to linger off the Pedir coast.

This was the advice given to Said Abu Bakar of Calcutta when he visited Achin with his brig the *Futtal Khair* in February, 1843. Having completed his business, he sailed for Penang, where he intended to dispose of his valuable cargo—sandalwood, coral beads, pearls and precious stones. The brig had not been under way two hours when a sudden storm forced her to seek shelter in the mouth of the Ryah River. While she was lying-to a sail came off from the shore. It proved to be the Rajah of Achin's long-boat with the Rajah's brother, Tuanku Abbas, [1] and his wife and children, on board, attended by thirty followers, all armed.

The longboat hailed the brig and came alongside. Tuanku Abbas informed Abu Bakar that he wished to go to Kuala Batu, on the Pedir coast, and offered to pay $150 passage money for himself and his people. Abu Bakar was on friendly terms with the Rajah. Doubtless he felt that it would pay to keep in with one of his relatives. Perhaps he was a snob and liked the idea of carrying royal passengers. At all events he protested that he was the Tuanku's servant, and that it would be highly improper for him to charge the Rajah's brother for his passage. Tuanku Abbas did not wound Abu Bakar's feelings by trying to insist on payment, but graciously accepted the offer and went aboard the brig, where the best accommodation was provided for him and his company.

On the following morning he regretfully informed Abu Bakar that he had not sufficient money with him to buy necessaries for the voyage, whereupon some of the crew were sent ashore for fruit, vegetables and other provisions, on which the royal party lived until the *Futtal Khair* reached Kuala Batu, thirty-five days later.

The Tuanku and his people then went ashore, and the next day invited Abu Bakar, his two sons, the mate and some of the passengers to a feast. Abu Bakar, pleasantly gratified by this mark of favour, accepted, but no sooner had he and his companions entered the Tuanku's residence than they were seized and confined in a prison

---

[1] *Tuanku*: a title given to Malays of high birth.

under an armed guard, while seven boats filled with warriors, under the command of one of the Tuanku's lieutenants, put off to the brig. The unsuspecting crew were made prisoners without difficulty, the British colours were hauled down, torn and trodden under foot, and the plundering of the vessel then began.

The sandalwood was first removed, then all the property belonging to the passengers and the crew, so that they were left with nothing but the clothes on their bodies. During the night Tuanku Abbas himself came aboard and ordered the clerk, Mami Kooti, to show him where the pearls and precious stones were kept. It must be supposed that Abu Bakar had been imprudent enough to babble of the treasure he had on board. By force of threats Abbas discovered the box, which was between decks under the captain's cabin. Some of the Tuanku's men broke it open in the clerk's presence and handed to their master a packet of pearls, one emerald, two diamonds, a gold necklace, a large packet of red coral beads, three cashmere shawls and a quantity of valuable cloths.

The work of plundering the brig took two days and a night. Tuanku Abbas did not leave her until she had been completely stripped; even her anchors and chain-cables were carried off. He appears to have intended to haul the vessel on shore and break her up, so that he could have her planks and timbers for building a new house. Abu Bakar was convinced that he meant to murder all the prisoners. There is no direct evidence of this, but it may well have been so, for he must have known that he would have been in an awkward position once he had let them go.

It was certainly fortunate for Abu Bakar that a fellow-countryman of his, Koonji Mahomed, who was trading at Pedir, heard of his plight and hastened to Kuala Batu to intercede for him. Koonji must have had some influence with the Tuanku, for soon after his arrival the prisoners were permitted to live in the *bali*—the public audience-hall which is part of every Malay court. They were still guarded, but for the first time were able to obtain food, which was provided by their friend.

Abu Bakar then implored Koonji to do what he could to save the brig and gave him a document empowering him to sail her to the nearest port. Thereupon Koonji borrowed $50 from one of the *Futtal Khair's* passengers, and with this sum succeeded in bribing the Tuanku's chief minister (*Shabandar*), a Kling, to persuade his master to let the brig go on a trading trip along the coast. The prospect of making something out of his prize before he broke her up appealed to the Tuanku (he appears to have been as guileless as Abu Bakar himself), and he gave his permission, but insisted that Koonji Mahomed should be responsible both for the charter-money and for the vessel herself.

Three nights after the *Futtal Khair* had sailed, Abu Bakar, with his two sons and the rest of the prisoners, succeeded in escaping while their guards were asleep. They made their way to Pedir, where they found Koonji Mahomed with the brig. Abu Bakar asked Koonji to take her to Penang and report to the authorities, while he himself went off to Achin in the hope of obtaining redress for his wrongs.

One may suppose that the Rajah was anything but pleased to see him. There is no evidence that His Highness was implicated in the plundering of the brig—indeed he had gone so far as to give Abu Bakar a warning in general terms. But like all Malay potentates he disliked trouble that was not of his own making and now he found himself in a tedious dilemma. He must have been shrewd enough to know that any orders he gave his brother to restore the looted cargo would be ignored, therefore he refrained from issuing them. At the same time he knew that if he refused to take action Abu Bakar would go off to Penang and perhaps return with British ships-of-war : a disagreeable prospect, however blameless he himself had been. Accordingly he procrastinated in a manner that would have done credit to Queen

Elizabeth, giving vague promises that he would have inquiries made and keeping Abu Bakar on tenterhooks for weeks.

Finally Abu Bakar lost patience and returned to Pedir. The Rajah, alarmed, sent orders that he was to be detained, but Abu Bakar slipped away in a trading vessel, and on July 15 reached Penang, where he lost no time in putting forward his case both to the Resident Councillor, and later to the Governor of the Straits. As he put it in his " humble petition," he threw himself and his misfortunes " at the feet of the authorities, and the Company, and under their flag, and looking to them for protection."

His account of his misfortunes was corroborated by the statement of Koonji Mahomed and the clerk of the *Futtal Khair* ; and the claim he submitted against Tuanku Abbas was as follows :

	$
Cost of the goods taken from the ship	5,547.62½
25 % advance, calculated as profits	1,386.90
Sailing expenses for the crew for 8 months at $200	1,600.00
Probable earnings of the Owner	1,200.00
	$9,734.53

It is unlikely that this claim was an under-estimate, and those who have had dealings with Indian litigants will smile at that meticulously calculated half-cent. He begged that his claims at the above rate might be demanded through the medium of the Honourable Company, and ended with the time-honoured phrase for all such applications, " For which kind act of humanity your Petitioner will ever pray."

When one considers that he had been in fear of his life for a week and kept as a suppliant for months, one cannot but feel that he was entitled to anything he could get.

♦   ♦

While the authorities were considering Said Abu Bakar's humble petition, news of another outrage on British shipping reached Penang.

On September 25, 1843, the brig *Robert Spankie*, commanded by a Parsee named Cursetji Framjee, with a crew of twelve, left Penang for the Pedir coast, and at the port of Murdu arranged for a cargo of betel-nut. Part of the load was delivered—$50 and seven balls of opium being paid for it—but the remainder was delayed and Cursetji, much to his annoyance, was forced to wait.

He and his supercargo, Murwangi, were on deck one afternoon when a large native boat came off, manned by thirty Achinese. On board was the Rajah of Murdu's brother (called the Rajah Muda, since he was the heir apparent) and a mysterious individual known as Haji Abdullah, an Englishman turned Mohammedan, who had been living at the court of Murdu for some time and had become the Rajah's chief adviser.

Cursetji knew Haji Abdullah, and, on learning that the Rajah Muda wished to visit the brig, he hoisted his flag and welcomed him and his people on board as unsuspectingly as Abu Bakar had welcomed Tuanku Abbas, and provided them with refreshments.

An hour later the Rajah Muda called attention to a fishing boat that was sailing past and asked the captain if he wanted any fish. Cursetji said he did, and he and Murwangi went to the side; whereupon the Rajah and his party set on them from behind with drawn weapons and cut them down. The crew, taken by surprise, were rounded up and kept on deck under a guard, while the bodies of the unfortunate Cursetji and his supercargo were flung overboard.

The pirates then started to loot the brig. The fishing

boat had been sent to the shore after the attack, and in the middle of the night three large empty boats came off and were loaded up with the plunder, which included the betel-nut, eight balls of opium, eighty-two bags of dates, eighteen pigs of lead, 140 axes, eight rings set with rubies and seven set with diamonds, three silver spoons, two silver watches, a box containing twenty-four razors, fourteen muskets, twelve handspikes, eight swords, four brass guns, and four kegs of gunpowder. All the ship's stores and fittings were taken, from copper boilers and compasses to teacups and saucers; also the personal belongings of the murdered men and the crew. By the time they had done with her the pirates must have stripped the *Robert Spankie* as bare as a rice-field after a swarm of locusts have been through it.

The loot was taken to the residence of the Rajah Muda, who went ashore next morning, leaving Haji Abdullah in charge of the brig and the prisoners.

Three days later the Rajah of Murdu sent for the mate of the brig, Sorabji, and the other native officers. Haji Abdullah took them ashore. The Rajah asked them why they had not made any attempt to resist the seizure of the vessel. They explained that they had been taken by surprise and were unarmed. His Highness then assured them that they should come to no harm and promised that he would send them back in the brig to Penang.

It is not difficult to imagine the relief with which those wretched captives heard these words. But that relief must have been matched by their astonishment when they heard His Highness declare that since Haji Abdullah had instigated the Rajah Muda to seize the brig and commit the murders he should be sent as a prisoner to Penang.

Sorabji and his companions then returned to the ship. The Rajah kept his word, for two days later Haji Abdullah was sent on board in chains, and Sorabji, having been given a letter from His Highness to the British authorities, was allowed to take the *Robert Spankie* back

to Penang, where the prisoner was handed over for
trial.

✧　　　✧

The delivery of Haji Abdullah to the East India
Company was an astute move on the Rajah's part. It is
clear that the question of ethics did not trouble him.
It was a matter of what was most expedient. Two
particularly vile murders of British subjects had been
committed, followed by the plundering of a vessel that
sailed under the British flag. Like the Rajah of Achin,
His Highness of Murdu must have seen that sooner or
later he would be called upon to answer for the misdeeds
of his brother and his subjects. Unlike the Rajah of
Achin, he had a convenient scapegoat at hand, and he
did not scruple to make the best use he could of his
advantage.

There is nothing to show what his relations with Haji
Abdullah really were; nor is there any evidence of
Abdullah's history save his statement before the magistrate in Penang: and that is meagre enough. He stated that
he was an Englishman and had been born in Canterbury,
but declared that he did not know his English name,
since he had been a Mohammedan for twenty-three years,
having been introduced into the faith of Islam while
still a boy, at the time when his father had become a
Mohammedan at Jeddah. He had been " in the Arab
country," he said ; " in Bengal and other places." That
he had performed the pilgrimage to Mecca is evident from
his holy title of *haji*, but he said nothing of this, nor did
he explain how he had come to hold a position of influence
at the court of Murdu.

It may be that the Rajah feared that this lone adven-
turer might become inconveniently powerful if his activi-
ties were to remain unchecked. It may even be that His
Highness genuinely believed that Abdullah, and not the
Rajah Muda, was responsible, and that he was shocked.
This is less probable, seeing that he made no attempt

whatever to return the loot and avoided any reference to its surrender in his letter, though he made out the best case he could for his brother, and the worst he could for the man of Kent.

He stated that the Rajah Muda was but twelve years old, not come to the age of discretion and, further, out of his mind. He had been but a pawn in the hands of the Haji Abdullah and the pirates, and they had taken him on board the brig to amuse him and had given him a bottle of brandy, the drinking of which had increased his madness. The letter stated explicitly that it was Haji Abdullah who killed the two Indians, and ended by declaring that although " the robbers " were not His Highness's own subjects "they shall be sent to our friend the Company if I can get them."

The statement of Sorabji, the mate, made before the Penang magistrate, does not bear out the youth and imbecility of the Rajah Muda : " He was a man of twenty-five years and upwards. I saw nothing of madness in his conduct." Being forward when the murders were committed, Sorabji did not see who actually struck the blows, but he deposed : " The prisoner, Haji Abdullah, was at the head of the party and considered generally as a *Panglima*, Chief Warrior, amongst them."

Jasu, the boatswain, corroborated the above evidence. He affirmed that the Rajah Muda was a grown man. He could not say decidedly that the Rajah had a drawn weapon in his hand, but he swore that Abdullah had, and that he had assisted the Rajah to get the cargo out of the ship and had been left in charge of the pirates.

The following is Haji Abdullah's statement, made to the magistrate after the usual caution :

" On the 29th day of the fast it was about 2 p.m. that the Rajah Muda sent for me. I told him I was sick. The Rajah then desired that I should be carried if I did not go. Thinking it most prudent to obey, I got a boat and went over to him. He was in a large Prow-Puckat of about ten Coyans burthen [1] and manned with about thirty men. The Rajah desired me to embark, and, on my asking him, said he was going to Samalungan. We got out of the river and there the Rajah said to me, ' We had better go to the Brig as it is evening, and there break our fast. [2] The captain, Cursetji, said to me, ' Is that you, Haji ? ' and having ascertained that the Rajah Muda was in the boat, he asked the Rajah on board.

" After talking some time and warming bread and having a goat killed, we were watching the going down of the sun. In the meantime a fishing boat being seen, the Rajah desired one of the Panglimas to hail it, and when it came on the starboard side Captain Cursetji and the other man were looking over the side when the Rajah himself threw a rope round them and ordered his people to murder them. I declare that I had nothing to do with the murder but tried to assist the crew."

Having made this statement Haji Abdullah was remanded in custody for trial before the Court of Judicature.

✧   ✧

After somewhat prolonged consideration Colonel W. J. Butterworth, the Governor of Prince of Wales' Island (Penang), Singapore and Malacca, decided to seek redress for these outrages on British shipping and British subjects, and on January 12, 1844, he addressed the following letter to Sir William Parker, Vice-Admiral of the Blue and Commander-in-Chief of Her Majesty's ships in the East Indies :

" I have the honour to transmit for your Excellency's information copies of depositions taken at Penang relative to the seizure of the brig *Futtal Khair* ; and the murder and piracy on board the *Robert Spankie* by the

---

[1] 10 tons, approx.

[2] From the date given by Abdullah, it is clear that the piracy was committed during the fast month of Ramadan, during which Mohammedans may not eat until sunset.

subjects of H.H. the Rajah of Achin; and with reference thereto I would suggest for Your Excellency's consideration the expediency of despatching two men-of-war, if they can be spared, in company with the *Diana* Steamer, in the first instance to Achin, for the purpose of demanding an interview with the Rajah, and subsequently, if need be, to the place where the outrages have been committed. The Owner of the *Futtal Khair* is now here, and will proceed with the expedition.

"I have every reason to expect that the Rajah will satisfactorily prove that he is in no way connected with the seizure of the *Futtal Khair*, or with the murder and robbery aboard the *Robert Spankie*; and that it will be necessary to counteract his weakness with reference to his own chiefs, rather than his strength, in opposition to us—but he is at least nominally answerable for the conduct of his subjects, more particularly one so near his own person as his brother, Tuanku Abbas.

"There is little hope, I fear, of obtaining restitution of the property pirated from the above vessels, but I think it should be demanded, as also the person of Tuanku Abbas and Rajah Muda; and in the event of H. H. declaring his inability to do either, I should suggest that the ships proceed to the places where these disgraceful acts of piracy were committed, and there exact an equivalent for the property destroyed, and the aforesaid persons, viz. Tuanku Abbas and Rajah Muda, taking such coercive measures for the purpose as shall be found expedient, even to the destruction of their villages, with a view at least of ensuring greater respect in future, to any vessel bearing British colours.

"Should Your Excellency concur in the view I have taken of this affair, and will spare either one or two vessels for the purpose of carrying it into effect, I shall be prepared to furnish a letter to the Rajah of Achin and to place the *Diana* Steamer under the orders of the officer despatched on this service, who will doubtless bear in mind that the whole object of the expedition is to foster and protect our commercial intercourse with Achin and the surrounding States."

As a result of this letter Admiral Parker instructed Commander the Hon. G. F. Hastings to proceed to Achin with the sloops *Harlequin* and *Wanderer*, and the East India Company's steamboat *Diana*, " for the purpose of obtaining restitution of the British property which has been plundered by the Achinese, or the sum of money which the Governor of the Straits considers as equivalent for the loss the owners have sustained by the piratical acts complained of." Commander Hastings was warned to guard against the treachery of the natives and the Admiral concluded his orders by saying : " I leave the details of this service to your discretion, satisfied that you will exercise a sound judgment, and will only add that if you fail in obtaining the redress demanded, you will be justified in destroying the villages and coconut trees, agreeably to the suggestion of the Governor of the Straits."

◇   ◇

The expedition sailed from Penang on January 20, 1844. Said Abu Bakar, the owner of the *Futtal Khair*, was on board the *Diana*, and among the *Diana's* crew was a seaman who had been serving in the *Robert Spankie* when she was seized. On board the *Wanderer* was Rajah Brooke. He had recently lost his mother, to whom he had been devoted, and had asked permission to accompany the expedition as a passenger, in the hope of finding in activity some anodyne for his grief.

The ships anchored in the Achin Roads on the evening of February 4, and on the following morning Commander Hastings set off to visit the Sultan, accompanied by Commander Seymour of the *Wanderer* and a force drawn from both vessels. Mr. Congleton, the commander of the *Diana*, had been sent on ahead to inform His Highness of the intended visit.

The town lay five miles up a shallow river. Once it

had been a celebrated Malay capital; now it was no
more than a few straggling huts and a small bazaar,
although its ruler still maintained some show of pomp.

Being intent upon conducting the negotiations in
accordance with Malay etiquette, Commander Hastings
waited with the boats until the final arrangements for his
reception had been made. Between one and two o'clock
he and Commander Seymour were ushered into the royal
audience hall and after some delay the Rajah made his
appearance. When ceremonial greetings had been exchanged Commander Hastings delivered a letter from
Governor Butterworth and formally made the required
demands. The Rajah requested until morning for his
answer.

The next day the naval officers again attended the
audience hall. The Rajah stated that he was anxious for
the Company's friendship, but that he was unable to deliver
up either Tuanku Abbas or the Rajah Muda of Murdu,
since he had no power over them or their rivers. He could
not be expected to pay the indemnity, since he knew
nothing whatever of the piracies, but he undertook to
send some of his officers with the expedition to Batu and
Murdu to assist in obtaining the redress demanded, and
gave a letter to the Rajah of Pedir, calling upon him to
render aid. His Highness agreed that the two chiefs and
their people deserved to be punished and expressed a hope
that Commander Hastings would take action against
them if they did not prove amenable.

His Highness could have said no less, and probably
could have done no more. No doubt the visit of the expedition to his capital was causing him some apprehension and his conscience may have been pricking him at
the thought that he had done his best to prevent Abu
Bakar from going to Penang.

Commander Hastings, however, decided to accept
his professions, realising that he spoke the truth when
he declared he was unable to control his own subjects,
and took leave of him in a friendly way, acquitting him,

as he stated in his subsequent despatch to the Admiral, "of being privy to either of the acts complained of."

While the naval party was at Achin, an interesting piece of information concerning Said Abu Bakar came to light. It appeared that while the *Futtal Khair* was visiting the capital Abu Bakar had sold the Rajah's *shabandar* two Arab boys as slaves. The *shabandar* himself volunteered this information (no doubt a nicely calculated piece of retaliation for Abu Bakar's having brought the British ships to Achin), and even produced the account showing that $35 had been paid for one of the slaves. Abu Bakar, knowing the attitude of the East India Company towards those who trafficked in slaves, must in his turn have suffered some uncomfortable moments when he learnt that his dealings had been revealed.

On leaving Achin Commander Hastings took his ships to Batu, and on the morning of February 10 ascended the river with the boats of the three vessels, manned and armed. They reached the village, three miles from the mouth, without opposition, and were there met by a flag of truce and a message from the Rajah of Pedir (with whom Commander Hastings had been in communication) asking them to await his arrival before taking action. Tuanku Abbas, it appeared, had left the village with his principal people on news of the squadron's approach.

While waiting, Commander Hastings landed his marines and small-arms party, with a field-piece of the *Wanderer's*, marched to the centre of the village and took possession of Tuanku Abbas's house, the boats having been placed in a position to be useful in case of need.

Shortly afterwards the Rajah made his appearance. He seemed most anxious to help, and even went so far as to put up a definite proposal on behalf of the Tuanku.

The indemnity claimed was $2,000 (Abu Bakar's account had been whittled down), and the Rajah suggested that Commander Hastings should accept $500 in cash and allow the balance to remain as a debt on security.

"I answered," says Commander Hastings in his despatch, "that it was impossible to lower the demands with which I was entrusted, but that if Tuanku Abbas would give himself up to me I might then be justified in making some agreement for the payment of the money, but that I could not lose time, and if within an hour or so my demands were not complied with I should commence destroying the village."

The Rajah withdrew and the officers began to examine the deserted houses. In some Abu Bakar came upon part of his looted cargo and personal property, and in the shops were found the stolen anchors of the *Futtal Khair*. These discoveries put an end to any doubt as to the guilt of the Tuanku and his party.

Three hours went by. Tuanku Abbas did not come. Probably no one had expected that he would. The Rajah returned with the information that he had been unable to effect a settlement. Commander Hastings then told the Rajah that he would carry out his threat to destroy the village, and requested His Highness to withdraw, since he had no wish to take life unless he met with opposition.

The Rajah and his people having departed, a fire-party was selected and in a few minutes Tuanku Abbas's settlement was blazing to the sky. Some of the sailors, having advanced beyond the cover of the marines, were attacked by a party of natives, and during the skirmish that ensued a few of the enemy were shot; after which the naval force returned to the ships and sailed for the Murdu River, anchoring off its mouth the same afternoon.

❖   ❖

At dawn on February 12 the boats were manned and armed, and made for the entrance of the river. This time, however, they were not to have so easy a task. The Rajah of Murdu threw all pretence of conciliation aside and, seeing that the handing over of Haji Abdullah had not served him, he decided to fight.

The following is Commander Hastings' account of the action that ensued :

"On arriving at the entrance we observed the natives in great force, waving and shouting, evidently to deter our approach, but as I could not get them to understand me, I ordered the boats to advance, and immediately we were assailed by a brisk fire of gingalls and musketry, and as we were the attacked party I had no hesitation in ordering the fire to be returned, which was instantly opened by the boats with their guns, the marines and small-arms party jumping from them at the same time through the surf, driving the enemy from the position they had taken up behind the embankments of the river.

" The boats were successful in finding the channel, and we advanced under a smart fire from the enemy, who concealed themselves on both sides of the river in thick jungle, the marines guarding the right bank and covering the boats in their advance towards the village.

" In the second reach of the river a heavy fire was opened on the boats from a stockade in which were mounted a few brass guns. The boats were gallantly pushed forward by their respective officers, and the stockade was carried, the guns being gained by Lt. Hodgson in the *Wanderer's* cutter, and embarked.

" Having searched the town, I ordered its destruction by fire, and in a short period the houses were in flames, the enemy still keeping up a most galling fire on the marines and boats. I deemed it best to advance and finish them, and in the reach behind the town they took up a strong position against our further advance. The marines immediately advanced to the attack, and with the assistance of the boats, they carried the position, the enemy contesting the ground with great obstinacy.

" Proceeding on some distance further, a house of considerable size was carried with but slight opposition, and from its appearance evidently the Rajah's. Having burnt it and many other houses on both sides of the river, and done great injury to their property, I directed the boats to take in their marines and return towards the vessels.

" Hardly five minutes had elapsed after the directions given on the other side were obeyed, before a most destructive fire was opened on our boats from the right bank of the river, which wounded many of our men, and seeing no chance against an enemy concealed as they were behind embankments but to drive them from such a position, I ordered the marines and small-arms party to jump from their boats and attack them. This service was gallantly executed by all the officers, seamen, and marines belonging to the respective vessels. I regret to say that during the attack, Lt. Henry Chads, senior lieutenant of the *Harlequin*, in encountering a native hand to hand with a sword, received two wounds, one of which nearly cut his left hand off, and the other severely injured his left side ; also the gunner of the *Wanderer* was severely wounded in three places by musket ball.

" After this sharp affair our route down the river was continued, the enemy annoying us by a severe fire from the jungle. We at length reached our vessels, and although I have to regret to Your Excellency the number of killed and wounded of both vessels (a return of which I have the honour to enclose), yet considering the nature of the ground, which is thickly covered with bushes and enclosures to the water's edge, I congratulate myself that the number was not greater ; but to punish these natives with greater severity a larger force would be requisite in such a country."

The number of serious casualties during the action amounted to eleven, two of whom subsequently died of wounds. The enemy were estimated to have had between fifty and seventy killed or wounded, their loss having been chiefly due to their exposing themselves recklessly on their stockade, in the manner of Malays, instead of picking off their attackers from the jungle.

Among those reported " seriously wounded " by the *Wanderer's* surgeon was Rajah Brooke.   In the return he is denoted " Passenger." He certainly worked his passage, for he took part in the attack with gusto, and in a letter to his friend John Templer, dated March 3, 1844, he described the action as " five hours' as pretty fighting as you would desire." Referring to his own wounds he said : " In charging the stockade I got a spear thrust which cut my eyebrow in two, a light but very bloody scratch which has slightly injured my beauty, and at the same time a shot inside my right arm which rendered me for the time *hors de combat* ; my eye is now well, and my arm so well that you may observe that I write as badly as usual." [1]

Thus did the British Navy extract retribution from the pirates of the Pedir coast.   Commander Hastings and his men did all they were sent to do, and they could have done no more.   Rajah Brooke's comments sum up the situation : " We could not well say," he wrote in the letter referred to, "that the Murdu people were either subdued or cowed.   Indeed, it is great odds against a small party of 150 men to send them among a numerous and not unwarlike population, and in utter ignorance of the country in which they are to serve."   Commander Hastings' admission of the transitory nature of the punishment he had inflicted may be gathered from the last paragraph of his despatch in which he says :

" I consider it my duty to state for the information of the authorities in the Straits, that from the bad characters of the different petty Rajahs of the Coast of Pedir, it is not safe at present for British vessels to trade at any of the ports to the eastward of Achin, except Pedir, and I shall warn vessels that I may meet of this fact."

◇   ◇

And what of Haji Abdullah, the nameless man of

---

[1] *The Private Letters of Sir James Brooke,* ii, 1.

Kent whom the Sultan of Murdu had so vainly sacrificed upon the altar of expediency ?

The end of his story is shortly told. We have seen the voluntary statement he made at the preliminary inquiry held at Penang. When finally tried before the Court of Judicature, his defence was on similar lines : he had been coerced into going aboard the *Robert Spankie* ; he had taken no part in the murders or the plundering of the brig ; on the contrary he had sided with the crew.

His defence availed him little, since he had no witnesses to support his tale, and there was evidence in plenty to contradict it. He was found guilty of being accessory to the murder of the Commander and Supercargo of the *Robert Spankie* and sentenced to be transported to the penal settlement at Bombay for life. On the face of it, he might have set up a plea that the Court had no jurisdiction, since the murders had taken place within territorial waters of an independent ruler, but he did not. There can be no doubt that material justice was done. Indeed, that nameless man from Canterbury may have considered himself lucky to have escaped the gallows, a fate he richly deserved.

One would have liked to know more of this strange character. Did he speak the truth when he told the magistrate that he did not know his English name ? Or was it shame that made him keep it secret, some queer loyalty to his own people ? And if his story were true, how had he lived all those years since his father had bereft him of his name and thrust him into an alien faith ? In what remote cities had he rested ? What deserts had he crossed ? What unchartered seas had he sailed ? Here was a man, one might suppose, who must have come to a knowledge of the Eastern mind deeper than Westerners may have. For twenty years he had lived among the followers of Islam; he spoke their tongue; he had made the pilgrimage to the holiest of their shrines. His lot had been cast in the lonelier places of the East, amongst men who had never known any white man but him : men

K

who were used to taking what they wanted, who were a law unto themselves. What had he learnt from his life amongst them? Perhaps so much that he might have made himself a king.

But was he a man whom life could teach? Often those to whom life shows most, learn least from what they see. It may be that he was one of those. Perhaps it was indeed true that he had forgotten his name and was a Malay not only by faith but in thought as well. He was certainly no supine forerunner of the modern beach-comber, content to exist upon the bounty of natives. That his devices could be as crooked as those of the most cunning Malay, we have seen, but he was a man of action too, and a man with some power to lead. Whether the plot to seize the brig was his or the Rajah Muda's one cannot say, but it is not hard to believe that, when it came to killing, his hand had been the first to draw a *kris*.

It would be foolish to sentimentalise about him, or to think of him hungering for the cathedral city he had known as a child. Had he captured the *Robert Spankie* after a good honest fight he might have attained a glamour of romance. As it is, Canterbury has small reason to be proud of this nameless son of hers, this treacherous guest who was himself betrayed; this pirate who fought by stabbing unarmed traders in the back. Although he suffered for his misdeeds, his punishment was probably less than he deserved. Nevertheless, I, for one, would have been glad to have had the writing of his life.

CHAPTER X

THE PIRATES OF JILOLO

H.M.S. *Samarang's* boats attacked by pirates off the coast of Jilolo
—Village burnt—The appearance of the pirate squadron—
Fierce encounter—Captain Belcher wounded—The pirates
make off—Dutch protest—Were Belcher's attackers really
pirates ?—Prize-money paid.

ON June 3, 1844, H.M.S. *Samarang* (Captain Sir Edward
Belcher), during the course of a voyage designed by the
Admiralty to secure a survey of the approaches to the
ports newly laid open by the new treaty with China,
was lying off the west coast of Jilolo (Halmaheira), one
of the Spice Islands.

Being detained by calms, Captain Belcher determined to take the opportunity of surveying part of the
Jilolo coast which was supposed to be incorrectly laid
down in the charts. Accordingly, leaving the ship in
charge of his senior lieutenant, Mr. Heard, he set out in
his gig, with his purser and assistant-surgeon and four
seamen, accompanied by one of the *Samarang's* barges,
commanded by Lieutenant Baugh.

About 10 a.m. the gig's party landed on a coral reef
which ran out a cable's length from an islet off the
main coast, leaving the barge at anchor fifty yards from
the shore. By pounding the brittle coral with crowbars,
a firm foundation for the instruments was obtained.
While the forenoon observations were being taken
several unarmed natives approached. They appeared
too cautious to respond to any friendly overtures and
presently stole away, but Captain Belcher was able to
gather from their conversation that they knew the
survey party to be English. This fact is important in
view of what occurred later.

Soon after Captain Belcher had obtained the meridian altitude of the sun he was surprised by a discordant yell behind him, and turned to see a party of some forty natives, all armed with spears and swords, advancing upon him from the island. Their leaders were dressed in scarlet, and from this Captain Belcher concluded that they must be Illanun pirates. As to their hostile intent there could be no doubt, for they came charging towards him, capering and yelling and hurling their spears.

Captain Belcher immediately ordered the chronometer and the light instruments into the gig. The natives, taking this move for a retreat, increased their pace, shouting with triumph. Captain Belcher gave his men the order to load their muskets and fix bayonets, at the same time directing the barge to close and cover them.

The natives continued to approach, and Captain Belcher directed his men to fire a volley over their heads ; but there was considerable delay before the muskets would go off, owing to faulty percussion-caps. Fortunately, however, the natives were not quick-witted enough to take advantage of this delay. They halted, but when Captain Belcher waved to them to retire they advanced again and did not retreat until they found the musket balls whizzing over their heads.

At this moment a large prahu appeared from the far side of the island and began to pull towards the barge, apparently with the object of cutting her off from the gig, but sheered off on seeing the muzzle of the brass six-pounder in her bow, and then hoisted a dirty Dutch flag. A voice hailed the gig in English, saying that the prahu belonged to the neighbouring island of Tïdore and merely wished to pass in peace and to go to a river in the north of Jilolo. But, on being allowed to proceed, she was no sooner out of range of the barge's gun than she began to make a circuit and succeeded in regaining the back of the island in spite of a Congreve rocket being fired over her.

Not wishing to lose his observations for securing the astronomical position, Captain Belcher did not pursue the prahu at once, but waited to obtain the afternoon sights; then packed up and made for the farther side of the island. On rounding the point he saw two boats making off, while the village whence they had escaped remained deserted. Mr. Hooper, the purser, was despatched with the gig to burn the village. This he did " in his usual good style," as Captain Belcher described it, and also destroyed six large prahus which he found hauled up on the beach.

Meanwhile the barge gave chase to the retreating prahus and captured both, the crews having run them ashore and taken to the jungle after a round of grape. After the arms, flags, and gongs had been removed, the two prizes were towed out to sea and burnt, and, having been rejoined by the gig, Captain Belcher pulled on about twenty miles to the south, and shortly after midnight anchored in a lonely bay, safe, as he thought, from further molestation.

All but the watch were sleeping, tired out after the exertions of the day, when across the calm sea came the faint sound of gongs. The officer of the watch, supposing that some feast was in progress on shore, at first paid no attention to this music, but as it grew nearer and nearer he gave the alarm, and there was barely time to furl awnings and clear for action before five large war-boats were sighted entering the bay.

The moon was just rising behind a hill in-shore, so that the party in the *Samarang's* boats were able to get a clear view of the newcomers without being seen themselves. As the prahus drew nearer they were seen to be the largest type of war-boat, about ninety feet in length, decorated at stem and stern with feathers and curling ribbons of bleached palmetto, with long streamers flying from their masts. Each prahu pulled about sixty oars, and had twenty fighting-men apiece. These warriors were apparently on the look-out for prey, for they were dressed in scarlet in the Illanun style, and were standing ready for action on the fighting-platform above the rowers.

With the moonlight shining in his eyes, the commander of the leading prahu actually sailed a few yards past the barge before he saw her. Then there was a sharp exclamation of surprise; an order was rapped out; the prahu's sail was lowered and she rounded-to while her captain gave a hail in Malay, followed by "Who are you?" in broken English.

"The captain of a British ship-of-war!" came the reply, both in Malay and English.

"Where is your ship?"

"Outside."

On hearing this the pirates (by this time Captain Belcher was certain they were no other) began stamping on the platforms, yelling their war-cries and hurling spears, exulting, no doubt, at the ease with which they were about to take these two unexpected prizes. The commander tried to turn his bow towards the barge, intending to bring his bow gun into action and then ram the barge by one effort of his oars, but the prahu's length prevented her from turning quickly and he failed.

On the other hand, escape from the bay was closed by the remaining four prahus, which had approached to within half a pistol shot and lowered their sails, so that Captain Belcher realised that it would be useless to waste time in further parley. He therefore opened fire on the leading prahu with the six-pounder, charged with round shot and cannister. The range was no more than twenty yards and the first discharge played havoc with the prahu, so that many of the crew leapt into the water, while those who remained pulled for the reef that jutted out into the bay from the shore and then took to the jungle. The remaining prahus then opened fire with their guns and showered volleys of spears at the boats. Pulling to within twenty yards of them Captain Belcher gave the second and third prahus four rounds each, so that they, too, made for the reef, heeling over as their crews tried to escape on one side. With the object of securing these three vessels the gig was directed to weigh the barge's anchor and to attach the cable to the prahus. They were then towed off by the barge and anchored by their own gear far enough off-shore to prevent the pirates swimming off and recapturing them.

In the meantime the fourth and fifth prahus, which had not suffered so much as the others, had pulled towards the reef, taken aboard the unwounded men who had landed and made off. Captain Belcher, leaving Mr. Hooper with the gig to guard the prizes, took the barge in pursuit. The prahus had a mile start, but the barge was faster and was not long in overhauling them. The prahus ran into another bay ; the barge followed, and after the second discharge of the gun the pirates ran their vessels aground and fled into the jungle, abandoning many dead and wounded. The wounded were all put in one of the prahus, which was disabled and left on the beach ; the dead were placed in the other, which was then towed out to sea and set on fire.

◇   ◇

By this time it was almost morning, but the adventures of the *Samarang's* people were not over yet, for as the dawn began to break over the sea they saw that another squadron of five prahus, even larger and more elaborately decorated than the first, had taken up a position in line abreast, with the obvious intention of preventing the barge from rejoining the gig.

The gig was not in sight. There was no saying what had become of her. To those in the barge it seemed more than likely that she had been taken unawares by the squadron that was now confronting them. Indeed, in the dim light they fancied they could see some of their comrades held as prisoners on the fighting-platform of the largest vessel, and, bent on rescuing them, Captain Belcher gallantly sent his barge straight at the pirate squadron, hopelessly outnumbered though he was.

In the largest of the prahus, which held the outside station, stood a gorgeously dressed figure. He and his companions performed a war dance on the platform as the barge advanced and the whole squadron yelled defiance, flinging spears and opening fire with their guns.

As it grew lighter Captain Belcher saw that he had been mistaken as to the figures he had seen in the pirate prahu. Whatever had happened to Mr. Hooper and his men, they were not prisoners, and so the barge's long gun began to pour a destructive fire of shot and cannister into the pirate craft from a range of twenty yards, supported by Congreve rockets and musketry. The pirates reeled under the attack, and some of them made for the reef, but the chief continued to fight his prahu until the last charge of cannister was in the barge's gun, the last rocket in the tube, and nearly all the percussion caps were expended.

Captain Belcher prepared to fire the last rocket, and ordered the barge to pull even closer to the prahu. As he stood in the stern, with the rocket-tube in his hand, taking aim at the chief, who was waving his *kris* in defiance, a well-directed shot from the prahu's brass gun struck the rocket-tube and, glancing on to Captain Belcher's thigh, knocked him overboard. Fortunately he had the presence of mind to cling to the barge's gunwale and thus supported himself until hauled in by two of his officers.

The pirates gave a yell of triumph when they saw Captain Belcher fall, but it was their last effort, for the barge fired the remaining charge in her six-pounder with such effect that they fled to the reef and abandoned their vessel, little knowing that their enemy's ammunition was almost completely exhausted.

With all this close-fighting it seems extraordinary that, besides Captain Belcher, the only other casualty should have been a marine, who was wounded in the neck. Captain Belcher's wound, however, was serious, the ball having entered his left thigh, passed out behind and re-entered the right, where it had embedded itself; and since it was urgently necessary to extract the shot as soon as possible the barge pulled for the ship, whose royals were by that time just visible above the horizon.

On seeing the barge retiring, the pirates returned to their vessels and began firing again, but without effect.

The barge reached the ship about 10 a.m., and although the crew had been on their oars for eight hours continuously, and in action for four, every man of them volunteered to go out again in search of the gig, whose fate was still in doubt. This time Mr. Heard, the senior lieutenant, was given command of the barge, and took with him the *Samarang's* two cutters. His orders were: " to seek for the gig, and, taking her also under his command, proceed to punish, or destroy, the remaining prahus; but on no account to land, or risk the crew, by bush-fighting." [1]

About 11.30 a.m. the second cutter discovered a sail in-shore; she was made out to be the gig. They closed with her, and discovered all was well. Mr. Hooper, finding that the barge did not return at day-break, had towed the three captured prahus to sea and burnt them. The largest was well stored with arms and gunpowder—some of the muskets having the Tower mark[2]; her brass gun was too heavy to embark in the gig. Before firing her, Mr. Hooper removed a woman and child and landed them on the reef. From

---

[1] Captain Belcher's official despatch.
[2] Some of these old Tower muskets may still be found stowed away in houses in the Borneo hills.

this woman's frequent ejaculations of "Papua!
Papua!" it seemed evident that she had been taken as
a slave on the New Guinea coast. Having burnt the
prahus, he had followed the course taken by the barge,
being guided by the sound of the firing; but when he
entered the bay the barge was gone, and, seeing several
prahus with flags flying and gongs beating, he concluded
that his shipmates had been overpowered, and was making the best of his way towards the ship when sighted
by the boat party. Mr. Heard directed him to return
to the ship and relieve the captain's mind, but, having
reported, the crew (who had scarcely rested since the
previous noon and had been pulling for hours under
a broiling sun) begged so hard to be allowed to rejoin
their companions that Captain Belcher consented.

After parting from the gig Mr. Heard made for the
scene of the last action, where he found a dozen prahus
moored within a reef behind a village, which was
inaccessible owing to the low water. The boats
immediately opened fire, to which the pirates replied
from a masked and entrenched battery, in which was one
heavy gun and several smaller ones of brass.

After an hour's cannonade on both sides the gig
rejoined the boat party, bringing further orders that there
was to be no landing and directing the boats to return
to the ship at sunset. "This order was not received
with pleasure," wrote Mr. F. S. Marryat, one of the
Samarang's midshipmen, "as we hoped to have the chance
of punishing the fellows a little more."[1]

As it was, nothing more could be done, for the
uncovered reef prevented a closer approach to the
village. Mr. Heard therefore pulled round the arm
of the bay, where he found two small prahus. These
were towed to sea and burnt, and the party returned
to the ship, which then made sail.

❖   ❖

[1] *Borneo and the Indian Archipelago*, p. 51.

This action had a curious sequel, which raised the question : were the people whom Captain Belcher attacked really pirates or was the fight and the ensuing loss of life due to some terrible misunderstanding ? The Dutch held that, so far from being pirates, the natives in question were actually employed by them to suppress piracy in those seas, and they made a vehement protest to the Singapore authorities, who seem to have felt that there was reason in their complaint. I have not been able to trace the original correspondence on this subject, and Captain Belcher does not refer to it, either in his official despatch or in the account he gives of the action in *The Voyage of H.M.S. Samarang*. I shall therefore take the next best evidence and quote from Mr. Marryat, who gives the substance of the Dutch arguments :[1]

" It is but fair," he says, " to give the arguments that were used against us, particularly as the authorities at Singapore appeared to think that we were to blame. They said, you were in boats and you touched at Gillolo ; the natives, accustomed to be taken off by the Illanoan pirates, were naturally jealous and suspicious, seeing no vessel. They came along, armed, to ascertain who you were. At 100 yards they stopped ; you signalled them to go away, and they advanced nearer to you, but they committed no act of hostility. You fired a volley at them, and they retreated. Here the aggression was on your side.

" At the same time, you say, a war prahu pulled round the point, and approached to within range ; when the prahu was close to you she ceased paddling and hoisted Dutch colours. You desired it to pull for the Gillolo shore, which it did. There was no aggression in this instance, and nothing piratical in the conduct of the prahu. After she had obeyed your orders to pull to the Gillolo shore, you wantonly fired a Congreve rocket at

[1] *Op. cit.*, pp. 52-4.

her; your conduct in this instance being much more like a pirate than hers. In the afternoon you pull along the Gillolo shore, and you discover a village; you send your boat ashore and set fire to it. Why so? You state that you were attacked by Illanoan pirates, who reside at Tampassook, some hundred miles from Gillolo, and you then burn the village of the people of Gillolo, and that without the least aggression on their part. Is it surprising that you should be supposed to be pirates after such wanton outrage? To proceed; you state that you then go in search of the prahu which you ordered away, and that on your way you captured a large canoe, which you take in tow, and afterwards perceive the pirates hauling their vessel into a creek. You attack them, and they run away, leaving the prahu in your possession, and as usual, after rifling the prahu and canoe, you set them on fire. Up to this point there has been nothing but aggression on your part; and it is not, therefore, surprising that you were supposed to be pirates, and that the communication was made along the coast, and the vessels employed against the pirates summoned for its protection. Again the prahus came out and surrounded you; they did not fire at you, but hailed you in English, requesting to know if you belonged to a ship. Now, if anything could prove that they were not pirate vessels, it was their doing this, and had you replied, they would have explained to you what their employment was; but you think proper to give no answer to this simple question, order them to go away, and then fire a loaded musket into them, which brings on the conflict which you so much desired.

"That these observations were true, it must be admitted, and the complaint of the Dutch, with the hoisting of the Dutch flag, gave great weight to them."

Mr. Marryat, then, inclined to the opinion that the Dutch attitude was justified; but that opinion may have been coloured by his personal animus against

Captain Belcher—which is evident in his book. On the other hand, in his account of the first encounter with the natives, he certainly does not mention any hostile action on their part beyond saying that they advanced with loud yells. Yet he was in the barge and had spears been thrown he must have seen them. Nor does Captain Belcher mention the spear-throwing in his official despatch—only in the published narrative. But he had reason to believe that the natives knew the party to be English, and the fact that their leaders were dressed in scarlet convinced him that they were Illanuns. This belief was subsequently confirmed by the master of a Dutch schooner, who assured him that no vessels of such size, or armed in such a manner, belonged to any of the petty authorities of the neighbouring States; and that they must have been Illanuns.

Against this, if the boats were Illanuns, was Captain Belcher justified in destroying the village? To me it seems probable that he was, for the Jilolo people were allies of the Illanuns and accustomed to join forces with them on their cruises. This is proved by Rajah Brooke's meeting with an Illanun fleet in the Sarawak River in 1841. In this fleet were several prahus from Jilolo, and their chiefs told the Rajah that since the Dutch had subjugated their country they had taken to a wandering piratical life : the old story of Dutch aggression and monopoly.[1] That the people whom Captain Belcher punished were employed by the Dutch for the suppression of piracy may have been true ; but it must have been a case of setting a pirate to catch a pirate, and, although vessels flying the Dutch flag would have been immune from attack, the Jilolo folk were doubtless glad enough to regard others as pirates that they might have an excuse for plundering them—and squealed when they burnt their fingers.

Moreover, further justification for Captain Belcher

[1] *The Voyage of H.M.S. " Dido,"* i, 194.

is provided by Spenser St. John, who, some time after
the episode, met at Sulu a man who had taken part
in the action. This person stated that the Sultan of
Jilolo had sent a fleet to take prisoner a tributary rajah
of New Guinea, who had been decoyed on board and
killed. On the return voyage the fleet had fallen in
with the *Samarang's* boats, which they mistook for native
prahus and attacked and were astonished at the reception
they received.[1]

By this evidence the boats were not Illanun, but
from Jilolo itself, and although the Dutch protest
was doubtless made in good faith on the information
of the disappointed warriors, it seems possible to acquit
Captain Belcher of having attacked peaceful natives
in mistake for pirates. This, at all events, was the view
of the Admiralty Court, when, on the return of the
Samarang to England, application for the award of
bounties was made. The affidavits showed that 1,580
pirates had been engaged in the action, of whom 350
had been killed; while twenty-seven vessels had been
destroyed or disabled. The Queen's Advocate, on behalf
of the Crown, admitted that a very meritorious service
had been performed and made no opposition to the application, with the result that £10,000 was awarded to the
officers and men of the *Samarang*, while for his wound
Captain Belcher obtained (according to Mr. Marryat)
a pension of £250 a year.

---

[1] *Life in the Forests of the Far East*, ii, 214.

CHAPTER XI

THE STRANGE CASE OF THE " PREMIER "

Captain Belcher receives news of the wreck of the *Premier*—
Captain and crew said to be detained at Gunong Tabor—
Lascars' statements—The *Samarang* reaches Gunong Tabor—
Friendly reception by the Sultan—The true story of the
Premier revealed—The captain's unwarrantable conduct—
Captain Belcher signs treaty with the Sultan—Proceeds to
Bulongan and rescues twelve lascars from slavery.

In November, 1844, Captain Sir Edward Belcher
took the *Samarang* in to Manila to refit, and while there
received the following letter, forwarded by Mr. William
Wyndham, the English trader at Sulu, from the master
of the British parque *Premier*:

> *Goonong Tabboo River,*
>   *10th Sept., 1844.*
> *To the British Consul or any European merchant at Sooloo or*
>   *Manila.*
>   *Gentlemen,*
>   *I take this opportunity of informing you the sad state*
> *we are now living in. On the 27th of July, 1844, the barque*
> *Premier from Hong-Kong, bound to the Island of Bally, in*
> *ballast and Chinese cash, for Rice, was wrecked on Pulo*
> *Panjang, and was obliged to take to our boats, but next day*
> *after leaving the ship, was taken in tow by a proa, and enticed*
> *us to go to Sultan Gooning's, as he would send us to Macassar*
> *soon ; but when we got there, he put us off from day to day,*
> *and made the excuse, that he would get all things from the ship,*
> *and send everything to Macassar with us in a proa.*
>   *We remained at his house five days, and was sent on*
> *board a proa in the river to live, where we had little to eat, and*

not a mat to lie upon. When he came from the wreck he had twenty or thirty proas loaded with all the iron and cash they could get ; and it was agreed with the Rajah of Balongan to divide the ship's crew. So the Sultan kept six Lascars and us seven Europeans ; the Lascars are all slaves, and we hear that he will sell us to the Sagi people, to be taken to the interior of Borneo, so as we will never be heard of more. Upon hearing this, I went to see if he would allow us to leave the island, and after some time he said we might take our own boats, he having the oars, rudder and sails, with our provisions, and boats' rullocks ; however, we made our escape in the night to Rajah's Moody's ¹ and there remain, but the Sultan is going to war with him if he does not give us up, and has told several people that he will murder us, so we are obliged to keep watch at night at the Rajah's house, and several attempts has been made to set fire to it. On the 12th (that is [in] two days) they go to war, and we are to use the large guns.*

We humbly beg, whoever may get these few lines, that he will use his power to take from this country any that remain alive of us to tell the whole of our sad fate. The names of the Europeans are

W. Brownrigg,	*Master.*
J. Watson,	*Chief Mate.*
J. Mathers,	*Second Mate.*
F. Potina,	*Seaman.*
H. Mathers,	*Apprentice.*
W. Parken,	*Apprentice.*
S. Mc'Dowell,	*Apprentice.*

The two latter sick.

We poor seamen beg for relief with all possible speed, and will ever be your obedient servants,

Wm. Brownrigg.

Pulo Mantan.

P.S.—Since I wrote, the Rajah came to me and said that he would send us to Coté in a fast pulling canoe this night

---

¹ *i.e.*, The Rajah Muda, the heir apparent.

(11th Sept.), so as to be out of the way of the Sultan, and to get to Macassar sooner.

We shall be obliged to fight our way down the river, and the Rajah has supplied us with musquets and ammunition.

                                                    W. Brownrigg.

This letter had been brought to Mr. Wyndham by six of the *Premier's* lascars, for whom he had paid ransom at his own expense, and then had sent on to the British Consul at Manila in the hope that some action might be taken by the authorities.

Captain Belcher lost no time in examining these men, and their statements disclosed a curious story. It appeared that the *Premier* had struck the reef, which was off the eastern coast of Borneo, at 11 o'clock at night. The Master (whom they knew as Milne, not Brownrigg) got one anchor out astern, but the cable parted. They worked at the pumps until 10 o'clock the following morning. The Master then fired guns to attract the attention of any passing vessel, and examined the ship, finding that there was a hole in her bow and that the water was pouring in fast; but the lascars insisted that her main keel was intact. No boats came to their assistance; there was not a sail in sight. Three boats— the cutter, the longboat and the gig were got out, and such articles as could be saved were put into them. The longboat had two casks of water, two small casks of beer, the carpenter's chest, the chief-mate's chest, and the lascars' bags. The cutter took one cask of rum, the Chinese copper cash, the arms and the captain's personal effects. She, however, was swamped, and her crew got into the longboat, lightening her to make her safe.

They quitted the ship at 3 p.m., but before leaving her the Master set fire to her, using a resin (*damar*) butt, which he placed on the main deck, near the mainmast, and also strewing the resin about the ship between decks, placing it on sticks to make it burn.

L

They reached an island off the Borneo coast the following night, and landed. The Master then said he proposed to go back to Zamboanga (near Sulu), but the lascars refused to go with him, saying that they wished to get to Macassar. He then shoved off, saying that those who wished to accompany him might do so. Only the Europeans went with him, the lascars, twenty-two in all, preferring to stay on the island. Four of them built a raft and put to sea, but were never heard of again; the remainder were taken off by a Malay prahu a week later, and were subsequently separated, twelve being delivered to a haji of Bulongan and six (those who eventually reached Sulu) going to the Sultan of Gunong Tabor, on the Pantai River, where they found the Master and other Europeans.

Having elicited these facts, Captain Belcher decided that he must not delay a moment in doing all he could to rescue his fellow-countrymen. He took the *Samarang* to Sulu, where the Sultan professed himself anxious to do all in his power to assist, and sent an officer in one of his own prahus to accompany the ship to Gunong Tabor.

The *Samarang* left Sulu on December 21, 1844, and four days later sighted the reef on which the *Premier* had been wrecked; and the same evening anchored within the mouth of the Pantai River. Gunong Tabor lay some distance up the river and was reached in the boats. The town was found to be closely stockaded and defended. On the approach of the boats the Sultan sent his Prime Minister to convey his welcome, and to inquire with what number of guns Captain Belcher would salute, and, after some discussion, it was arranged that the *Samarang's* party would return the Sultan's salute of twenty-one guns to the English colours.

These formalities having been carried out, the sound of music was heard, and a moment later a procession

was seen filing through the gates of the town towards
the boats. It was headed by a standard-bearer carrying the red and white colours of Gunong Tabor, followed
by two armed warriors ; then came the Prime Minister,
who marched beneath the State canopy, a huge umbrella
of scarlet silk fringed with gold lace; after him, two
musicians, one playing a flageolet, the other an English
brass drum (which it was discovered later had come from
the British settlement at Balambangan years before).
These men were dressed in red bordered with yellow,
with cowls over their heads. A bodyguard of armed
men brought up the rear.

The procession advanced to the landing-stage,
and the Prime Minister invited Captain Belcher to accompany him to the palace. Placing himself on Captain
Belcher's left side, taking his left hand and passing the
right hand under Captain Belcher's right arm, the
Prime Minister conducted his guest to the canopy.
The other officers, similarly escorted, followed, and the
procession set off to the royal audience hall, a large
building on the right of the palace, open on all sides,
the floor being covered with mats. Gaily painted
Chinese chests, on which were lain small yellow cloths
with scarlet patterns embroidered in gold, served as
seats.

The Sultan, whom Captain Belcher describes as
" a fine, well-shaped, intelligent young man of about
five feet eleven, and thirty years of age, most elegantly
habited in scarlet and gold embroidery," advanced to
meet his guests and welcome them to his territory.
" There could be no doubt of the genuine cordiality
of our reception," wrote Captain Belcher. " It was
eagerly kind, and the anxiety of the Sultan to prove his
friendship was manifested in every possible manner." [1]

Such was the attitude of the ruler whom Captain
Belcher had darkly suspected of robbing his ship-

---

[1] *The Voyage of H.M.S. "Samarang,"* i, 216, 217.

wrecked fellow-countrymen. It is pleasant to be able
to relate that these suspicions were ill-founded. In
these grim annals of treachery, pillage and bloodshed,
the Sultan of Gunong Tabor, at least, stands out as an
honest man, true to his professions of friendship, an
agreeable example of the Malay prince at his best.

It appeared that he had kept a journal in which he
had entered the receipt or delivery of every article
saved from the wreck. He had also set down the con-
versations he had had with the Master of the *Premier*,
whom he, too, had known as Milne, and he was able
to show that all the shipwrecked Europeans had been
taken away by a Dutch schooner-of-war two months
previously. He produced a document from the Dutch
captain as evidence, and stated that he himself had sent
the six lascars to Sulu without asking ransom; the
ransom had been demanded by the captain of the prahu,
not by his authority. This statement was subsequently
found to be correct.

His Highness told Captain Belcher that Captain Milne
and the other Europeans had become very troublesome.
He had suggested their going to Sulu in the boat that
took the lascars, but they had declined, as it appeared
that their pride recoiled against being associated with
the native crew. In fact, Captain Milne had sworn
that he did not care what became of the unfortunate
lascars, saying, " Do what you please with them; sell
them," as though they had been slaves.

As the Europeans had insisted on remaining, the
Sultan had provided them with fowls and rice, the best
he could obtain, and had treated them as equals; for
this he had not even received thanks. Finally, they had
become so sullen and discontented, and their drunken-
ness and foul language had so incensed his own people,
that he had put them on board a prahu lest they should
come to harm. They had then started to intrigue with
his rebellious cousin, the Rajah Muda, who had induced
them to join him in his fort three miles away, promising

THE SULTAN OF GUNONG TABOR.

[From *The Voyage of H.M.S. "Samarang."*

to send them safely to his uncle the Sultan of Koti. Had they gone to Koti, said the Sultan, they would certainly either have been murdered or held to ransom, and to prevent this he had blockaded his cousin's fort until the schooner arrived, when the whole party were allowed to go free.

The Sultan complained that so far from thanking him for his efforts, Captain Milne had showed his ingratitude by demanding back a writing-desk which he had presented on his first arrival ; but this had been given back, together with every other article that had come out of the ship, as the Sultan was able to prove by the receipts he held.

Why Captain Milne (or Brownrigg) took such trouble to set fire to his ship there is nothing to show.   Captain Belcher considered his action " highly injudicious and unwarrantable.   In the first place the vessel became a beacon to attract the pirates of this region; in the second, he was bound to save the property as far as he was able.   Had he not acted as he did, the masts, sails, etc., would have been saved, and the Sultan of Gunong Tabor would have been satisfied with reasonable salvage."[1]

The Sultan told Captain Belcher that Milne's action " divided his power," for the ship and her stores became " as fish," everyone taking what he could catch.

" Everything I could find to restore," said His Highness to Captain Belcher, " I was glad to send away, because it reminded us of bad men ; but the iron of the vessel, which my people had cut out of the wood where the fire had bared it, and had been worked into spear and kris blades, I was unable to recover.   But I am so happy that you have come to give us better thoughts of your countrymen ; we must be friends ; I must have an English flag."

Finding that His Highness had no agreement with other nations which bound him to more than friendly

---

[1] *Op. cit.*, 241.

reception and permission to trade (for the Dutch had not yet annexed this part of Borneo), Captain Belcher drew up the following treaty :

" The Sultan of Gunung Taboor is anxious to enter into friendly relations with Her Majesty the Queen of Great Britain, and is willing to execute a formal Treaty of Friendship and Commerce whenever Her Majesty the Queen of Great Britain will send any duly authorised person.

" The Sultan of Gunung Taboor engages, that the subjects of the Queen of Great Britain shall always meet with friendship and protection within his dominions.

" On the part of the Queen of Great Britain, Sir Edward Belcher, commanding Her Majesty's Ship *Samarang*, engages, that similar friendship and protection will be accorded to the subjects of the Sultan of Gunung Taboor, should they visit any of the ports belonging to Great Britain."

This treaty was signed by both parties and His Highness, standing up before his people, locked his right thumb in Captain Belcher's and declared that they were brothers. A royal salute was fired from the ship's boats to complete the ceremony.

The Sultan informed Captain Belcher that the remaining twelve lascars were probably still at Bulongan, a town some distance to the south, and offered to give all the assistance he could in their recovery. Taking with him the Sultan's chief naval officer with a prahu and escort, Captain Belcher then took leave of His Highness and having reached the mouth of the Bulongan in the *Samarang*, ascended it as far as the town in the ship's boats.

The Sultan professed his friendship, but was obviously a weaker potentate than His Highness of Gunong

Tabor, and apparently in the hands of his chiefs, who did not relish the idea of handing over the lascars without compensation. Finally, he declared that some of them could be produced in two days, but others were in the interior and could not be handed over in less than six. Captain Belcher, suspecting that the Sultan's ministers designed to tire his patience by repeated delays, after the fashion of Malay nobles, replied that having come thus far to find these subjects of his Queen, he would remain there until every one of them was produced, and reminded the Sultan that during the period of waiting he would expect His Highness to support the boats' crews.

This had a stimulating effect, and on the evening of the second day ten lascars were handed over, and they were followed on the fourth day by the remaining two.

The Sultan appeared glad to be rid of the lascars before they involved him in further trouble, but Captain Belcher did not leave until he had concluded a treaty with His Highness similar to that made with the Sultan of Gunong Tabor.

Captain Belcher then quitted Bulongan with the rescued lascars, whose joy at their unexpected release was extreme. The whole affair is a good example of the jealous care with which Great Britain is wont to watch over her subjects, and Captain Belcher's zeal and diplomacy is a contrast to the callous indifference of those wretched men's own Master. What became of him, or why he called himself Brownrigg when his name apparently was Milne, we are never likely to know. He certainly did not deserve to command another ship.

On the other hand, by his prompt action, Captain Belcher attained his object without violence and merely by a show of strength. The Sultan of Gunong Tabor had certainly shown himself more humane and enlightened than most Borneo princes of his day, and even the Sultan of Bulongan had surrendered the lascars when called upon. Captain Belcher felt assured that these people had been better treated than they would have been anywhere else in Borneo, and the visit of the *Samarang's* boats left behind an impression from which nothing but good could come. " I firmly believe," he wrote, " that they now entertain a greater dread of the force we could bring against them than if we had destroyed their towns. No such power has been exhibited, but I have reason to know that they have magnified it in imagination to such an extent that any distressed British subject will, in future, meet with a *home*, instead of that *revenge* which harsher measures would have inevitably entailed." [1]

---

[1] *Op. cit.*, p. 246

CHAPTER XII

THE SULTAN OF BRUNEI

The city of Brunei—The Sultan's pedigree—Rajah Muda Hassim, the friend of the English—Pangeran Usop's slave-dealings with Serip Usman of Marudu—Rajah Brooke and Captain Belcher visit Brunei—The British flag insulted—Captain Belcher's ultimatum to the Sultan—The Sultan promises the cession of Labuan Island.

IT is customary to call Brunei the Venice of the East. The description is a facile one, but apt, inasmuch as Brunei is a city of waterways: more than that, most of its houses are built actually over the water at a point where the river forms a wide and shallow estuary. The State of which this city is the capital is still ruled by a native Sultan, with a British Resident as adviser. It is a British Protectorate, and for administrative purposes forms part of the Straits Settlements.   To-day its area is scarcely 3,000 square miles, but a century ago the Sultan's sovereignty extended over the territory that is now Sarawak, and over much that is now held by the British North Borneo Chartered Company, although even then the power of Brunei, like that of other independent Malay kingdoms—Achin, Malacca, Bantam, Johore—was on the wane.   Pigafetta, the historian of Magellan, gives a glowing description of the splendours of the Brunei Court when he visited it in 1521.   He estimated the houses at 25,000, although this is almost certainly an exaggeration.   But immense numbers of Chinese had settled in the town, and the extensive trade with China brought the State a prosperity which dwindled when the European powers began to take an interest in the Archipelago.

However, in 1840, there were said to be still some 30,000 inhabitants in the city, which was divided into four parts by two main waterways that intersected each other in the form of a cross. Three of these divisions consisted of strong wooden houses, built on piles over the water, and so close together that there was barely room for a canoe to pass between them. The fourth part of the city was built on the river-bank, and here was the mosque and Sultan's palace. The palace, like the other houses, was built on high piles driven into the mud, so that at high tide it had lapping water beneath it, and, at low, an expanse of stinking mud. The roof was of thatched palm-leaf and the floor consisted of slats of the hard nibong-palm, set about a quarter of an inch apart.

On a fine day at high water the city must have looked like a picture from a fairy tale : the houses seemed to be floating like water-lilies on the surface of the river, and above them fluttered banners and streamers of every colour, indicating the rank and office of the princes and nobles above whose roofs they flew. As evening drew on, the throbbing of drums and the music of gongs made melodies across the water. But it was in the mornings that Brunei could be seen at its best. Since there were no shops, the daily market was held in canoes, which thronged into the city at sunrise, bearing their produce from every part of the river. They gathered in the main waterway of the city and were made fast to each other, so that they formed long lanes through which the housewives of Brunei could paddle their own crafts and examine the wares for sale with as much convenience as if they had been on shore.

The ruler of Brunei at this time was Sultan Omar Ali Suffedin, whose family had provided the throne with twenty-five reigning princes, a fact of which His Highness was extremely proud. Since his relationship

THE CITY OF BRUNEI IN 1840.

[From *Life in the Forests of the Far East.*

with other members of the royal family had an important
bearing on contemporary history, it will be well to show
how he traced his descent from his great-grandfather,
Sultan Omar Ali.

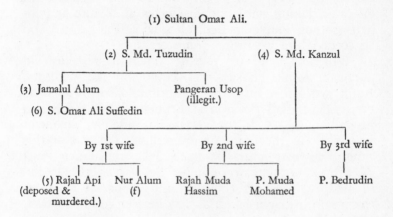

On the death of Rajah Api, who had no legitimate
issue, his brother, Rajah Muda Hassim, became, by
the Brunei law of succession, the rightful heir to the
throne, but he resigned his claim in favour of his nephew,
Omar Ali Suffedin, retaining the office of Prime Minister,
which he had held during the previous reign to the
satisfaction of the people, with whom he was very popular.
His influence was greater even than the Sultan's, and
since he was an enlightened prince he might have been
a power for good at the court had it not been for his
cousin, Pangeran Usop.

Usop, being an illegitimate son of the former Sultan,
Mohamed Tuzudin, could not succeed to the throne.
But he was as unscrupulous as he was ambitious. He
became intensely jealous of Rajah Muda Hassim, and
determined that, come what might, he and not his
cousin should be the power behind the throne of
Brunei. There is little doubt, indeed, that he designed
to contest the succession itself.   Muda Hassim's attempts

to conciliate him were of no avail. A man like Pangeran
Usop is not to be put off by the bestowal of secondary
offices and showy marks of distinction, and the result
was that, sick and tired of the intrigues of the Brunei
Court, Muda Hassim withdrew to the province of
Sarawak, taking with him his wives and suite and his
half-brother, Pangeran Bedrudin, while Pangeran Usop
succeeded him as Prime Minister.

While engaged in putting down a rebellion in
Sarawak, Muda Hassim met James Brooke, with the
result we know. In the meantime, Usop was busy
consolidating his position at Brunei. With the Sultan
he had an easy task, for Omar Ali Suffedin's character
was weak to the point of imbecility. He was at this
time over fifty years of age. His appearance must
have been unprepossessing, for he was short, fat and
bloated, with a deformity in the shape of an extra
thumb on his right hand, as may be seen in his portrait.
He could neither read nor write, and to the Europeans
who met him he appeared incapable of mental concen-
tration. Even the most serious matters of State could not
hold his attention for more than five minutes together.
In manner he was heavy and inclined at first to be timid
with strangers, but when his initial shyness had worn
off he would talk and joke incessantly. He was, in
fact, easy-going and good-tempered, and not unduly
cruel as Malay princes went; and he combined a certain
generosity with an insatiable avarice for personal
possessions. This avarice he carried to a degree which
astonished those who came to his court, and when
foreign visitors had handed over handsome presents
for His Highness's acceptance, he was not above begging
for the share which had been reserved for his ministers
and nobles. Not without cause was it said of him that
he had the head of an idiot and the heart of a pirate.
His treatment of the captain and people of the *Sultana*,
already related, is a fair example of his rapacity, and if
he did not connive at piracy he was certainly glad

enough to pocket some of the profits that came from slave-dealing.

This suited Pangeran Usop very well, for he had formed an unholy business agreement with Serip Usman, a half-bred Arab who had settled in Marudu Bay and built a fort some distance up the Marudu River. Usman had no title whatever to the territory he occupied, but he had gathered round him a band of some 2,000 cut-throats and rapscallions, and this force enabled him do to as he pleased, while his holy descent, and the fact that he was married to a daughter of the Rajah Muda of Sulu, gave him prestige among the piratical settlements of Illanuns at Tempasuk and else-where along the north-western coast of Borneo, so that they made common cause with him.

One of his objects in settling at Marudu was to possess himself of the valuable edible birds'-nests caves on the neighbouring islands. He was in the habit of leading his raiding expeditions in person, and he levied tribute on nearly 5,000 families in the Marudu district; nor did he scruple to attack European trading ships if a chance occurred. He was both robber and receiver of stolen goods; but he specialised in slaves. His influence in Sulu had led to an alliance with the Balanini, who, when they were about to set out on a cruise, would obtain from him their supplies of provisions: salt, guns, shot and powder. On their return they would pay him at the rate of five slaves for every hundred rupees' worth of goods they had received. It will be remembered that a large number of the slaves taken by the Balanini came from Brunei, and Usman hit on the astute and profitable plan of re-selling these victims to Pangeran Usop, who, having paid 100 rupees apiece for them, would restore them to their relatives at the price of 200 rupees a head.

Usop was thus in the way of building up a comfortable fortune by this traffic in the flesh of his own country-men, and it may be supposed that the Sultan, so long as he received what he considered to be a due proportion of the earnings, put no obstacles in his way.

So that Usop for a time continued on his course of intrigue and oppression, until his tyranny caused the populace to long for the return of Muda Hassim, under whose control they had been content. This trend of popular opinion made Usop hate his cousin more bitterly than ever. He grew to look upon him as his enemy, and took every opportunity of creating suspicion against him in the mind of the Sultan, whose half-witted amiability he found easy to sway. Matters reached a crisis when news came of Muda Hassim's alliance and friendship with James Brooke; for Brooke was known to be on the side of law and order and pledged to suppress piracy. That was the last thing that Pangeran Usop wanted, for it would have meant the end of his traffic in Brunei slaves. He therefore gave out that Muda Hassim and Bedrudin were under Brooke's thumb and had become traitors to their own country; that they would help the English to take Labuan, and that the taking of Labuan would be but a step to the annexation of the whole Brunei kingdom.

At first little credit was paid to these statements, anyhow, by the people as a whole. But Pangeran Usop was a shrewd man. He knew, just as newspaper proprietors know to-day, the cumulative force of reiterated statement, and gradually his propaganda began to take effect. Muda Hassim, whose intelligence service kept him posted as to what was going on, having first treated Usop's activities with disdain, began to see that, with the populace as well as the Sultan becoming influenced against him, his position might become serious, and, finally, he determined that he must return to Brunei to refute the charges that were being brought against him.

Now it was perfectly true that Rajah Muda Hassim was friendly to James Brooke and the English. He was also in favour of the occupation of Labuan. Thus far Pangeran Usop was right. But Muda Hassim was no traitor to his country. On the contrary, having more vision than the average Brunei noble, he believed that nothing but good could come from association with a Power which would stamp out piracy and encourage trade, and in a letter presented to Rajah Brooke, and addressed to Her Majesty Queen Victoria, he promised his co-operation to that end.

In October, 1844, Rajah Muda Hassim and his brother Pangeran Bedrudin, with their wives, were taken to Brunei in the steamer *Phlegethon*, whose commander gave up his cabin for their accommodation—presumably he made the offer before he realised how extensively the two princes were married. When the party was embarked at Kuching the most elaborate precautions were taken that no male eye should behold the faces of these ladies. The awnings were spread and the after-part of the ship screened with heavy canvas. The sailors were ordered to remain in the fo'c'sle. Late at night the royal barge came alongside by torchlight and, one by one, each of the ladies, carefully covered by a sarong, was smuggled aboard and carried below. "Twenty-four of these poor creatures," wrote Captain Belcher, "were thus crammed into a space not sufficient for half the number, and, at the moment of their embarkation, a special request was made ' to look another way.' Any disregard of such an intimation, to their own people, would have entailed instant visitation of the *kris*, and we noticed that all the crew of the Rajah's vessel not immediately concerned in their removal, kneeled, stooping with their heads to the bow of the barge. Mr. Brooke and myself were seated abaft the gun on the stern of the vessel, and I observed that he not only abstained most punctiliously from looking in the proscribed direction, but earnestly enjoined me to obedience." [1]

These unfortunate people suffered so severely during the voyage that one actually died in her confined quarters below, but although Muda Hassim was urged to allow them up on deck, that they might breathe some fresh air, protected by screens, he would not consent to their removal.

❖   ❖

Rajah Brooke, earnestly anxious to support Muda Hassim, proceeded to Brunei with Captain Belcher in the *Samarang*. Their arrival caused a panic among Pangeran Usop's party. The batteries were put in a state of defence, and as one of the *Phlegethon's* boats, taking Pangeran Bedrudin up the river to Brunei, passed the fortified island of Cherimon, near the river mouth, it was told to " keep off," and insults were hurled at the British flag. The steamer herself, however, reached the capital without further incident.

On the following day Captain Belcher embarked Rajah Muda Hassim in the *Samarang's* barge, attended by the armed boats of the *Phlegethon*, and landed him in state at the Sultan's audience hall, a three-sided building open to the water. On a platform before the entrance were mounted six brass guns, and above the carved roof, whose gables were decorated with large wooden horns, waved the red and yellow standard of Brunei.

The party was received at the entrance to the hall by a group of chiefs, handsomely dressed in gold-embroidered silks and satins, who ushered the visitors into the main hall, the walls of which were decorated with shields and hangings of coloured cloth.

The natives who filled the chamber sat cross-legged on the matted floor, preserving a respectful silence ; and an aisle was kept clear between them leading

[1] *The Voyage of H.M.S. " Samarang,"* i, 172.

to the throne at the far end of the room. This throne was an affair of painted wood, gilded and carved, and on close inspection suspiciously reminiscent of a Chinese bedstead; upon it, sitting cross-legged, was the Sultan, to whom the party were presented one by one. The Sultan received Muda Hassim with favour; ostensibly, at all events. Chairs were then placed in a half-circle in front of His Highness, and on these the Europeans seated themselves. Pangeran Usop did not appear. It must have been a gloomy morning for him, since none knew better than he how easy the Sultan's putty-like mind was to mould, and he now had to stand aside while the detested Muda Hassim reasserted his former influence.

The Sultan was dressed in a loose jacket and trousers of heavily-embroidered purple satin, a close-fitting vest of gold cloth, with a light cloth turban on his head, which was bald. In his sash was thrust a gold-headed *kris* of beautiful workmanship. His expression was a mingling of suspicion and simplicity; and he used the extra thumb on his right hand to fill his mouth with betel-nut, in which he indulged to excess.

Immediately below him were his two personal attendants, with his betel-nut box and his weapons. Within the half-circle formed by the Europeans were Serip Yussif, one of the principal ministers, Muda Hassim, and Bedrudin, all sitting cross-legged. On each side and below the throne hundreds of armed guards were stationed, those in front sitting with drawn swords, those behind holding long spears, tipped with tufts of scarlet hair.

The discussion was carried on through Mr. Williamson, the interpreter, the speakers being Captain Belcher, Rajah Brooke, Serip Yussif, Muda Hassim and Bedrudin, the Sultan occasionally nodding to signify his approval of various remarks made by his ministers. The whole conversation, although not secret, was carried on in

M

so low a tone as to be inaudible to any but those seated nearest to the throne.

Captain Belcher pointed out that on entering the river that morning one of his boats had been insulted from the forts on Cherimon Island, although flying the white ensign at the time. In consequence of this incident, he demanded that proper respect should be accorded the British flag ; that the forts should be dismantled, and that Rajah Muda Hassim and Pangeran Bedrudin should be reinstated in offices becoming to their rank.

Serip Yussif, who bore the English no love, expressed unqualified disapproval of these demands. The Sultan himself said little. As it was doubtful whether anything short of compulsion would be effective, the conference ended by Captain Belcher indicating the steamer which lay abreast of the palace, and reminding the Sultan and his ministers that a few broadsides would blow the whole town to destruction. With this parting remark, the Europeans rose to depart, saying that they would wait until the following day for an answer.

The situation held a distinct element of danger. The European party—only eight in number—had taken a high hand and they were surrounded by hundreds of armed natives who could and would have fallen upon them at a signal from the Sultan. But although more than one chief would obviously have liked to despatch the white men then and there, they dared not do so, and the party passed unmolested between them to the platform outside, which they found thronged with Muruts, hill folk, who had come down from the mountains to render assistance to the Sultan in the event of hostility on the part of the British. They were armed with long knives and shields which they brandished, occasionally giving a loud yell ; but in spite of their threatening attitude, they allowed the party to pass unharmed to the *Samarang's* barge.

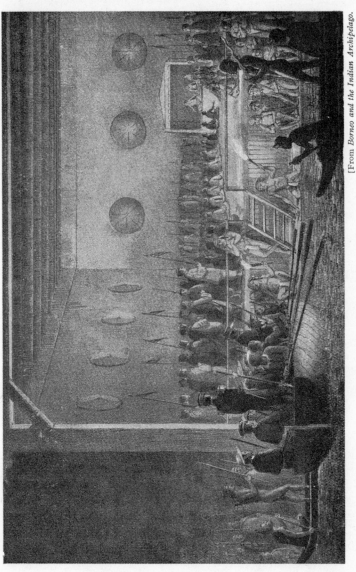

THE SULTAN OF BRUNEI'S COURT.
(Signing the Treaty with Great Britain.)

[From *Borneo and the Indian Archipelago*.

The time limit having expired without His Highness having complied with Captain Belcher's demands, it was decided that no more time should be wasted in useless discussion; the Sultan must be brought to terms at once. Apart from any other consideration, the safety of the Europeans themselves demanded it, since in consequence of the people's indignation at the attempt to coerce their ruler, their attitude hourly grew more menacing.

At 7 p.m. the British party went to the audience chamber. They were unarmed, for they felt that any attempt on their part to defend themselves against so many hundreds would inevitably be unavailing, and that the natives would be far more impressed by indifference to danger.

So much for the moral effect; but in case this should prove inadequate, two of the *Samarang's* officers kept the barge lying on her oars abreast of the audience chamber, with a charge of grape and cannister in her six-pounder, and its muzzle covering the Sultan himself during the whole of the interview.

It was a curious situation. Inside the audience chamber, which was packed with armed men, were five Europeans dictating their own terms to the Sultan; the platform outside was crowded with wild and fierce Muruts, ready to leap to instant action at the first sign of trouble; and every native in the city not only anxious for a fight, but armed and waiting for it.

Those in the barge and the steamer were equally prepared. The discharge of the barge's six-pounder would instantly have killed the Sultan and scores of his followers; and in the main street the steamer lay with a spring on her cable, her half-ports up and her guns loaded. One of them was trained directly on the Sultan, while a man stood ready with the lighted tow in his hand, and every seaman and marine on board held a musket ready loaded.

Rajah Muda Hassim and his brothers were present

at the conference; also Pangeran Usop. Muda Hassim began by suggesting to the Sultan, in terms of perfect courtesy and respect, the dangers of heeding the councils and advices of Pangeran Usop, the latter replying to these charges with the same courtesy with which they were made—both men masking their hatred beneath a veneer of extreme politeness.

Finally, the Sultan, motioning Muda Hassim to him, said: " My father enjoined me at his death to be guided by your counsel, and I intend to be so "; then, feeling suddenly ill, he retired, after having desired Rajah Brooke to consider Muda Hassim as acting for him. The latter immediately assumed control, and, after calling Pangeran Usop to account for his dangerous and foolish acts, sent him with the other ministers to the Sultan for His Highness's consent to the immediate razing of the batteries on Cherimon. This consent they obtained, and Muda Hassim at once issued orders for the batteries to be demolished before dawn.

His Highness also agreed to Captain Belcher's demand that Rajah Muda Hassim and Pangeran Bedrudin should be installed in offices becoming their birth and rank, and a document, addressed to the Queen of England, was then drawn up and the seals of the Sultan and Pangerans were formally attached. It ran as follows :

This Document is addressed by the Sultan, and the Rajah Muda Hassim, as Rulers of the Territory of Borneo, to the Queen of England. The Sultan, and the Rajah Muda Hassim, desire to gain the friendship and aid of the Queen of England for the suppression of piracy and the encouragement and extension of trade ; and to assist in forwarding these objects, they are willing to cede to the Queen of England the Island of Labuan, and its islets, on such terms as hereafter may be arranged by any persons appointed by Her Majesty. The Sultan, and the Rajah Muda Hassim, consider that an English Settlement on Labuan will be of great service to the natives of the coast, and will draw a considerable trade from the

*northward, and from China ; and should Her Majesty the
Queen of England decide upon the measure, the Sultan, and the
Rajah Muda Hassim, promise to afford every assistance to the
English Authorities.*

Rajah Brooke subsequently remarked upon the
coolness shown by the natives, who, although well
aware that the steamer's guns were trained upon them,
showed not the slightest emotion and carried on the
conference with quiet self-possession.

Pangeran Usop was let off lightly, to his evident
relief, being merely relegated to an inferior position.
This leniency was probably owing to the presence of
Rajah Brooke.

Having attained their object, the British party
rejoined the *Samarang*. The ship then sailed for Labuan
and anchored in the new harbour, which Captain
Belcher named Port Victoria, in honour of the Queen,
feeling confident that before long the island would be
British Territory. [1]

It must have been a happy day for Rajah Brooke,
for at last, after long and patient endeavour, events
were shaping as he had planned. As he wrote in his
Journal :

" A port like Labuan and Balambangan would, beyond
doubt, give an impetus to trade, merely from the freedom
from all restrictions which the natives would enjoy ; and
piracy being *checked*, the countries which now lie fallow
would, from their proximity, be induced to bring their
produce into market. This limited extension is of little
moment compared with the results which must attend
our using a beneficial influence over the native governments, for the purposes of affording protection to the

---

[1] Labuan is the Malay word meaning harbour, anchorage. The island has
an area of twenty-six square miles.

poorer classes, insuring safety to the trader, and, without
any guarantee, holding out a fair prospect of success to
the planter or the miner. The slightest acquaintance
with the N.W. coast of Borneo would prove to any
observer, the ease with which these objects might be
effected. The native governments are everywhere fallen
to decay, and the capital of Borneo requires protection
and assistance." [1]

Yet two years were to pass, and much blood was to
be spilt, before the Union Jack was hoisted on Labuan
Island.

---

[1] Mundy's *Narrative*, ii, 24-5.

CHAPTER XIII

THE DOWNFALL OF PANGERAN USOP

Pangeran Usop and Serip Usman form an alliance—Admiral
Cochrane's promise to attack Marudu—Arrives off Brunei
with his squadron—Pangeran Usop's defiance—Panic in a
man-of-war—Usop's house fired on—His flight—The Sultan
signs his death warrant—His execution.

EARLY in 1845 Rajah Brooke was appointed Her
Majesty's Confidential Adviser in Borneo, and was
directed by Lord Aberdeen to go to Brunei with a letter
addressed to the Sultan and Muda Hassim on the subject
of the suppression of piracy.

He set off on his mission in a despondent frame of
mind. To his thinking there had been too much talk
and letter-writing, and too little action, on the part of
the British authorities, and he saw his own tremendous
efforts for peace in Borneo being wasted by the apathy
of his own people. For two years desultory negotiations
had been in progress, with no sign of any definite
conclusion. The British Government would neither
definitely support the Sultan, nor attack the openly
defiant pirates ; consequently Rajah Muda Hassim and
his party were fast losing faith in the British will or
ability to help them. Pangeran Usop, naturally, was
astute enough to make the delay serve his own ends,
while Serip Usman made no bones about expressing his
contempt for the British Navy from his stronghold at
Marudu. The position was so critical that it was to be
feared that at any moment Usman, aided by Usop,
might attack and seize Brunei, when there would be
an end to all chances of a peaceful understanding and
to all his hopes for Borneo's future.

On his arrival at Brunei, however, Rajah Brooke found that Muda Hassim was doing his utmost to fulfil his engagements. Although his position was not made easier by the fact that the Sultan suspected him of plotting to depose him (an idea probably suggested to him by Pangeran Usop), he had addressed a letter to the Illanuns of Tempasuk, informing them of the treaty with Great Britain for the suppression of piracy; he advised them to mend their ways and ordered them not to visit Brunei until they could satisfy him that they were no longer pirates. A letter of similar purport had been despatched to Serip Usman; but instead of having the desired effect, it did but rouse the chief of Marudu to further defiance, and three months later he and his men had plundered and burnt a schooner which had been wrecked off the Borneo coast. Her crew were never heard of again.

Muda Hassim's stand against piracy had inevitably tended to strengthen the alliance between Usman and Usop. If Usop chose to invite Usman and his followers to Brunei, there was little doubt that they could make themselves masters of the town; and there appeared to be a possibility of Usop taking just that step. On the other hand, Muda Hassim was the favourite of the people and had the support of at least three-fifths of the population; and in the event of Usop calling in Usman and the Illanuns of Tempasuk, Rajah Brooke would have supported him with forces from Sarawak. But that would have meant civil war in Brunei, which was just what Brooke wished to avoid. It was a difficult situation. A decisive move by the British Government might have settled it once and for all; but nothing was done and the Sultan himself remained a mere pawn in the game. The real issue lay between Pangeran Usop and Rajah Muda Hassim.

❖ ❖

Muda Hassim was so far able to influence the Sultan

that a letter, of which the following is a translation, was
presented to Rajah Brooke on his arrival at Brunei,
dated March 4, 1845 :

*The Sultan and the Rajah Muda Hassim have received
the letter brought by our friend, and we beg to acquaint our
friend, that in accordance with the appointment of the Queen
of England, we receive our friend as Her Majesty's agent in
Borneo. We now acquaint our friend that we adhere to our
former declarations, conveyed lately through Captain Sir
Edward Belcher, but at the same time, we beg our friend and
Captain Bethune will, pending these negociations, take measures
to protect Borneo from the pirates of Marudu, under Sheriff
Houseman, who is, as we well know, in league with some of the
Pangerans of Borneo, ill-disposed to our government, in consequence of our agreement with the English and of the measures
we have taken to suppress piracy.*

*We, likewise, through our friend, as Her Majesty's agent,
beg to convey our continual assurance of friendship to the
Queen of England, and to express our hope, that through his
assistance we shall be enabled to settle the government in
Borneo, to suppress piracy, and to foster trade for the well
doing to both countries.*[1]

Mr. Brooke's drooping spirits revived somewhat on
the receipt of this letter, for he believed that it would
be sufficient to stir the British authorities to take action
against Serip Usman. On leaving Brunei, therefore, he
went to Singapore for the purpose of interesting the
naval Commander-in-Chief, Rear-Admiral Sir Thomas
Cochrane, in the affairs of Borneo. He had several
interviews with Sir Thomas, who promised that, when
his engagements permitted, he would visit the north-
west coast of Borneo and attack Marudu.

But the weeks passed and the squadron did not
come. Rajah Brooke, with the impatience of a man

---

[1] *The Private Letters of Sir James Brooke*, ii, 55.

of action, hated waiting and once more became despondent, as the following extract from a letter to his friend, John Templer, shows:

Brune, May 22, 1845.

It is not to be wondered at, that the bad faction, headed by P. Usop, are making head, and our good friends dropping from want of support. Muda Hassim and Budrudeen are threatened from without by Sheriff Osman, the pirate chief, because they have declared for the suppression of piracy. Within P. Usop conspires against their power—the sultan is doubtful—and the mass of the people on both sides lukewarm and confused. The position in which they are now placed is entirely our doing, and if the sacrifice be complete, or the town convulsed by civil war, it can only be attributed to our slowness and inaction—for I would answer with my life to control the wrong, and defend the right with thirty well armed Europeans.

You must know, that since we last left this place for Singapore, the American frigate, "Constitution," has been here to offer immediate protection, and a treaty of friendship and commerce, on the grounds of the coal being ceded to them, and the right of exclusive trade granted. It is probable that from the badness of their interpreter (who was formerly my drunken servant), that the demand for exclusive trade has been erroneously understood; but independently of this, had the American officers remained here longer, and been better versed in native politics, there can be no doubt that both the sultan and P. Usop would have formed this alliance, or become sufficiently intimate to gain them to their party, merely out of spite and opposition to Muda Hassim and Budrudeen.[1]

Sir Thomas kept his word, however, and on August 8, 1845, a British squadron appeared at the entrance to the Brunei River. The Admiral's flag was in H.M.S. *Agincourt*, and the remainder of the squadron consisted of the *Vestal*, the *Daedalus*, the steam-sloop *Vixen*, the

---

[1] *The Private Letters of Sir James Brooke*, ii, 64-6.

brigs *Cruiser* and *Wolverine*, and the East India Company's paddle-steamers *Pluto* and *Nemesis*. Such a force had never been seen in Borneo waters before.

The steamers, carrying a large body of seamen and marines, ascended the river to the city. Rajah Brooke accompanied the Admiral, who was met when he landed by the Sultan and conducted to the audience hall. Sir Thomas assured the Sultan that he had brought his ships to destroy the pirates who had been threatening Brunei, and added that he would punish any turbulent men in Brunei who troubled the government. His Highness expressed his thanks, looked pale, and trembled. Then Sir Thomas took his leave, the band struck up, the marines presented arms, and the British party returned to the *Pluto*. "What touched my heart at the close of the audience," wrote Rajah Brooke in his Journal, "was Pangeran Usop seizing my hand from behind. Poor devil, I pity him; but measures must advance, and he has deserved his fate, whatever it may be."[1]

The Admiral's next move was to call upon the Sultan and Muda Hassim to punish Pangeran Usop for having retained in slavery the two lascars of the *Sultana*, British subjects, in spite of the agreement between Brunei and the British Government for the suppression of piracy. The Sultan replied that he had been faithful to his engagements and that he disowned the action of Pangeran Usop, but was not sufficiently powerful to punish him. Since the offence had been committed against British subjects, His Highness expressed (though not without some reluctance) his willingness that the Admiral should take what steps he thought fit for the punishment of his refractory minister.

This was exactly what the Admiral wanted. With some solemnity he agreed to the Sultan's proposal, although it was clear that, if the Pangeran proved

---

[1] Mundy's *Narrative*, ii, 36.

obstinate, it was not going to be easy to use force against him without doing damage to other houses in the town.

It seemed that Usop had no intention of giving in without a fight. He had retired to his house, which was in a position overlooking the town. There he stayed. Everyone was well aware that he knew what was toward, but he remained quiet. About ten o'clock that night, however, Muda Hassim came to Rajah Brooke and in some excitement informed him that Usop had been loading the guns that defended his establishment. The Rajah passed on this intelligence to the Admiral and precautions were taken aboard the three steamers against a surprise attack.

During the night an incident occurred which for a few minutes made it seem that Muda Hassim's anxieties were to be justified. It cannot be related better than in Rajah Brooke's own words:

"Aboard the *Vixen* there were between four and five hundred men, marines and bluejackets, from the various ships, and in the course of the night, one of those extraordinary panics occurred, which deprive men of their senses for the time being, and, it would appear, affect the best-disciplined and steadiest of troops. At dead of night, a marine officer, suffering from nightmare, screamed out, and seized the next sleeper, who seized the next, and so on, the clamour spread. Someone sang out: 'We are boarded by Malays!' and the panic became general. The men, unarmed, rushed aft, knocking each other down in the scuffle, each man taking his neighbour for an enemy, each expecting a kris to be at his throat, and each pummelling, struggling, and punishing every body and every thing within reach. This confused mass of men, deaf to the voice of their officers, rushing aft, invaded the admiral's screened sleeping-place. The stokers, to increase the confusion, rushed up with shovels; the fore-hatchway was blocked up with struggling bodies, jammed in hot haste, some ascending, some descending. Officers sleeping below, rushed up, some with shirt and sword, others with shirt, and chair armed. The confusion, having arrived at its height, gradually subsided. The men heard their officers, being tired of thrashing each other, and order was at length restored. The marine sentry was found walking quietly on his beat, and on being taxed, exclaimed, 'Lord bless you, Sir, there's no one aboard, it's only Mr. R.— dreaming.'"[1]

Pangeran Usop himself remained quiet during the night. The following morning he was ordered to appear before the Sultan, but refused to obey the summons. When one thinks of the force he must have seen arrayed against him from the windows of his house, one cannot but admire his spirit. Perhaps he had escaped retribution so often that he did not believe that the British, who had delayed so long, would ever take serious action against him, and no doubt he counted on the humanity of Rajah Brooke. So he remained behind his guns, hoping, as many another desperate bluffer has hoped before and since, that his hand would not be called.

But Sir Thomas was not a man to be played with. The British Navy had been slow in taking action, but now that it had come it meant business. At about 2 p.m. the steamers took up their position before Usop's house. The marines were landed, ready to advance. Usop was then given twenty minutes in which to surrender. Still he did not come.

When the time limit had expired, the Admiral ordered the *Vixen* to fire a single shot over the roof of the Pangeran's house. This device, so often employed by a would-be humane adversary, has the disadvantage that the person attacked is unaware of the intention of the attacker. For all he knows, the shot may have been intended to hit him and just gone wide. Such may have been Pangeran Usop's impression of the work of the

---

[1] *The Private Letters of Sir James Brooke*, i, 81-2.

Vixen's gunners. At all events he made so bold as to
return the single shot with three from his own batteries.

This was too much for the patience of the Admiral.
Up went the signal " Commence Action," and the *Vixen*
fired a salvo in earnest. That was the end. His bluff
called, Pangeran Usop decided upon instant flight, and
the marines advanced without further resistance. Fortunately the house was in a detached position and no
damage was done to any other property.

On Pangeran Usop's premises was found a vast store
of gunpowder and twenty-two guns. Twenty of these
the Admiral presented to the Sultan and Muda Hassim ;
the remaining two he retained to provide compensation
for the two lascars whom Usop had so unwarrantably
detained. The Brunei chiefs, with a moderation as
creditable as it was unusual, refused to take any of the
property found in the house, but this was soon looted
by the populace of Brunei, who had no scruples about
taking advantage of the late Prime Minister's downfall.

Sir Thomas apparently imagined that having
destroyed Pangeran Usop's house he had rendered him
powerless. At all events, having completed the work
of destruction he sailed with his squadron for Marudu.
But Usop was not done with yet. Two days after the
Admiral's departure he returned with 200 natives he
had summoned to his banner, seized a hill behind his
demolished house, and began an attack on the city.
Pangeran Bedrudin hurriedly collected a force and after
some stiff fighting drove him off. Bedrudin pursued
the fleeing rebels, but on approaching their camp he
found that Usop's followers had deserted him and that
Usop himself had fled. His wives, children, gold, and
other property fell into the hands of Bedrudin, who
returned to Brunei the same evening in triumph.

By his flight Usop lost all his former prestige in
Brunei, so that he would scarcely have found a dozen

men to follow him had he returned. All his life he had been a boaster, but now his boasting could avail him no more. "His mouth was brave," exclaimed the Bruneis, "but his heart was timid. He should have died as other great men have died, and not have received such shame. He should have amoked, or else given himself up for execution."

Such was the public comment in Brunei, and it is interesting as disclosing Malay psychology. It was the instinct of the crowd to down still further the man who was already down. For that Pangeran Usop possessed an uncommonly fine supply of what is vulgarly known as "guts" it would be difficult to deny. He had defied the guns of three steamers, a British Admiral, and 500 British bluejackets and marines. Having been forced from his position he had returned, and had his followers had any heart for the fight he might quite possibly have taken Brunei and given a great deal of trouble before he was dislodged. As it was, he preferred discreet flight to senseless death by amok and, accompanied by his brother, he repaired to the neighbouring district of Kimanis, of which he was the feudatory lord, demanding the protection of the local chief, who was his vassal.

The chief of Kimanis protested his loyalty and would probably have harboured him had he not received a few days later his overlord's death warrant signed by the Sultan and countersigned by Muda Hassim and Bedrudin. This document bore the seals of the signatory princes, followed by a short outline of the rebellious actions of the two outlaws, and a paragraph stating that the Sultan had made a treaty with the Queen of England, and that if any persons harboured traitors accused of piracy, the English would help His Highness to burn their towns.

The chief of Kimanis decided that it would be impolitic to ignore so dire a threat, but the execution of the order was not so easy. For Pangeran Usop was taking no chances, even in the territory of his avowedly

devoted vassal. He always went armed, and when he
bathed or slept his brother stood guard with a drawn
kris. Usop himself performed the same office for his
brother. For days the chief waited, tending his lord,
bringing him his food, holding his clothes while he
bathed : but never able to surprise him. Three of the
chief's relatives sat watching continuously, seated on
mats in respectful attitudes, waiting for a chance to
catch one or other of the guests off his guard, but
hour after hour they sat in vain.

On the tenth day after his arrival Usop was standing
on the landing stage by the river, naked *kris* in hand,
watching over his brother while he bathed. Suddenly
he called for a light for his cigarette. The chief of
Kimanis saw his chance. He brought a piece of fire-
wood with a lump of charcoal on it that was scarcely
glowing and presented it to his lord. Usop tried to
get a light but failed. Without thinking, and intent on
lighting his cigarette (even as you or I) he laid down
his *kris* and took the wood in his hand. It was a fatal
mistake—the kind of mistake a hunted man never makes
more than once. The chief of Kimanis seized the
opportunity his cunning had contrived. He flung his
arms round Usop and pinioned his hands to his side.
The relatives leapt from the mats on which they had
sat watching for so long and secured the Pangeran's
unarmed brother.

That was the prelude to the end. The mode of
execution was the usual one for State offences. Each
prisoner was given a mosquito net in which he wrapped
himself. He then seated himself upon the ground and
gave the signal that he was ready for death. A cord
was placed round his neck and he was strangled. It is
said that death was instantaneous.

CHAPTER XIV

THE BATTLE OF MARUDU

Admiral Cochrane's squadron in Marudu Bay—Serip Usman's stronghold—The strength of the British expedition—The advance held up by the boom—The flag of truce—The action begins—Gallantry of the pirates—The boom forced—The marines carry the first battery—The capture and burning of the forts—Guns and booty taken—The episode of the wounded woman—British casualties—Captain Talbot's leadership criticised—The ruins of the fort to-day—The magic pebbles.

ON hearing that Sir Thomas Cochrane's squadron was approaching Marudu Bay after leaving Brunei, Serip Usman is said to have exclaimed:

"I care not for all the ships of the British Navy. Let them come!"

Pieces of purple such as this must come easily to one who believes himself secure from harm, and this was Usman's enviable position, for he had long since performed the mystic rites which procure invulnerability, and having proved his immunity from the effects of shot and sword on many an expedition, both to his own satisfaction and to the awed respect of his followers, he had no reason to have any personal fear in the coming fight. Nor is there much doubt that he imagined his position to be impregnable. It was certainly a strong one, sufficient to daunt any native expedition; and Usman had had no experience of actions against a disciplined European force.

The situation he had chosen for his stronghold was some five miles up the Marudu River (now known as the Langkon), immediately behind a sharp bend, so that it was not visible from a distance. On a tongue of land

N

formed by the main stream and a tributary he built one fort; another and larger one on the right bank, and placed a floating battery on the left side of the river. Behind the forts were the dwelling-houses of the settlement, roofed with palm-thatch.

These defences were protected by a double boom, thrown across the river 200 yards below the forts and formed of enormous tree-trunks, which were bolted together by means of large iron plates and bound round and round by the iron cable of a large vessel; the ends of the cable were fastened by numerous turns to the stumps of trees on either bank. The result was a barrier that was as ingenious as it was formidable. No craft of any size could pass either through or over it, though a cut in the right bank permitted the passage of a small canoe.

On this boom were trained the principal guns of the forts—four eighteen-pounders, two twelve-pounders, three nine-pounders. Twenty-two smaller brass guns were used for defence elsewhere. Under his command Usman had ten Arab captains, each of whom had one hundred tried warriors. With this force, and behind these well-contrived defences, Serip Usman awaited the British admiral's attack.

The squadron entered Marudu Bay on August 17, 1845. The following day Sir Thomas Cochrane transferred his flag from the *Agincourt* to the steam-sloop *Vixen*, and she, in company with the East India Company's steamers, *Pluto* and *Nemesis*, and the ships' boats, proceeded up the bay and anchored as close as possible to the entrance of the Marudu River. The same afternoon the attacking force embarked in the ships' boats, twenty-four in all. The expedition was commanded by Captain Charles Talbot, of H.M.S. *Vestal*, and consisted of:

41 naval officers
5 marine officers
303 petty officers and bluejackets
197 N.C.O.'s and marines

───

546

───

Nine of the boats were gunboats, and shortly after sunset the expedition was joined by a boat from the *Pluto*, carrying the *Agincourt's* field-piece.

Captain Talbot's instructions from the Admiral were to "proceed up the branch of the Maloodoo stated by the pilots to be in the occupation of Scheriff Osman; and should their statements prove correct, to ascertain as far as possible the strength of his position and amount of force, either attacking the Scheriff on his refusal to surrender, should he feel equal to the enterprise, or falling back to some suitable position, while he communicated with me in the event of his not considering his force sufficient to guarantee success."[1]

The force anchored for the night just inside the bar of the river, and next morning at daylight, after a light meal of biscuits and water, set off up-stream in two divisions, the launches and pinnaces with guns leading, guided by two Sarawak Malays who knew the position of Usman's stronghold.

The dense mangrove which fringed the bank and the windings of the river prevented Captain Talbot from seeing far ahead, and as the force began to draw near the objective he took one of his officers with him and went on to reconnoitre. On rounding the bend of the river which screened the forts he suddenly came in full view of Usman's position, saw the two forts, bright with fluttering banners and thronged with armed men

───

[1] Sir Thomas Cochrane's despatch to the Admiralty, dated August 26th, 1845.

in full war-dress ; saw the batteries bristling with guns ; saw that formidable barrier lying across the stream. A single glance must have been enough to show him that there was no hope of the boats forcing a way through ; yet the position of the smaller fort was such that it could be attacked only by the river, while the large fort, above which flew Usman's standard—a tiger on a red ground—appeared to be defended by another stream on the right bank[1] (in reality it was but a shallow creek) which seemed to preclude its being assaulted from a flank. Captain Talbot made up his mind that there was nothing for it but to hack a passage in the boom. He retired and ordered the main force to advance. It was by then about 9 a.m.

As the leading boats reached the boom, a canoe shot out from the main fort ; in it sat a young chief in a scarlet coat, his silken head-cloth decked with feathers. He carried a flag of truce and hailing Captain Talbot said that he was sent by his chief to inquire the object of the expedition. Captain Talbot replied that he required the unconditional surrender of the forts and the person of Serip Usman himself. He offered to meet Usman, either within or without the boom, provided that the latter brought all his force with him. The chief went back with this message and returned to say that Usman must decline Captain Talbot's offer, but proposed that two senior officers, in gigs, should come through the boom and enter the fort to negotiate. Captain Talbot, who was not to be trapped by so obvious a ruse, refused, and instructed the messenger to say that unless the original demands were complied with in fifteen minutes he would bombard the forts.

As soon as the flag of truce had retired, Captain Talbot, scarcely expecting that his demands would be complied with, decided to waste no time. Cutters with axes were brought up to the boom, where the gunboats

---

[1] The reader will remember that the true right and left banks of a river are those seen as one faces down-stream.

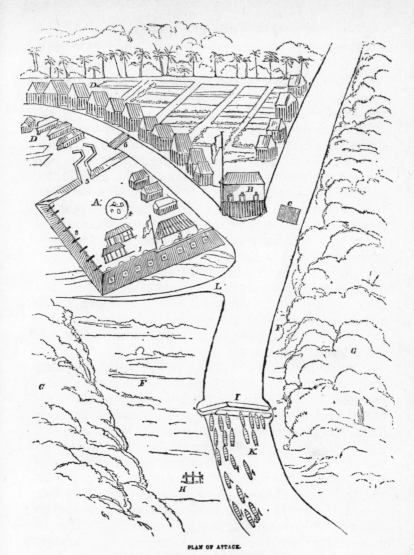

PLAN OF ATTACK.

REFERENCES :

A. Enemy's Stockade—
    1. Eight-Gun Battery
    2. Eight Gingals mounted
    3. Serip Usman's House
    4. Cemetery
    5. Entrance to Stockade
    6. Wooden Bridge
B. Three-Gun Battery

C. Floating Battery
DD. Malay Village
FF. Cleared Jungle
G. High Jungle
I. The Boom
L. Creek
H. Rocket Battery
K. Boats of the British Squadron

were in line abreast. The small-arms division in the other boats were ordered to anchor by the stern (it being flood tide) ready to advance as soon as an opening was made.

As soon as they saw the sailors' axes busy the pirates opened a heavy fire with the guns they had trained on the boom. The boats, crowded with men and jammed within the narrow confines of the river banks, presented an easy target, and at the first shot two men were killed and three wounded in one boat alone. Among the first to fall mortally wounded was Leonard Gibbard, senior mate of the *Wolverine*, while working at the boom, axe in hand.

After their first round the enemy's guns were thrown out of position, which they did not easily recover, and their fire was briskly returned by the gunboats, while a rocket party which had been landed on the right bank did considerable damage, one rocket entering a loophole and killing a whole gun's crew.

Usman himself was plainly visible to the attacking party, directing the fire with great courage and coolness. Nor did his followers lose heart in face of the well-directed storm of shot and grape that poured in amongst them, and as soon as one man was shot down his place was filled. The chiefs, brilliant targets in their coloured war-coats, leapt on to the battlements and stood recklessly brandishing their swords, encouraging their men and hurling defiance at their enemies. Nor was this devil-may-care spirit shown only by the chiefs, for when a shot brought down Usman's own standard a volunteer immediately swarmed up the stump of the flagstaff, erected the broken post, clung on like a monkey until he had got the flag securely lashed, heedless of the bullets that were whizzing past him, and then coolly slid down unhurt.

❖   ❖

Meanwhile the party at the boom, terribly exposed,

[From *Views in Borneo, Sarawak, and Labuan.*

CUTTING THE BOOM AT MARUDU.

were working desperately with their axes, but it was not until fifty-five minutes after the action had started that they had cut a gap wide enough for the smaller boats to pass through.

The first boats through this gap were two cutters filled with marines, who speedily carried the three-gun battery, which, being on high ground, commanded the main fort. By a well-directed fire from this position they soon emptied the fort of its defenders, who could be seen swarming through the village and fleeing for the jungle behind. Usman fought gallantly to the last, standing on a wing of one of the principal embrasures. But his invulnerability was not proof against the fire of those marines, and he fell shot through the neck, his body being carried away by some of his followers.

Meanwhile boat after boat was passing through the gap in the boom. While they did so the pirates abandoned the smaller fort and soon were in full flight. Close upon their heels came the victors. The village was soon cleared and patrols were pushed up both banks of the river, but met with no opposition. Had the pirates first held the village and then made a gradual instead of a headlong retreat, they could have inflicted considerable loss on their enemy, for Lieutenant Pascoe of the *Vestal*, describing the advance, said : "After all our battalion drill at Penang in May and June last, I cannot say much for the order and regularity of movement in our bluejacket brigade, nor did the marines appear to be much better in hand. On leaving the boats to advance, all was helter-skelter, as though going to a Fair."

As it was, only a few straggling fugitives were encountered. One of those, Serip Mahomed, the bearer of the flag of truce, had sufficient spirit to turn and face his pursuers. As he was in the act of hurling his spear at Mr. Pascoe, a bluejacket brought him down with a bullet that went through his shield and penetrated his forehead, while the spear fell within a few feet of its target.

In the forts and about the village the carnage was frightful. Many of the dead and wounded had, like the Serip himself, been carried away, but enough remained to show what frightful execution the Navy's guns had done within the narrow confines of the fort. Bajaus and Illanuns in their bright dresses and golden charms lay on every side; two or three Serips in turbans and white flowing robes; many slaves forced to fight against their will, amongst them a captive Chinese.

Not a few of the dead pirates were dressed in armour, some in coats of fine chain, others in makeshift mail, fashioned from the leaden linings of tea chests; some had brass helmets upon their heads. These helmets were eagerly seized as souvenirs by the light-hearted blue-jackets and marines, and it is said that some of the party would have been in danger of being cut down by their comrades as pirates had they not shouted out in time, " Avast there, shipmate, I'm *Agincourt* ! "

Three large war-boats and several smaller vessels were captured and burnt. Twenty-five brass cannon were seized as loot and the heavy iron guns (said to have been taken from a ship) were spiked. The other booty included two magazines of gunpowder, large stores of camphor, china ware, bales and boxes of English manu-factured goods, and some French prints. Had evidence been needed to prove Serip Usman a pirate there was plenty available. The boom itself had been fastened with the chain cable of a vessel of something like 400 tons; other chains were found, also a ship's longboat, and many articles of ships' furniture and equipment, in-cluding two bells, one of which was ornamented with grapes and vine leaves and marked *Guilhelm Ludwig, Bremen*. This vessel was supposed to have been wrecked off the coast of Borneo in the previous year, but nothing had ever been heard of her crew.

Once the forts and the village had been cleared the order was given to " Burn and destroy." This order seems to have been issued with lamentable lack of forethought, and to have been carried out with that singular lack of discipline which characterised the whole action, for no firing-party was detailed, and, as anyone who has been in a similar position knows, an unconditional order to "burn" is a very dangerous one to give, so excitable is the influence that leaping flames invariably have on even the best trained troops. They seem to rouse some exultant maddening impulse for destruction that slumbers in every man's heart, be he savage or civilised. On this occasion the order had just that effect. Every sailor and marine improvised a firebrand, which he began to flourish with indiscriminate fervour, setting light to the first building at hand and glorying in the blaze he created from the dry timber and bamboo and the palm-thatched roofs. So that whereas a careful commander would have begun by firing the buildings farthest from the boats and working back to the river, the whole of Serip Usman's stronghold went up in flames about the same moment and several of the parties very nearly cut off their own retreat.

Mr. Pascoe, who was in charge of one of these parties, had the forethought to look inside each building before he allowed his men to fire it, lest any wounded fugitive should be within. In one house he discovered crouching in a corner behind some boxes an old woman with two little children, one of whom was very ill. With some difficulty he removed them to the river bank, and leaving them under a shady tree returned to his work of supervision. On his return half an hour later he found that the old woman had slipped across the river with the healthy child, leaving the sick one behind. It was handed over to the care of a female prisoner, who was subsequently set free.

By the time the work of destruction was over it was past midday. The bluejackets and marines had had nothing since their light meal at daybreak, and now every man became his own butcher and cook, catching the goats and poultry that roamed everywhere and roasting them in the embers of the smouldering buildings for the midday meal. Then about 2 p.m. the whole force re-assembled at the boats and returned down-stream, reaching the ships soon after sunset.

◇   ◇

The following day a party under Commander Giffard, of the *Vixen*, completed the work of destruction. While thus employed some of the sailors came upon a young woman who had been a slave in Usman's house-hold. Her right arm had been shattered at the elbow by a grapeshot, and she was holding a little girl of two years old in her left. She was in great pain and suffering badly from thirst. The arm was carefully bandaged and she was taken on board the *Vixen*, where the surgeon saw that amputation would be necessary. As she stead-fastly refused to have the little girl taken away from her, the operation had to be performed with the child clinging to her left arm. When it was over she began to gesticulate excitedly with her left hand, speaking in short, urgent sentences, but since no one could understand her, Rajah Brooke was fetched. It was then discovered that, not understanding the necessity for the operation, she had thought that the British intended to cut off the right hands of all their prisoners, and she was begging that they would take her only remaining hand rather than hurt her child. The necessity for the amputation was then explained to her, and she was assured that every care would be taken of her and the child, and they afterwards accompanied Rajah Brooke to Sarawak.

Other prisoners made it evident that the losses of the pirates had been even greater than had first been supposed, for the slaves had had orders to pitch the dead into the river as they fell, or else to carry them off into the jungle, it being considered a terrible disgrace for the bodies to fall into the hands of the enemy. It was also proved fairly conclusively that Usman had either been killed out-right or had died of his wound, though his body had been carried off in the same way.

The British casualties amounted to six killed and fifteen wounded. In his official despatch to the Admiralty, Sir Thomas Cochrane, commenting on these losses, observed : " When the great strength of the position is referred to, and that the force was for one hour exposed to the steadily-sustained fire of eleven heavy guns, within little more than 200 yards of our own position, it is rather astonishing than otherwise, and a source of thankfulness, that the casualties were not more numerous."

This is perfectly true, and the lightness of the casualties can be attributed only to the appalling marksmanship of the Serip's gunners—for if ever there was a target to gladden the heart of a gunner it was that press of boats, crowded with men, packed against the boom at a range of 200 yards. The gallantry displayed by both officers and men during that hour was superb, but Captain Talbot's leadership is open to criticism. The forts were but five miles from the mouth of the river, and it should have been possible to send up native scouts to reconnoitre the position before ever the advance began. They would have discovered that the stream on the right bank was but a creek, knee-deep, so that the small-arms division could have landed, marched towards the main fort and assaulted it while the boom was being cut. This would probably have ended the action much earlier, for all experience of such encounters shows that natives, however strong their defences, will not wait when they see cold steel approaching them. Lieutenant Willcox, of the *Vixen*, actually volunteered to examine this ground after the advance had been held up by the boom, but his services were not accepted, although in the end some of the parties from the boats that were in the rear did land on this bank in their eagerness not to be late for the action, marched through the creek, and were among the first to reach the fort.

Then the expedition carried an extraordinary number of officers—no less than one to every ten men. This probably made for confusion ; it certainly did not make for better discipline, as was shown by the incident of the boats of the small-arms division dashing for the opening in the boom, while the haphazard method by which the destruction of the town was carried out might have had serious results.

However, success is the only thing that really matters in warfare. The action, despite the leadership, had been successful; the objective had been carried; within a few hours the power of Serip Usman had been broken and his stronghold had ceased to exist; and Sir Thomas was able to suggest to their Lordships that Captain Talbot's report would "convey a gratifying narrative of his success, and prove the soundness of my judgment in selecting this officer for the important duty confided to him."

Had Serip Usman himself escaped, the action might have had less valuable consequences than it did, for a man of so active and dominating a personality would have soon gathered together another band and made a fresh stronghold elsewhere. As it was, not only he, but his son had been killed, and the remnant of his followers retired to Bongon, a village nearby, and later formed a settlement in the south-west of the island of Palawan. But they gave no further trouble, and from that day to this there has been no other pirate settlement in Marudu Bay.

The remains of Usman's stronghold may still be seen (though they are not easy to find) amidst a tangle of jungle not far from Langkon Rubber Estate. I paid a visit to them some years ago and found within the crumbling ramparts two tombstones which I was told marked the graves of the Serip's son and of that royal lady, his wife, who was reputed to have had the power of walking on the sea. She had refused to be consoled for the loss of her lord, and having died of a broken heart had been buried on the spot where he made his last stand. On the grave I noticed a number of little white pebbles. My guide told me that they had been brought from Sulu specially to place on the grave of this daughter of the royal house. These stones had magic properties, he said, for water in which they were placed acquired curative properties. Natives would come from far and near to possess one, and, strangest of all, no matter how many were taken their number had never grown less throughout the years.

CHAPTER XV

THE MURDER OF RAJAH MUDA HASSIM

The Sultan gives Muda Hassim the title of Sultan Muda—The
evil influence of Haji Saman—The plot against Muda Hassim
and his brothers—Muda Hassim's house attacked—His end—
Pangeran Bedrudin's last stand—Sends his ring to Rajah
Brooke—Bedrudin's slave boy brings news of the massacre
to the Rajah.

THE death of Pangeran Usop had far-reaching consequences, for his daughter had married the Sultan's
adopted son, Pangeran Hassim (not to be confused with
Rajah Muda Hassim), who shared his father-in-law's
hatred of the British, and determined to avenge his fate.

After the flight of Usop from Brunei the power of
Muda Hassim and Bedrudin had been in the ascendant, so
that the Sultan had formally appointed Muda Hassim his
successor, and given him the title of Sultan Muda.   He
had not taken this step without considerable reluctance,
and probably he would not have taken it at all had he seen
any other course open to him, since, quite apart from his
dislike for Muda Hassim, he secretly wished to secure the
succession for his own son.   He had hated having to
sign the death warrant of his old favourite and adviser,
Usop, and the shrinkage of his personal income, owing to
the cessation of profits from slave-dealing, must have
caused him acute annoyance.

It was not difficult therefore for Pangeran Hassim to
play upon his father's weak and vacillating mind, particularly since he received support from those of the nobles
who had always looked askance at the Sultan's concessions to the English.   The leader of this party was a
man of low birth, one Haji Saman, who had wormed

himself into the Sultan's favour by flattering him and listening to his grievances. And it was Saman and his confederates who pointed out to the Sultan that by one well-planned coup he could sweep from his path his inconvenient and pro-English uncles, the Sultan Muda, Pangeran Bedrudin, and Pangeran Mohamed, and at the same time enrich himself by seizing their possessions.

An appeal to the Sultan's greed never failed. For a while he hesitated, never having made a quick decision in his life; then gave way, and under his royal signet issued the order for the assassination of more than a dozen of his own family.

Once the royal approval had been secured, Saman and his fellow-conspirators did the rest. Without warning, and in the dead of night, forty or fifty armed men surrounded the house of Muda Hassim, set fire to it in several places and then began a general attack. Muda Hassim, however, succeeded in escaping to the opposite side of the river in a canoe, taking with him his wife and children and several of his brothers. Saman's men followed, but with the aid of a small body of attendants who had come to his rescue, Muda Hassim defended himself for some time. His brothers fell, some killed, some wounded, and at last he found himself at the mercy of his assailants. He persuaded them to allow a message to be sent to the Sultan, begging that his life might be spared. This entreaty the Sultan refused. Seeing that death was inevitable, Muda Hassim then retreated to a vessel which chanced to be moored to the river bank, and, having placed a cask of gunpowder in the cabin, he laid a train, and then summoned the survivors of his people. When they had joined him he fired the train and the whole party was blown up. He himself, however, was not killed by the explosion, but, determined not to be taken alive or butchered by his enemies, he ended his life by blowing out his brains with a pistol.

While Saman's assassins were attacking the heir to the throne another gang was assaulting the house of his brother Bedrudin. Although taken completely by surprise, Bedrudin fought bravely at the head of the few followers who happened to be in the house. One by one his companions were cut down, overpowered by numbers. Bedrudin, after fighting desperately and killing several of his assailants, was shot in the left wrist; his shoulder and chest were cut open by a knife wound, so that his right arm hung useless, and he had a cut on his head and face. A young woman of his harem, Nur Salum, fought with him and was wounded by his side, and this girl, with Bedrudin's sister and a slave called Japar, his personal attendant, remained by him, although both wounded, when the rest of his companions had either been killed or had fled. In the darkness and confusion these four escaped to a distant part of the house, which stood on piles over the water.

Bedrudin directed Japar to open a cask of gunpowder which was standing in the room and to scatter the powder in a circle on the floor. Then he took from his finger a ring—it was Rajah Brooke's own signet ring, with the Brooke crest upon it, which had been given him as a present. Calling Japar to him, he gave him the ring, bidding him escape from Brunei by sea, make for Sarawak and hand the ring to Rajah Brooke. He was to beg the Rajah not to forget his friend, but to tell the Queen of England of his fate.

Japar swore that he would obey his lord's commands. Bedrudin bade him go, and the boy dropped through the loose flooring of the house into the water below. Then Bedrudin fired the gunpowder, putting himself and the two women for ever beyond reach of the Sultan's treachery.

Thus two enlightened princes were removed from the Brunei scene. Both had been men of vision, friends of England, friends of Brunei too: perhaps the best friends Brunei ever had. It was thanks to Muda Hassim that Rajah Brooke was able to turn Sarawak from a tropical wilderness, in which the cheapest thing was human life, into a land of peace and order. Had it not been for the gallantry of young Bedrudin, Pangeran Usop would have made himself master of Brunei. Bedrudin had always particularly endeared himself to Europeans, for he was a pattern of courtesy, gracious, handsome and dignified. More than that, he was that rare thing, a Malay noble who, in the midst of the intrigues and crooked politics of the Brunei court, could remain faithful to his promises and loyal to his friends.

Nor was it only he and his brother who perished that dark night; for no less than thirteen members of the royal family—the Sultan's uncles, nephews and cousins—met their deaths by that atrocious plot, the like of which is not to be found in Malay annals, sinister though some of their stories are. [1]

It was Japar, Bedrudin's slave boy, who brought the news of the murders to Rajah Brooke. After leaving his lord's house he hid in the city, waiting for a chance to get away to Sarawak, but before he could make his escape he was discovered and taken before the Sultan, who, seeing the ring on his finger, took it from him and ordered him from his presence. Japar then found sanctuary with Pangeran Muda Mohamed, the only one of the princes who had escaped death—having been wounded in several places he had saved himself by flight, and had ultimately been given the Sultan's protection.

Japar had been two months with Muda Mohamed, unable to escape to Sarawak, when news was received that a British warship was anchored at the mouth of the Brunei River. This was H.M.S. *Hazard* (Captain Egerton), which had called at Brunei quite unaware of

---

[1] I have always imagined that this incident must have furnished Joseph Conrad with certain episodes of *The Rescue*. Those who know the book will recall that Tom Lingard's friend, the native prince, was called Rajah Hassim, and that the name of the Rajah's faithful attendant was Jaffir; they will recall, too, how Rajah Hassim gave Jaffir the ring to take to Lingard, and how Hassim and the lady Immada were blown up in the hulk.

the murders that had taken place. Knowing what the captain's fate might be if he ventured into the city, Muda Mohamed despatched Japar to the ship, bidding him tell the captain what had happened and warn him not to trust himself in the city, since the Sultan was erecting forts to defend the river and was determined to hold no further intercourse with Europeans. Having given his warning, Japar was to entreat the captain to take him to Sarawak so that he might deliver Bedrudin's last message to Rajah Brooke.

With great difficulty Japar succeeded in escaping from the city, and reaching the *Hazard*, where he delivered his message. It was well he did so, for soon after his arrival two of the Sultan's ministers appeared bearing Muda Hassim's flag, and inviting Captain Egerton to accompany them to the town. Had he gone, there is no doubt that he would have been killed; as it was, he declined the invitation and made for Sarawak, taking Japar with him.

The *Hazard* reached Kuching on March 30, 1846, and for the first time Rajah Brooke heard of the fate of his friends from Japar's lips. His feelings are best described in his own words, taken from his Journal, under the entry of April 1, 1846 :

" It is impossible for me to describe the indignation which I feel at this almost unheard of butchery of every member of the royal family known to be well-inclined to the British policy. This infamous act has sealed the most flagrant breach of treaty entered into with Her Majesty's Government with the blood of the Sultan's nearest relatives, and His Highness has now openly declared that he is prepared to fire upon the British flag whenever it shall appear near the defences which he is erecting.

" Had this dreadful event arisen out of any source of internal struggle for sovereignty or power, however much to be regretted, it would not have rendered me so miserable as this fearful intelligence has now done. Surely Her Majesty's Government will well consider the case. It is beyond a doubt that the treachery and bad faith of the Sultan has resulted entirely from the fidelity of the Rajah Muda Hassim, and of Pangeran Budrudeen, to their engagements and the treaty entered into with the British authorities in these seas. Nor can I forget that these princes and their families returned to the capital, at the express invitation of the Sultan, in H.M.S. *Samarang*, and were subsequently reinstated in their former position, under the authority of a British naval officer. What other object can the Sultan have in placing himself in a position of such decided hostility to the British Government than a determination to have again recourse to the former atrocious system of piracy and murder?

" No less than thirteen of the members of the royal family have been massacred; and that the vicious sovereign gave his consent, if he did not directly order these murders, is clear on the face of the evidence before me.

" Had I the power I would myself destroy both the city and the Sultan, or at least would depose him; then, if possible, I would rescue the son of Muda Hassim and his surviving brothers, and place them in a fresh locality, and commence *de novo* with a better government under my own supervision.

" Possibly Her Majesty's Government may decide either on the punishment or deposition of this traitor to his engagements, and this murderer of his family. Should it be so, it will be necessary to consider what then will be the next best course to pursue—how yet to save the country from a return to its evil ways. We cannot recall the past, but if decisive measures are speedily taken, the small remnant of the royal family, and others not implicated in the Sultan's guilt, may, under protection, be formed into a government favourable to British interests, and to the interest of commerce generally; but one step is absolutely necessary to be taken— the British Government *must* act decisively if they wish to retain a shadow of character with the inhabitants of

the Archipelago, or to suppress piracy. Desultory
efforts can do nothing, and I am sorry to say we have in
part reaped the fruits of long delay. However, to rail is
now useless. My object must be to repair. The loss
of Budrudeen is irreparable to his country, and to me
everything as a friend ; yet, in a British point of view,
the massacred may be turned to advantage and be the
means of forming a government, a nominal government
entirely at our command.

" If we take possession of either Labuan or of Balambangan this new settlement will attract a large number of
working classes in Brunei, and at once open that part of
the country to the enterprise of the British merchant.
Only act and with vigour, and every thing may yet be
done. I am inclined to believe that the Commander-
in-chief will view the subject in the same light as I have
done, for he has a personal knowledge of the intricate
question of Borneo politics, and I am very certain from
the known decision and character of Sir Thomas Cochrane, that, should he concur in the opinion which I have
expressed, he will act at once and vigorously against the
atrocious Sultan, and inflict upon him the punishment he
really appears to have sought at his hands. Sir Thomas
will surely consider that the fate of these fine princes has
been drawn upon them solely through their connection
with the English, and that the existing government at
Brunei has completely laid aside the mask, and shame-
fully broken all the solemn engagements entered into last
year. For myself I feel confident that the Sultan will
now throw off all his reserve, and that he will act against
us in every way both openly and in secret. It behoves
me, therefore, to be on my guard both to strengthen my
position, and to counteract his treachery. . . .

" I can write no more, My poor, poor friends, how
sad and melancholy has been your fate ! Never, never
can I forget it. The regret, the indignation which I
feel overpowers me." [1]

---

[1] Mundy, ii, 87-91.

CHAPTER XVI

THE CAPTURE OF BRUNEI

Admiral Cochrane returns to Brunei—Sultan's preparations for
defence—His attempt at treachery—The attack on Brunei—
The batteries carried—Guns captured—Sultan flees to the
jungle—New Government established.

AT the time when news of the murder of Muda Hassim
and his relatives reached Sarawak, Sir Thomas Cochrane
was at Madras, but on receiving despatches from Rajah
Brooke he proceeded to Sarawak in H.M.S. *Agincourt*
with all speed, arriving there on June 24, 1846, in company with H.M.S. *Iris*, H.M.S. *Hazard*, and the steamers
Spiteful and *Phlegethon*.

Sir Thomas found Kuching buzzing with reports and
rumours of the activities of the Sultan. Many natives,
escaping from the bloodthirsty tyranny of the Brunei
nobles, had sought refuge in Sarawak, and all agreed that
the piratical party now had the upper hand. The city
had been put into a state of defence. Five thousand
warriors were under arms to protect it. The Sultan had
a personal bodyguard of five hundred picked men. The
batteries on the island of Cherimon, destroyed by the
influence of Muda Hassim, had been set up once more,
and heavy brass guns had been erected on a mud flat in
the centre of the town. Even allowing for the exaggeration of the bazaar, there was no doubt that the
Sultan was defiant and meant to put up a fight.

Sir Thomas stayed only one day at Kuching and
sailed with Rajah Brooke on June 25. When it became
known that the Rajah was to accompany the expedition
against Brunei, the greatest interest and anxiety was
shown by the population. The head men of every class

and race, as well as large numbers of Chinese, Malays and Dayaks, assembled to bid him farewell ; and as he stepped into the waiting boat and waved his last good-bye to his subjects an onlooker would scarcely have needed further proof of the popularity of his paternal government—that newly-founded government which was so strange a contrast with the ancient one he was setting out to put to rights.

❖　　　　❖

After an excursion up the Rejang River, the squadron entered the Brunei River on July 6. Its composition was now as follows : H.M.S. *Agincourt, Iris, Ringdove, Hazard* and *Royalist* ; H. M. steam-sloop *Spiteful*, and the Honourable East India Company's steamer *Phlegethon*, giving the Commander-in-Chief an available land force of 230 marines and 500 seamen.

The captains of the squadron dined with the Admiral that day, and while they were still on board the flagship a large prahu was sighted coming down the river, decked with banners. As she came nearer two magnificently-dressed personages were seen to be sitting under an enormous yellow damask umbrella, surrounded by numerous attendants. The prahu paddled boldly alongside the *Agincourt*, and the gentlemen came on deck. They declared themselves to be pangerans, sent by the Sultan to welcome the Commander-in-Chief and delivered a letter from His Highness.

This was a long, rambling epistle, deploring the fact that the captain of H.M.S. *Hazard* had not seen fit to come to the capital on the occasion of his recent visit, or to receive the presents sent him by the Sultan. His behaviour had apparently been caused by a lying story told him by Japar, the follower of Pangeran Bedrudin, and the letter went on to say that " Pangeran Muda Mohamed, with many compliments, requests his friend the Admiral not to believe anything Japar may have stated." To this document were affixed the seals of the Sultan,

Pangeran Mumin (the Prime Minister), and Pangeran Muda Mohamed.[1]

Having read the letter, Rajah Brooke proceeded to interrogate the bearers, for he was not satisfied that they were the men of rank they purported to be, and was almost certain that the seal of Muda Mohamed, whom he knew to be friendly to the English, must have been obtained by force. He very soon elicited from the two emissaries a sinister message which, they said, they had been ordered to deliver verbally : that while the Sultan would be delighted to see the Admiral at the capital, His Highness could not allow him to come up attended by more than two small boats.

So obvious an attempt at treachery would scarcely have deceived a child, and the Rajah recommended that the two self-styled nobles should be detained on board. This was done, and the arms and guns having been taken aboard, their prahu was secured astern for the night.

The following morning Sir Thomas shifted his flag to the *Spiteful* and proceeded up the river with the *Hazard* and *Royalist* in tow. For a ship of any size the navigation of the Brunei River is extremely intricate, the soundings and currents being very irregular, but the previous afternoon the Admiral had made a reconnaissance as far as the island of Cherimon, six miles from the river mouth. There he had found two large batteries under construction, but not yet finished, and had had the narrow channel abreast of the island surveyed and buoyed off. The greatest depth of the channel at high water was thirteen feet, while the *Spiteful* and *Hazard* drew fourteen and a half, but the bottom was soft mud, and by lightening the ships of every spare article on board it was hoped to get them over. The *Spiteful*, going ahead at

---

[1] A translation of the original may be found in Mundy, ii, 140-2.

full speed, succeeded in forcing her way through the mud
for over a hundred yards ; the *Royalist* followed her, but
the *Hazard*, less fortunate in warping, took the edge of
the shoal and remained hard and fast, all efforts to get
her off being in vain.

The *Spiteful* and the *Royalist* anchored off Cherimon
Island, and next morning they were joined by the
Phlegethon with the gunboats in tow. The *Phlegethon*
carried six twenty-four- and twelve-pounders, which had
been fixed on the bridge connecting the paddle-boxes ;
howitzers and field-pieces were forward, ready to act on
either bow.

At 9.30 a.m. the signal was made for the whole force
to proceed, the *Phlegethon* leading, with 200 marines and
400 seamen ready for action. The city was another six
miles above the island, and at 10.30, on rounding a bend
of the river, there about half a mile wide, the *Phlegethon*
got sight of four batteries, two directly ahead, in a raking
position, on ground rising sheer above the river, the
others, flanking ones, on either bank ; the latter did not
appear to be manned.

As the steamer neared the batteries ahead the colours
(chequered yellow and white) were hoisted and the
gunners, dressed in scarlet, were seen ready for action,
with lighted matches in their hands. It was subsequently
ascertained that Haji Saman, the Sultan's adviser and the
instigator of the murders of the princes, was in command
of the position. The river at this point was staked across,
and while the *Phlegethon* was carefully sounding her way
through the piles the Brunei gunners opened fire at a
range of 1,000 yards. The shot—round and grape—
passed between the steamer's masts but did not strike her,
and she replied by bombarding the position for fifteen
minutes, after which Captain Rodney Mundy of the *Iris*
shoved off in the gunboats, pulled for the shore and
stormed the batteries without the enemy putting up a
serious resistance. The flag was captured, and all the
guns were spiked except three brass eighteen-pounders

THE "PHLEGEHTON" UNDER FIRE FROM THE BRUNEI FORTS.
July 8, 1846.

[From *Views in Borneo, Sarawak, and Labuan.*

of great beauty, while the magazines and ammunition were destroyed.

The expedition then proceeded on its way up-stream and anchored half a mile below the city, when all hands went to dinner. By 1.30 they were on their way again, and as the *Phlegethon* opened up round the point below the city she came under the fire of no less than eighteen guns from the hill forts, and from the battery in the city itself. The first shot, a thirty-two-pounder, passed through the paddle-box, breaking part of the wheel, and, entering the galley amidships, killed a cook. This was followed by showers of grape and cannister, aimed with such precision that within five minutes another man had been killed and several wounded; but the steamer's return fire subsequently upset the Brunei gunners' aim and she pushed on without further loss. Even so, nine grape-shot penetrated her iron side below the water-line, abreast of the foremast, and had the vessel not been divided into compartments she would almost certainly have been sunk, for the foremost compartment was found to be full up to the hatches.

Once the steamer was in position, Captain Mundy again shoved off in the gunboats to attack the batteries at close quarters, but the *Phlegethon's* fire had been a settler, and before the boats could reach the shore the gunners had fled in every direction.

"Nothing could be more contemptible," wrote Captain Mundy in his Journal, "than the defence made by those wretched Borneans. We had always understood that the Malays were a brave and determined race, and from the strength of their positions, the calibre and number of their guns, and the really efficient preparations which they had made, an average amount of courage would have greatly crippled our force before we could have reached the town. It is, however, probable that the rapid movement of the steamers directly at their forts, and the admirable arrangements made by the Commander-in-Chief for securing the immediate landing

of an imposing force under cover of the rockets and gunboats, completely paralysed the enemy from the first
moment of our advance." [1]

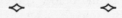

As soon as the *Spiteful* and *Royalist* had taken up
their berths abreast of the city battery the marines were
landed and marched to occupy the hills overlooking the
Sultan's now deserted palace.   When Captain Mundy
landed at the city battery he found that it was armed with
ten brass guns of large calibre ; and that over every one
the word IRIS had been chalked in large letters—an
innocent endeavour on the part of one of the seamen of
that ship to show that he had been first on the scene.
The guns were Spanish, and elaborately ornamented, the
largest measuring fourteen feet six inches, cast in the time
of Charles III of Spain—a beautiful piece of workmanship
which, as Rajah Brooke remarked in a letter, was "really
worthy to be placed in St. James's Park." [2]

" So ended the 8th of July," wrote Captain Mundy.
" Thirty-nine pieces of cannon, mostly of large calibre,
fell into our hands, nineteen of which were brass.   The
Sultan, his boasted army, and all the inhabitants had fled.
Not a native was to be found in the capital, and as the full
moon rose over the desolate buildings, she showed the
white tents of the marines encamped on the heights in
strong relief against the dark jungle beyond, and at the
same time threw her rays over a city which, having
flourished 500 years under Mohammedan rule, now fell
before the arms of a Christian power." [3]

---

[1] Mundy, ii, 150.

[2] I have not been able to discover what became of this cannon.   Mundy
records, *op. cit.*, ii, 151, that Brooke wanted to present it " to the Yacht Club
at Cowes, and see it placed on the terrace in front of the roads."   This, however,
was never done.

[3] Mundy, ii, 151.   Some of the captured guns were melted down to make
cannon for the Crimea.

THE CAPTURE OF BRUNEI, 1846.

[From *Rajah Brooke's Journals.*

From the information of prisoners it was ascertained
that the Sultan, with his bodyguard of 500 men, had
retreated to the village of Damuan, about thirty miles
from the capital, where His Highness was said to have
determined to fortify himself and make a stand. An
expedition consisting of 160 marines and 300 seamen
under Captain Mundy was sent in pursuit of him, but
although they did succeed in reaching Damuan after
considerable difficulty, owing to the heavy rains and
swampy condition of the country, they could not come
up with the Sultan, who retreated before them, and
having destroyed his temporary stronghold they re-
returned to Brunei, leaving His Highness still at large.
Haji Saman had also escaped—by sea—leaving his wives
and children behind him.

Meanwhile Pangeran Mumin, Pangeran Muda
Mohamed and a few other friendly chiefs returned from
the jungle and had an audience with the Commander-
in-Chief, Mumin finally agreeing, at Sir Thomas's suggestion, to take up his quarters again in the city, and,
assisted by Muda Mohamed, to try to persuade the inhabitants to return.

The Commander-in-Chief's assurances that the lives
and property of the populace would be respected had a
good effect, and within a few days the city was crowded
with people returning from their hiding-places in the
jungle, bringing their possessions with them. Confidence was completely restored, and the flagship's band
was a source of great interest and amusement to the
natives, who would pack round the *Spiteful* in their
canoes all the time it was playing.

On July 19, seeing that the new government showed
every prospect of shaping well, Sir Thomas summoned
Mumin, Muda Mohamed and the other chiefs and
requested Rajah Brooke to read to them a proclamation
in Malay which had been drawn up for the benefit of the
Sultan. The purport of it was that if His Highness
would pledge himself to return and govern his people

justly, abstain from acts of piracy and remain loyal to his engagements with the British Government, no further action would be taken against him; but that if he failed in any particular, the Commander-in-Chief would return and burn his city to the ground.

The Brunei nobles assented to this document, and undertook to have it delivered to His Highness. This matter settled, Sir Thomas, considering that he could do no more at Brunei, anyhow for the present, took his departure and rejoined the flagship. The squadron then stood across the channel for Labuan. The operations had been successful in every way, and not only had the murders of Muda Hassim and his relatives been avenged, but it seemed the foundation-stone of a new, better-governed and more prosperous Brunei had been laid.

CHAPTER XVII

HOW LABUAN BECAME BRITISH

Admiral Cochrane destroys pirate nest at Tempasuk—Captain
Rodney Mundy pursues Haji Saman—His strongholds taken
and burnt—Captain Mundy's audience with the Sultan—
Promises of good behaviour—Captain Mundy instructed
to take possession of Labuan—A stormy audience—The treaty
signed—Hoisting of the flag.

On leaving Labuan on July 25, 1846, Sir Thomas
Cochrane's squadron proceeded along the north-west
coast of Borneo. On reaching Ambong it was found
that the whole place, which had been a thriving little
town when Sir Edward Belcher had visited it in H.M.S.
Samarang two months previously, had been looted and
burnt to the ground by the Illanun pirates who had their
stronghold at Tempasuk, ten miles to the north, the
reason given being that the headman and people of
Ambong had shown themselves friendly to the British;
and the Illanun chief had sworn that the same punishment
would be the fate of every other place that might elect
to trade with Europeans.

All this had taken place but a couple of weeks previously. Sir Thomas, ever indefatigable, promised that
he would avenge this piece of flagrant defiance. Depositions were taken, guides procured, and two days later
the signal was made to "prepare boats for service," and,
led by the *Phlegethon*, the squadron was soon making for
Tempasuk.

In the afternoon Sir Thomas and Rajah Brooke
landed, and protected by the armed boats of the flagship, had a meeting with the Illanun chief, who was told
that if within twenty-four hours he did not present himself on board the *Agincourt* and give assurances of future

good conduct his stronghold would be attacked and destroyed.

The twenty-four hours passed, but the Illanun did not come. Captain M'Quhae of the *Daedalus*, with a force of 250 seamen and marines, was then sent up the river. His orders were to obtain a peaceful submission if possible ; but he found the pirate stronghold deserted and could not get into communication with the chiefs. He therefore burnt the principal buildings and destroyed the war-prahus, while Captain Mundy inflicted similar punishment on Pindassan, another Illanun haunt ten miles to the northward, the following day.

The site of Serip Usman's forts in Marudu Bay was next visited, but the whole place was found to be still deserted. Then the main squadron stood away for the China coast, leaving Captain Mundy with the *Iris*, *Hazard*, and *Phlegethon* to attend to affairs on the Borneo coast. His orders were to revisit Brunei, and if possible to enter into negotiations with the Sultan ; to attack Haji Saman, wherever he might be found, and then to revisit Tempasuk and Pindassan and to expel the Illanuns should they have made any attempt to rebuild their forts.

Captain Mundy's reflections on parting from his chief are worth quoting : " No officer can regret being left in command, yet am I sorry to part with our chief. Sometimes, perhaps, I may think that His Excellency's hours of rising are inconveniently early, and may disapprove of this habit as having a tendency to draw the captains from their cots at a period of the morning not quite agreeable ; perhaps, also, I might venture the opinion that, occasionally, the squadron may be a little overworked; but, as the Admiral never spares himself, there is not much cause for a growl, and I willingly record the admiration of my brother officers and myself at the skill and great nerve he has displayed in navigating so large a force along this dangerous and unsurveyed coast." [1]

❖   ❖

[1] Mundy, ii, 209.

It was not long before Captain Mundy received news that Haji Saman had fortified himself on the Membakut River, a few miles from Kimanis, where Pangeran Usop had met his death. Captain Mundy decided to attack him at once, and on August 16 the boats of the squadron, with a force of seventy bayonets under the command of Lieutenant Little, crossed the bar of the Membakut, Captain Mundy and Rajah Brooke accompanying it in the gig of the *Iris*.

News of the expedition had been noised abroad, and they were soon joined by a fleet of forty war-prahus, with a force of some 500 men, from the neighbouring rivers, their chiefs all professing themselves anxious to rid the district of the unwelcome but still powerful fugitive who had come amongst them.

Haji Saman appeared to have made himself master of the river—and it could not have been a difficult matter for so forceful a personality to bend the pagan inhabitants to his will—for on the way up-stream the expedition encountered two successive positions on the banks, each fortified and defended by Saman in person, but evacuated when the boats came to close quarters. One of these positions was an enormous house, 300 feet long, but it was speedily carried and burnt.

The expedition bivouacked for the night, and next morning, after five hours' pull, reached the head of the river and there came upon Haji Saman's third and last stronghold.   As they rounded a bend and sighted it the foremost boat gave a cheer ; a few strokes more and the guns and rockets came into action.   The enemy opened fire both with musketry and blowpipes, but once the marines and bluejackets had landed the natives remained true to type ; for it will have been noticed in these annals that never once did a native force, however strong, and however well protected by defences, stand against a bayonet charge. With his men went Haji Saman, following the example of his royal master, to seek security in the jungle, and that was the last occasion on which he ever troubled British arms.

The position destroyed (the remains of it may still be seen on Membakut Rubber Estate) the whole force retraced its course down-stream and regained the *Phlegethon* by sunset, the casualties during the operations having been one man killed and fourteen wounded. The native allies were given a feast on the steamer's quarterdeck, and before they left Rajah Brooke drew up a bond to which all the chiefs willingly subscribed. It promised that all the peaceable tribes should protect each other against their neighbours, and each independent chief engaged to protect the persons and property of shipwrecked or distressed Europeans who might be driven on that iron-bound coast. It was a beginning, at least, for making the coast safe for peaceful traders; and it must never be forgotten that it was thanks to the early efforts of the first Rajah Brooke that this part of northern Borneo, although beyond the limits of Sarawak, entered the first era of peace it had ever known.

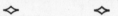

On the following day the *Phlegethon* took Rajah Brooke on to Brunei. Captain Mundy spent some days cruising in the neighbourhood of Membakut and Kimanis, and dropped anchor in the Brunei River on August 26. There he received the following letter from Rajah Brooke, who had just left for Sarawak:

Brunè,
August 25, 1846.

My dear Mundy,
We arrived here on the 19th, and found the "Hazard" off Cherimon. After well weighing all matters, I resolved (villain though he be) not to reject any advances from the sultan, and, as I expected, I received a most humble letter from his Majesty, in answer to which I intimated by message (for I declined any personal interview), that he was permitted to return

THE CAPTURE OF HAJI SAMAN'S FORT.

[From *Rajah Brooke's Journals.*

to the city.   He arrived accordingly, and with many oaths and protestations of sorrow swore that he would do anything for pardon.

I informed him that his request for pardon must be made to the English Government, and that he was bound to re-ratify his broken engagements.

This he did, and also sent a letter to the Queen to the same effect.   I next made him proceed in state to the graves of his murdered relatives, and then demanded justice on the murderers of the royal family.   Having no more time I quit the city to-day, and leave His Highness to chew the cud of mortification.

You should keep up the funk *I have established, and all will be right.*

I have quite a menagerie of old women and young children on board the " Phlegethon," with a few men, the unhappy survivors and dependants of Muda Hassim's family.

Believe me,

Yours very sincerely,

James Brooke.

To Captain Rodney Mundy, R.N.

Captain Mundy decided to go up to the capital at once, but sent an officer ahead of him to assure the Sultan that His Highness need have no cause for apprehension.   On his arrival, however, he learnt from Pangeran Mumin that the Sultan had once more retired into the interior on hearing of the approach of the ships' boats.   Mumin's hand trembled as Captain Mundy shook it in greeting, and he made abject excuses for his sovereign's lack of confidence, obviously fearing that it might mean a renewal of hostilities.

Captain Mundy repeated his assurances, however: the Sultan had nothing to fear so long as he abstained from piracy and acts of violence.   He promised that he would not interfere with the government of the State beyond seeing that treaties were respected and commerce unmolested.   In short, let them do well and he was their friend, let them do evil and he would burn and destroy

P

their city. He told Mumin plainly how dissatisfied he was at the Sultan's conduct, and said that he would return to Brunei in a month, when he trusted that His Highness would grant him an audience and arrange terms for peace.

❖   ❖

The next weeks Captain Mundy spent revisiting the north-west coast of Borneo. At Ambong he learnt that the Illanuns from Tempasuk and Pindassan had given up any idea of rebuilding their settlements and had betaken themselves to Tunku, on the east coast, and having completed the pacification of the Membakut district and made certain that Haji Saman should have no opportunity of making further trouble, he returned to the Brunei River.

This time the Sultan appeared to be in a very different frame of mind, for he sent a deputation to welcome Captain Mundy, with a gracious message that he would be glad to receive him at the capital.

Accordingly, the following morning, September 19, the ships' boats set off for the capital once more. They were drawn up in line opposite the palace, and a guard of marines landed on the terrace leading to the audience hall.

At eleven o'clock Captain Mundy arrived in the *Iris's* galley. The Sultan received him at the entrance of the audience hall, and the marines, drawn up in a position that directly enfiladed the Sultan's divan, presented arms, making their muskets tell. The old monarch started and trembled at the sound. He was no doubt in a highly nervous condition, and for all the assurances he had received his dark mind was probably troubled by a suspicion that Captain Mundy might act as he himself would have done—have recourse to treachery when an opportunity occurred. He recovered himself, however, and since a show of courtesy comes naturally to all Malays, good and bad, he graciously offered Captain

Mundy his hand and led him to a seat, though he continued to glance distastefully at the marines.

After presenting his officers, Captain Mundy informed His Highness that he wished to speak in private. The Sultan rose at once and led the way through a long corridor to an open chamber, which looked on to the river. He then ordered a large wax taper to be lighted and placed before them, explaining that this was witness of the pureness of his heart and of the inviolability of the oath he was prepared to take to " his sister, the Queen of Europe."

Captain Mundy then said that he would not interfere with his government in any way so long as the Sultan appointed ministers who would be friendly to Europeans, countenance lawful trade, discourage piracy and observe treaties. The British flag had been fired on; what redress would be considered sufficient he did not know, but at least His Highness's former evil counsellors, some of whom were still in the city, should be punished.

The Sultan, now crestfallen and humiliated, feared one thing above all : that the British Government would use its power to depose him and set another prince upon his throne. With humility, therefore, he replied that he was ready to submit to any terms the Admiral or Rajah Brooke might dictate, and swore that in future he would fulfil the terms of his engagements, and that his government should be strictly just.

Captain Mundy answered that all depended on His Highness's own conduct, and added that it would be much more agreeable to him to protect Brunei than to burn it to the ground—as its fate would be if the counsels of evil men again prevailed. Then, after listening to further protestations from the Sultan, he took his leave. Doubtless His Highness watched those marines embarking in their boats with much relief.

❖   ❖

After cruising for some time off the coast of Sarawak,

Captain Mundy took his squadron to Singapore. There, on November 25, H.M.S. *Wolf* brought him the following instructions from Sir Thomas Cochrane:

> *Your first proceeding will be, on your arrival off the Borneo River, to wait upon the sultan and acquaint his Highness that her Majesty the Queen is now desirous of availing herself of the treaty entered into in November, 1844; and that you have received instructions to carry her Majesty's wishes into effect.*
>
> *The judgment and discretion you have already evinced since my departure from the coast of Borneo persuade me that, in the relations that will hereafter take place between the squadron under your command and the sultan and his ministers, your own conduct (and you will take measures to secure the same on the part of the officers belonging to it), will be governed by the utmost circumspection, urbanity and forbearance, that his Highness's misconduct, and consequent humiliation, shall only be brought to his recollection through the contrast offered in the present tranquillity and increase of dignity he enjoys by his friendly relations with Great Britain.*
>
> *Having made your preliminary arrangements with his Highness or his ministers, you will proceed to take formal possession of Labuan, with the usual ceremonies observed on such occasions; and if you have the means of doing so at hand, you will erect in a conspicuous place a stone column, stating the day, month, year, and reign in which the possession was made. You will be careful not to incur any expense upon the island without authority to do so; but should you make any discoveries either in its vegetable or mineral productions, the possibility of obtaining a sufficiency of good water, or any other of its capabilities not already known and reported on, you will communicate the same to me, and should the opportunity offer, you will make further examination into the very promising coal which Mr. Brooke and myself discovered on the mainland in the vicinity of Moarra island.*
>
> *You will, in conformity with the instructions contained in Viscount Palmerston's letter, station at Labuan one of the*

*sloops under your command, and the steam ship which will
shortly be added to your force, assigning to them the duty of
suppressing piracy along the coast, from the Sarawak to the
north point of Borneo, and visiting yourself this part of the
district under your immediate command from time to time as
circumstances may render necessary.*

*As Mr. Brooke, her Majesty's Political Agent in Borneo,
has been intimately associated with all my proceedings connected
with the island, you will communicate with him before visiting
Brune, and afford him the perusal of this dispatch; availing
yourself of any views or suggestions which he may offer to you as
to the best mode of carrying out the foregoing instructions. His
long residence in the country, and intimate acquaintance with the
manners and customs of its inhabitants give great value to his
opinions, and of which I have frequently availed myself, with much
advantage to the public service.*

Thos. Cochrane.

To G. Rodney Mundy, Esq., Captain of H.M.S. "Iris."

Now the treaty entered into between the Sultan and
Sir Edward Belcher stated that " the Sultan was willing
to cede to the Queen of England the island of Labuan
and its islets, on such terms as may be hereafter arranged
by any persons appointed by Her Majesty."   But Captain
Mundy's instructions were " to take formal possession of
Labuan," no mention being made either by the Commander-in-Chief or by Lord Palmerston of any equivalent.
The question that immediately suggested itself to Captain
Mundy was—how would the Sultan and his ministers
react to the demand for unconditional surrender of the
island ?   Knowing the avarice of the Sultan, it did not
appear likely that His Highness would regard the terms
with any enthusiasm.

However, Captain Mundy sailed for Sarawak with
the *Iris* and the *Wolf*, and having held a conference
with Rajah Brooke (who shared his misgivings, but
counselled firmness), he reached the Brunei River on
December 15, 1846.

At daylight on the following morning he despatched Lieutenant Heath of the *Iris* with the ship's boats to the capital. Mr. Heath was a Malay scholar and was given a document which he was to translate sentence by sentence to the Prime Minister. In this Captain Mundy gave the gist of his own instructions, and at the same time set forth the indignation felt by the British Government at the Sultan having fired on the Queen's flag, adding significantly that it would greatly depend upon the attitude of His Highness and his ministers towards the cession of Labuan whether or not pacific relations would be renewed.

This was putting the screw on with a vengeance, and it may be said that Captain Mundy definitely exceeded his instructions in opening the diplomatic game with this scarcely-veiled threat. On the other hand he had been set an extremely difficult task : modern opinion might consider it almost immoral. But if his Government wished to make capital out of the murders the Sultan had connived at, and get the island of Labuan for nothing instead of having to pay for it, that was not Captain Mundy's concern. He was at Brunei to carry out his orders, and to carry them out with as little friction as possible ; and he firmly believed that violent opposition to his demands (for they were little else) could best be kept in check by keeping the possibility of another visit from the British Navy before the eyes of those of the Sultan's advisers who were still ill-disposed.

❖   ❖

Mr. Heath returned the same evening. He had been received by the Sultan himself, who declared that he was ready to see Captain Mundy, and was prepared to sign the treaty when it was laid before him.

So far all seemed well, although perhaps Captain Mundy, knowing the man he was dealing with, thought it a little too good to be true. At all events, on Friday, December 18, he ascended the river to the capital.

Pangeran Mumin met him at the landing-stage. As before the Sultan received him at the entrance to the audience hall, which was crowded with ministers, nobles and courtiers, all armed with the kris.

Captain Mundy wasted no time but immediately asked permission for Mr. Heath to read aloud the treaty which had been sent for His Highness's seal and signature. The clauses of this succinct document ran as follows :

1. Peace, friendship and good understanding shall subsist for ever between Her Majesty the Queen of Great Britain and Ireland, and His Highness the Sultan of Borneo, and his respective heirs and successors.

2. His Highness the Sultan hereby cedes in full sovereignty and property to Her Majesty the Queen of Great Britain and Ireland, her heirs and successors for ever, the island of Labuan and its dependencies, the islets adjacent.

3. The government of Her Majesty the Queen of Great Britain and Ireland hereby engages, in consideration of the cession above specified, to use its best endeavours to suppress piracy, and to protect lawful commerce, and the Sultan of Borneo, and his ministers, promise to afford every assistance to the British authorities.

The first article appeared to give satisfaction ; the second, to Captain Mundy's surprise, caused no demur, anyhow at first. But the third article was actively resented by the nobles, who either directly or indirectly owed much of their income to piracy and slave dealing. Instead of receiving the assurance that the British Government would suppress piracy and protect commerce as a set-off against the cession of Labuan, they would obviously have given much to be rid of it.

An animated discussion lasted for nearly an hour. Captain Mundy wisely sat silent and let them talk.

Finally Mr. Heath said: "The nobles want cash in exchange for the cession."

"I have no instructions to entertain such a proposition," replied Captain Mundy.

Then said the Sultan: "This day is Friday, a day kept holy to the Prophet; I cannot sign any paper on it."

Captain Mundy: "No objection was made to Lieutenant Heath when I proposed the Friday."

His Highness: "The former treaty was different from this. We require money in return."

Captain Mundy: "When your Highness fired at the British flag you broke that treaty, and peace has not since been made. The Admiral and Mr. Brooke expect your Highness to sign this as a proof of the sincerity of your promises when I was last here."

The Sultan fell silent, but among the nobles the discussion went on interminably; one of those discussions to which there seems no reason why there should ever be an end. At last Captain Mundy began to lose patience. He turned to the Sultan and exclaimed firmly in Malay: "*Bobo chop! Bobo chop!*"

It was vile Malay, but doubtless His Highness grasped the meaning—that he was to send for his seal and be done with it. It is equally probable that Captain Mundy's tone brought him back from the realm of academic discussion to the world of actualities, which embraced that distasteful guard of marines which was there again at the entrance to the hall. Whenever he looked up he could see it from where he sat. He rose, saying: "I promised and I will keep my promise." Then he left the hall accompanied by several of his nobles.

Twenty minutes went by. The British officers sat waiting in silence. His Highness did not return. Finally Captain Mundy suggested to Pangeran Mumin that the tide had turned, and requested him to send a message to the Sultan. This was done, and in a few minutes His Highness reappeared, carrying the royal seal in his own hand. With him came a host of attendants bearing wax tapers, hammers, and Chinese paper. The great seal was held over the candle and blackened, and then its impression was stamped upon the treaty. It is not difficult to imagine the relief with which Captain Mundy must have affixed his signature as representative of the Crown.

That the Sultan's act found little favour with some of the nobles was clear enough, for many of Haji Saman's party were there that day. Captain Mundy marked their looks of defiance, and fixed his eyes steadily on each in turn. They met his gaze with a cool and haughty stare.

Before Captain Mundy took his leave the Sultan requested five minutes' private interview, and asked confidentially whether the Queen would interfere with his government at Brunei. Captain Mundy reassured him on this point, and proposed that the next time the *Iris* appeared in the river His Highness should pay her a State visit, when he should be received with royal honours, and thus both his subjects and his enemies would know that he was in alliance with the English nation.

This proposal so gratified His Highness that he said that he would come to Labuan for the ceremony of hoisting the English flag, if his presence was particularly required, but that, since he was always sea-sick, he hoped he might be excused. Captain Mundy tactfully replied that he could not hear of His Highness crossing the open sea in his State barge, and presented him with a handsome silver-mounted telescope. Then, bidding adieu to the princes and nobles, he stepped into his gig, the battery saluting with fifteen guns and the drums and cymbals beating lustily. The news of the cession had already spread abroad, and as the ships' boats began to move down the river hundreds of canoes flocked round them with joyful acclamations, showing that the populace of Brunei, at least, knew they had nothing to fear and everything to gain by the establishment of a British colony at their doors.

❖   ❖

The *Iris* and the *Wolf* proceeded to Labuan, where preparations for the ceremony of hoisting the flag were begun. The day fixed was December 24, and by that time clearings had been made, tents pitched, wells dug, guns landed and the flagstaff beached and stepped at a distance of twenty yards from the shore.

Early on the morning of the 24th, a large granite slab was erected on the rising ground close to the flagstaff, where its inscription may be read to-day :

THIS ISLAND

WAS TAKEN POSSESSION OF
ON DECEMBER 24th, 1846,
IN THE NAME OF HER MAJESTY

VICTORIA,

QUEEN OF GREAT BRITAIN AND IRELAND,

UNDER THE DIRECTION OF
HIS EXCELLENCY REAR-ADMIRAL

SIR THOMAS COCHRANE, C.B.,

COMMANDER-IN-CHIEF,

BY

CAPTAIN G. R. MUNDY,

COMMANDING

H.M.S. IRIS.

At eight o'clock top-gallant yards were crossed, and the ships dressed for the ceremony. At noon forty marines and 140 bluejackets landed and took up their positions. Pangeran Mumin, with a number of nobles and attendants, had arrived the previous day and had been saluted with thirteen guns. At two o'clock Captain Mundy, accompanied by Commander Gordon[1] of the

---

[1] This officer died of malaria on January 7, 1847, before the ships left Labuan, and was the first European to be buried on the island.

HOISTING THE UNION JACK ON LABUAN.
December 24th, 1846.

[From *Views in Borneo, Sarawak, and Labuan.*

Wolf, landed and received him on the beach; then led him through the file of marines to the raised platform close to the flagstaff, where the officers of the *Iris* and the *Wolf* had already assembled. Mumin took his place under his orange umbrella, while the nobles and chiefs gathered on the gravelled space below. The crews of the prahus, amounting to several hundred men, were invited to draw near, and Captain Mundy then delivered the following oration, which was translated into Malay by Mr. Heath:

" I make known to all present, that this day I take possession of the Island of Labuan, and of the small islands around, in the name of Her Majesty the Queen of England.

" We now, therefore, stand on British territory.

" The quiet and good people of every nation will be protected in their lawful commerce by the English men-of-war, and pirates, both by sea and land, will be utterly destroyed, and their towns burnt to the ground. The Queen of England and the Sultan of Borneo are henceforth friends. The English admiral will therefore destroy all piratical vessels that make war against the Sultan, or that molest the coast."

A midshipman then hoisted the Union Jack. At the same moment the British ensigns—white, blue and red— were run up at the tents. The ships and batteries fired a royal salute, while the marines and bluejackets kept up a roll of musketry. Then three cheers were given for Old England and Her Majesty, responded to by the men still on board the ships manning the rigging.

Thus, in ten minutes, was Labuan taken possession of in the name of the British Crown.

CHAPTER XVIII

THE DESTRUCTION OF A PIRATE FLEET

The steamer *Nemesis* falls in with a Balanini squadron off Brunei
and gives chase—The pirates anchor to receive attack—Desperate fight lasting seven hours—Six pirate prahus escape—
Five destroyed—Survivors captured and brought to Brunei—
Spanish expedition against the Balanini—The chief who
surrendered to save his wife and family.

In May, 1847, Rajah Brooke went to Brunei with instructions from the British Foreign Office to negotiate
with the Sultan a treaty that would place the trading
arrangements between Great Britain and Brunei on a
more satisfactory basis than they had been hitherto.

He accomplished his object, and on May 27 His
Highness put his seal to a treaty that not only regulated
trading relations, but allowed British subjects accused of
offences in Brunei to be tried by Her Majesty's representative and bound the Sultan not to alienate any portion
of his dominions without the sanction of the British
Government.

Having concluded these negotiations the Rajah left
Brunei in the East India Company's steamer *Nemesis*,
commanded by Mr. Wallage, bound for Singapore.
Commander Charles Grey of H.M. brig *Columbine* was
also on board with a company of his men, who had
formed an escort to Rajah Brooke at Brunei.

While the steamer was making her way down the
Brunei River it happened that a Balanini squadron,
composed of eleven prahus, was cruising along the coast
outside. The largest of these boats mounted six guns,
of which one was a brass nine-pounder, and all of them
were protected by flat, musket-proof boards (*ampilan*)

fitted to the gunwale. The total force on board was about 350. The squadron had parted from the main Balanini fleet several weeks previously. It had almost circumnavigated the island of Borneo, and, having raided some of the Dutch settlements and carried off a number of slaves, it had attacked Sirhassan Island in the Natunas, but had been repulsed. Landing subsequently in a secluded bay, the pirates had repaired their vessels and had burnt alive one of the Chinese prisoners who had proved recalcitrant. Thence they had stood over to the Sarawak coast and had discussed plans for attacking the rising settlement of Kuching, Rajah Brooke's head-quarters. But on learning that some British ships-of-war were anchored off the town they decided to continue their voyage north to Brunei, where they could always count upon capturing slaves amongst the unwary fishermen.

❖　　　❖

On the morning of May 30, this fleet was in full chase after a fishing boat, which was endeavouring to escape to Labuan, when they were sighted from the mast-head of the *Nemesis* as she rounded Muara Point.

As soon as the pirates discovered the steamer they abandoned the chase of their quarry and began to pull away to the west. But the *Nemesis* gained upon them, and by eleven o'clock Rajah Brooke was able to satisfy himself that they were Balanini pirates. Here was the chance he had been awaiting for many years. He held a hurried council of war with Mr. Wallage and Commander Grey, and it was decided to attack the pirate fleet forthwith.

The armament of the *Nemesis* consisted of two thirty-pounders and four long-sixes, and besides her own complement of eighty officers and men (British with the exception of six natives), she was fortunate in having on board the *Columbine's* party, consisting of fifteen seamen and eight marines.

In their attempt to escape, the pirates pulled across the extensive Muara Shoal where, owing to the small depth of water, the steamer could not follow but was forced to make a deviation of three or four miles before she could follow the course taken by the prahus. Then, however, she began to overhaul them rapidly, and the pirates, seeing that they had no further hope of running from her, determined to take up a strong position and fight, and with that object made for a small bay in the island of Pilungan, where they anchored in line, with their bows to seaward, about ten yards apart. Then, having joined their boats together with hawsers, they awaited the approach of their enemy. It is impossible not to admire their undaunted resolution, for none of them, it may be supposed, had ever seen a " fire-ship " at close quarters before, and as the *Nemesis* bore down upon them with her paddles churning she must have seemed a formidable foe indeed.

By one o'clock the steamer was within a few hundred yards of the prahus, and in two fathoms of water. The Rajah decided to give the pirates a chance of surrendering. A boat had scarcely been lowered, however, when they began the action by opening fire with their guns all along the line, killing one man on board the *Nemesis*, which promptly replied, and steaming up and down the pirate line poured in a destructive fire of round shot, grape and cannister from her thirty-pounders at a range of 200 yards.

The Balanini fought with great resolution, but after two hours' cannonade several of the prahus were severely damaged. Seeing that the crews were beginning to abandon these vessels Commander Grey decided that the moment for an assault at close quarters was come.

The *Columbine's* cutter, manned with her crew and the marines, put off from the steamer, followed by the two cutters of the *Nemesis*, each armed with a brass five-pounder. Commander Grey himself took charge ; with him were two naval cadets, both greatly excited at the prospect of their first action.

The cutters pulled to the left of the Balanini line, allowing the steamer to continue to pour in her grape with much effect; although most of the round shot fell in the jungle behind owing to the heavy ground-swell. Although the boats on the left were by now in a half-sinking condition, the pirates put up a desperate resistance, even fighting hand to hand in the water until cut down, and it was only after a protracted encounter that two of the prahus were secured.

The remainder continued to fight, until at four in the afternoon three of the prahus on the extreme right, taking advantage of a breeze which had sprung up, cast off the hawsers, and crowding all sail, bore away to the eastward while the remaining crews ran their six crippled vessels ashore and fled into the jungle.

Thinking the boat party would no longer require his assistance, Mr. Wallage gave chase to the escaping prahus while Commander Grey went forward to secure the prizes that were lying on the beach. But no sooner did the pirates see the *Nemesis* steaming away than they dashed out of the jungle, and yelling their war-cries, once more manned five of their deserted prahus, and having launched them with extraordinary rapidity made a bold attempt to pass out to seaward of the cutters.

Commander Grey took his three boats after them, and tried to cut off the largest of the prahus which, with a smaller one attached to her, was in the rear. Seeing his movement, the other pirates returned to support their companions. Those in the cutters, now badly out-numbered, would have been in danger of being over-powered had not Mr. Wallage perceived their perilous situation. Giving up his chase he put about and made for the scene of the fight, but as soon as the pirates saw the steamer bearing down upon them again they began to pull away to the westward, closely pursued by the cutters. Meanwhile some of the pirates who had remained behind in the jungle, seeing the cutters engaged, had re-manned the sixth prahu on the beach and pulled away in the opposite direction, making the fourth to escape to the eastward.

By this time it was five o'clock. Those of the boat-party who had been wounded—the colour-sergeant of marines and six men—were put on board the steamer and the chase was continued until 8 p.m., by which time three of the prahus were overhauled and destroyed, the remainder making their escape in the darkness. The *Nemesis* returned to Labuan the same evening.

Thus ended an action which had lasted seven hours, in the course of which the *Nemesis* had fired 160 round of shot and nearly 500 charges of grape and cannister. She was hit several times by the pirate guns, but the shots failed to penetrate the iron. Two men were killed and six wounded on the British side, while between forty and fifty of the pirates were left dead upon the island beach, besides ten killed in the prahus. The pirates had about 100 prisoners on board their vessels and many of these unhappy creatures were killed or wounded by the fire from the *Nemesis*, for during the action their masters had forced them up from below and made them sit on the decks, fastened in couples by rattan collars. Of the pirates themselves not one was taken alive, a sufficient proof of the desperation with which they must have fought.

On the morning after the fight the six prahus which had escaped all put in for water at the north point of Labuan—unbeknown to the *Nemesis* and H.M. brigs *Columbine* and *Royalist* which were lying at anchor in Victoria Harbour. They then made for the Sulu Sea, but only three of them survived the passage, the remainder being so badly disabled that they foundered off the Borneo coast. Between forty and fifty of the pirates, together with some of their prisoners, succeeded in reaching the shore. The pirates were captured by a force of Bruneis the Sultan had sent out, while a number of the prisoners, mostly Chinese and Malays, after wandering in the jungle for many days, succeeded in reaching the capital. On their arrival they were kindly treated and subsequently, by orders of the Sultan, arms were put into their hands and they were confronted with their late masters and told to take vengeance on them. This, however, one and all declined to do.

The reason for their refusal is not clear, for they appear to have suffered indescribable cruelties at the pirates' hands. But refuse they did, whereupon His Highness directed his own people to carry out the executions, and they, mindful of their fellow-countrymen who had been carried into slavery by the Balanini, rushed at the pirate prisoners and cut them down on the spot. In those days there were no protracted trials at the Court of Brunei, and the Sultan was thus able to prove himself true to the engagements of the treaty he had so lately signed, without any great trouble to himself.

The pirates who returned to their stronghold on Balanini Island were far from being broken in spirit, and it is said that the families who had lost their relatives in the action went to Sulu and begged the Sultan to fit out an expedition to avenge the defeat. Not wishing to see a British squadron at his front door, the Sultan refused, but that did not deter the Balanini from continuing their marauding cruises, particularly along the coasts of the Philippines, for although the action off Labuan had taught them to keep clear of steamers, their strength had not been seriously depleted. It was the old story of isolated actions having little lasting effect.

The Balanini became such a scourge in the Philippines, however, that in the spring of the following year (1848) the Manila Government decided to send a strong punitive expedition against their main stronghold.

Before the attack the Spanish commander gave orders that no quarter was to be given, and told his men

Q

that he was determined to carry the pirate fort at all costs. The entrance of the lagoon was forced, and three times the Philippino troops charged, but each time were driven back with great loss, even though half the fighting-men of the pirate force were away upon a cruise. Then the Spanish officers and artillerymen dashed to the assault. They penetrated the outer defences of the fort and won the inner stockade, when to their horror they found the pirates killing their women and children to prevent them falling into the hands of their enemies. This wholesale butchery was not stopped until the Spanish commander promised quarter to the men. Upon this they submitted, and were marched off as prisoners to the ships, while the fort and settlement were destroyed.

The Manila Government prudently removed these prisoners, with their wives and families, to one of the northern islands of the Philippines, and there set them to cultivate the land. Among those who were thus trans-ported were the wife and children of a well-known Balanini chief who had been absent at the time of the attack. On his return from the cruise he found his house burnt and his family gone. He immediately went to Zamboanga, the nearest Spanish settlement, and gave himself up to the authorities, saying that he was tired of the wandering life he had led, and asked for nothing better than to live as a peaceful agriculturist with his family and friends.

He was taken at his word and sent to the penal colony in the north, where he joined his wife and set to work planting rice. A close watch was kept over him at first, but he toiled with such good will that just before the rice crop was ready to be harvested this vigilance was relaxed, since it seemed to the authorities that no one would abandon the produce of a year's labour.

But they had yet to learn the cunning and ferocious determination of this pirate stock. For in allowing himself to be sent to the penal settlement the chief had

had no other object but to rescue his wife and family. For a year he waited his chance, and when it came he seized it, regardless of the risk he ran. At dead of night, taking a few companions to whom he had unfolded his plan, he fled with his wife and children to the seashore. There he seized a boat and embarked, and although hotly pursued escaped back to his former haunts.

Pirate or not, he was a stout fellow, and people have had medals for doing less.

CHAPTER XIX

THE LAST OF THE SARIBAS

The Saribas again take to piracy—Their defiant message to Rajah
Brooke—Commander Farquhar's expedition against them—
News of a Saribas fleet at sea—Commander Farquhar takes
up position at the mouth of the Batang Lupar River—Pirate
fleet approaches the river—Night action—Pirates' heavy
losses—The expedition ascends the Batang Lupar and the
Kanowit—Destroying pirate strongholds—Defeated chiefs
attend peace conference at Kuching—Political persecution
of Rajah Brooke.

FOR some years after the expeditions of 1843 and 1844
the Saribas and Sekrang gave little trouble. It seemed
as though they might really abandon piracy for good and
all. But as time went by and vigilance was relaxed, the
memory of the lesson taught them by the British Navy
became less vivid in their minds and once again they
began to raid.

Rajah Brooke was absent in England in 1848, and
on his return he found that the Saribas had been on the
war-path. In the following year Captain Keppel, then
commanding H.M.S. *Maeander*, was again appointed to
suppress piracy on the coast of Borneo, but was unfortunately recalled to China before he could undertake
any extensive operations. No sooner had the *Maeander*
sailed than the Saribas began to fit out a large fleet for sea,
having been further encouraged by the absence from
Sarawak of Rajah Brooke, who by this time had been
appointed Governor of Labuan. They captured several
trading boats, and burnt three villages, slaughtering at
least 400 persons, men, women, and children.

One day a young Saribas Dayak, who had been a
member of one of these raiding expeditions, was brought

into Kuching as a prisoner, having been picked up on the trunk of a palm-tree, some distance out at sea. It appeared that he had left the main Saribas squadron and had gone inland on a little excursion of his own, with the object of securing some heads for his personal aggrandisement, and on his return had found that the boats had sailed without him. Fearing to trust himself to the people whom his fellows had lately so barbarously ill-used, he had trusted himself to the palm-log and pushed out into the stream, hoping that the tide would carry him up the river; but, as it happened, the ebb carried him out to sea, where he was found by a fishing boat from Kuching and brought in for judgment. After detaining him for a few days Rajah Brooke sent him back to his chiefs with a caution that if they did not abandon their piratical ways they would be attacked and remorse-lessly punished once more.

So far from giving heed to this warning the Saribas set out on another expedition, and with a fleet of over seventy prahus made a raid on the villages along the banks of the Sadong River. They chose their time well, for the men were out in the fields, busy harvesting the rice crop, and the women and children were left un-protected. The fleet swept up the river on the tide. The leading prahu stopped abreast of the first home-stead; the warriors dashed on shore, and in a few moments secured the heads of their sleeping victims. While they were about this work the rest of the fleet pushed on, and as they came to each successive house the leading boats stopped and repeated the performance of their fellows.

In this way they secured over one hundred heads and much booty. Only one house of all those attacked made a successful defence. The headman of the village happened to be prepared with fire-arms ready and powder dry. His people had only just begun work when they saw the pirate craft sweep up the reach. Twenty-seven of them got back in time to the long village house—

raised on posts above the ground like all Borneo habitations—and pulling up the ladders they kept the pirates at bay, shooting down the first three that landed, so that the remainder thought it prudent to push on up the river to the next village.

After the main fleet had quitted the river with their heads and booty a few more desperate characters remained behind. They dressed themselves in the clothes of their victims, and thus disguised dropped down the river in the small canoes they had found abandoned on the river banks. On coming to a village they called to the women (in the Sadong dialect) to come out of their hiding-places, saying that they would take them to a place of safety. Only too often was this ruse successful. The unhappy women rushed out with their children in their arms to meet the fate of those whose heads were already heaped in the pirate prahus.

On their return to their strongholds the insolence of the Saribas so far increased that they had the audacity to send Rajah Brooke a message, asking him " if he were an old woman and afraid of them, since he did not attack them as he had threatened."

The Rajah realised that, although no British man-of-war was available to help him, some action must be taken if further sacrifice of life and property were to be prevented, for he knew well that the longer he delayed the more daring would the pirates grow. Accordingly, on March 25, 1849, he set out with a flotilla of 98 prahus and a force of about 3,200 men, including four boats from the East India Company's steamer *Nemesis*. He was able to inflict some punishment on the pirates and prevented the union of the Saribas and Sekrang fleets by defeating a Sekrang force of 150 prahus.

The Sekrang were driven back to their own river, but none knew better than Rajah Brooke that the result of such engagements could not be lasting, and he welcomed the coming of H.M.S. *Albatross* (Commander Farquhar) which arrived to take the place of the *Maeander* in Borneo waters in May, 1849. Preparations for a fresh expedition against the Saribas and Sekrang were at once begun, and on July 24 a combined European and native force sailed from Kuching. It consisted of H.M. brig *Royalist*, commanded by Lieutenant Everest, the Honourable Company's steamer *Nemesis* (Commander J. Wallage), three boats of H.M.S. *Albatross*, the three boats of the *Nemesis*, the *Royalist's* cutter, and the *Maeander's* small steam-tender *Ranee*. Rajah Brooke embarked in his new native-built boat, the *Singh Rajah* (Lion King) and was accompanied by seventeen prahus manned by Sarawak Malays, while numerous detachments of Dayaks under their chiefs joined the expedition, bringing the native force up to seventy fighting prahus and 3,500 men.

Early on the morning of July 24 the *Nemesis* started with the *Royalist* and the *Ranee* in tow, the *Albatross* being left at Kuching. The European boats followed, and this division of the force anchored on the night of the 24th off the entrance to the Sarawak River. The native boats dropped down with the ebb-tide, with streamers flying from their three slender masts and gongs beating. The Rajah's prahu brought up the rear.

On the morning of the 25th the *Nemesis* took in tow the European force, and standing out sufficiently to avoid the shoals, brought them to the entrance of the Batang Lupar at 5 p.m. The boats were anchored in line across its mouth, and the *Nemesis*, proceeding up the river with the *Royalist*, left her off the Linga branch. Then she returned to the boats and proceeded with them, early on the morning of the 26th, towards the Saribas, off which she anchored at 3 p.m. to await the arrival of the native force.

On the evening of July 28 news came in that a large pirate fleet had left the Saribas early on the morning of the 26th, and had stood to the northward. It had thus slipped out but a few hours before the arrival of the expedition. The native who brought this information had only escaped capture by breaking up his boat and hiding himself in the jungle, whence he saw the fleet sail past. He stated that the pirates' immediate object was the capture and plunder of a large settlement on the Rejang River.

The Rajah and Captain Farquhar immediately determined to intercept their return, and measures were promptly taken to this end. Since it was known that the custom of the Saribas was to escape into the jungle rather than stand out to sea when attacked, the Rajah, with twelve large well-armed prahus and two men-of-war cutters, made for the Kaluka, a river more to the north-east, with an inland communication with the Saribas. They took up a position across its mouth, concealed from the outside by a bend at its entrance, with fast scout-boats keeping a look-out in the offing, so that with the main fleet at the entrance of the Batang Lupar both approaches to the pirates' stronghold were cut off.

The intervening land between the mouths of the Batang Lupar and the Kaluka is a flat sandy promontory, running out to sea for a couple of miles, and known as Tanjong Maru. Outside the southernmost point of this flat, called Buting Maru, the *Nemesis* anchored in midstream; the men-of-war's boats, and forty native prahus under the Datu Tumanggong of Sarawak, extended from her in an oblique line towards the mouth of the Batang Lupar, the European boats being nearest to the steamer. A dozen prahus took up their position on the opposite side of the river; a few others were detached here and there.

❖   ❖

Meanwhile the pirate fleet was continuing its cruise unchecked. It consisted of 150 prahus, few carrying less than thirty fighting men, some as many as seventy, while nearly all the great chiefs, both Malay and Dayak, of Saribas and Sekrang were on board. They attacked several villages in the neighbourhood of the Rejang River and captured two trading vessels laden with sago, and another lately out of Singapore with a cargo of cotton goods. These were plundered and burnt.

Then, hearing that there was an expedition on the look-out for them, they turned homewards and towards evening on July 31, one of the Malay scout-boats signalled that the pirate fleet was approaching the mouth of the Kaluka in two divisions.

A rocket was immediately sent up to warn the *Nemesis* and Rajah Brooke formed up his division in a compact line across the entrance to the river. The pirates were sweeping forward at a great rate on the strong flood-tide when the leading boats saw that the entrance was guarded and gave the alarm. The whole fleet then changed its course and steered for the Batang Lupar entrance, passing Rajah Brooke's squadron at long gunshot range. The cutters of the *Royalist* and *Albatross* went off in pursuit, leaving the Rajah to occupy his position, which was too important to be left unguarded.

By this time the light was failing and the pirates did not sight the *Nemesis* for some time. When they did so, however, they became aware, for the first time, of the extreme peril of their situation : both entrances to their river closed against them and in front of them a more formidable enemy than they had ever encountered yet—the dreaded fire-ship.

It was too dark for the watchers on the steamer to make out the low-lying pirate craft, but suddenly across the water came three shivering strokes on a deep-toned gong. Those in the *Nemesis* heard it, and Rajah Brooke, although eight miles away, heard it, too. Everyone knew what that signal meant. It was the commander of the pirate fleet summoning his chiefs to a council of war.

For almost twenty minutes no further sound broke

the stillness of the night, while the expedition awaited
the pirates' next move.   Then a great yell of defiance
came shrilling over the sea.   It was followed by the
splashing of thousands of paddles, ever growing louder.
No scouts were needed to tell Commander Farquhar,
who was on board the *Nemesis*, that the pirates had
decided to force the Batang Lupar entrance.

A rambling exchange of shots now began, accompanied by the discharge of musketry, which increased as
the fleet drew nearer.   The darkness was greatly in
favour of the expedition, for the pirates could not see the
danger into which they were running.   As they swept
up to the Batang Lupar entrance they encountered the
Datu Tumanggong's detachment; when they turned
they were faced by the ship's boats.   The blue lights
burnt by the boats and the glare and noise of the rockets
that by now were hurtling through the air threw them
into greater confusion.   They soon became too panic-
stricken to use their arms with any effect, and had no
thought of anything but escape.   Finding themselves
surrounded, they made a dash for Tanjong Maru, but
failing to force a passage many of them ran their *bangkong* on shore, abandoned them and fled into the jungle,
fearing to be attacked from the Kaluka side by Rajah
Brooke's division.   Others in detached parties tried to
escape out to sea, and seventeen of the larger vessels,
attempting to get past the steamer, were destroyed.

The action then developed into a series of encounters
which extended from the Batang Lupar to the Kaluka, a
battle line of almost ten miles.   The loss, both of life
and boats, was almost entirely on the pirates' side, but
it was not until dawn that the full extent of the terrible
punishment inflicted became apparent.   On the eastern
point of Buting Maru lay eighty deserted prahus.   Along
the beach, as far as the eye could see, was strewn the
wreckage of the great pirate fleet.   Boats which had

[From Illustrated London News.

THE BATTLE OF BANTING MARU.

been swamped were floating bottom upwards, carried backwards and forwards by the tide. The sea was dotted with bodies in full war-dress.

Many of the crews were seen to be still clinging to the wreckage or swimming in the water, but although orders were issued that mercy was to be shown to any who wished to give themselves up, these orders were difficult to carry out, for the pirates themselves neither gave quarter nor expected it. They had taken to the water with their weapons, and the casualties suffered on the British side were mostly caused by the sailors' efforts to save their enemy from drowning. Over eighty prahus were captured with their guns and considerable booty. In one boat was discovered the mangled and headless body of a woman captive whom the pirates, finding themselves forced to abandon, had slaughtered and mutilated in wanton cruelty rather than allow her to escape.

It was estimated that some 3,000 escaped into the jungle after abandoning their boats. Had Rajah Brooke wished to cause the utmost destruction he might have landed on Buting Maru and caused great slaughter among these fugitives ; but he stayed his hand. The exact number of the pirates' losses is difficult to calculate exactly. Two months after the action Rajah Brooke was given the following figures by some of the Saribas themselves :

Killed during the action	300
Killed after the action while on their way home	50
Died of wounds in the jungle, or after reaching their homes	450
	800

Commander Farquhar subsequently claimed that ninety-eight prahus had been captured or destroyed and that the crews of the pirate fleet had amounted to 3,430 "at lowest computation," of whom at least 500 were killed during the action, and an equal number by the native auxiliaries. On his claim the Judge of the Court of Admiralty certified the number at 500. The following is the statement of the distribution of the prize money:

	£
Amount of head-money claimed and paid to the Commanders, officers and men of the ships *Albatross*, *Royalist* and *Nemesis* (less charges), for the night affair of 31st July, 1849	
500 men killed, at £20 per head ..	10,000
2140 men not killed or taken, at £5 per head	10,700
	£20,700 [1]

✧   ✧

On the morning of August 1 a council was held, and it was decided to follow the pirates up the Batang Lupar. Accordingly, on the afternoon of August 2, the whole force anchored near the entrance of the Paku branch, the scene of the action in 1843. Here the steamer and the heaviest prahus were left behind, and the lighter boats, with some of the captured *bangkong*, continued the advance, the steam-tender *Ranee* leading the way, attended by the man-of-war boats, and followed by a dense mass of native craft, whose occupants were all eager for plunder.

As the expedition advanced they found the pirates had resorted to the usual means to check their progress, scores of trees having been felled across the stream; so that it was frequently necessary to land parties on either bank to cut a boat passage through these barriers.

---

[1] Parliamentary Return, No. 114/1852. The prize money was claimed according to the provisions of 6 Geo. IV, Cap. xlix, sect. 1.

In one place nine huge trees had been felled, one so immense as effectually to arrest further progress. For the purpose of clearing away these obstacles a party of Dayaks landed, headed by three sons of the chief of Lundu. Out of a foolish contempt for their enemies they took neither fighting-jackets nor shields. Advancing carelessly they penetrated too far into the jungle, and while drawing some bamboo caltrops from the ground they were pounced upon by a number of the enemy, who were lying in ambush. Before help could reach them two were cut down, and the head of one was taken.

When the chief of Lundu reached the *Nemesis* after the loss of his two sons he found that one of his nephews had just been killed by the accidental discharge of a musket. The poor old man, completely overcome by the misfortunes of the day, burst into tears and holding up three fingers intimated that the loss was more than he could bear. Having obtained permission from the Rajah, he returned home with his followers, taking with him the bodies of his sons and nephew for burial.

The expedition destroyed the new fort that had been built at Paku, and then, having rejoined the steamer, made for the Rejang River with the object of punishing some of the scattered tribes of Sekrang which lived on one of its tributaries, the Kanowit.

One dark night some of the Malays came upon a Saribas Dayak who was floating up with the tide in a canoe made from tree-bark sewn together with strips of rattan. He was a lonely straggler from the fleet, but made a desperate resistance and severely wounded one of his captors. He was taken on board the *Nemesis*, and since he refused to give any name the sailors called him Saribas Jack. He fully expected that sentence of death would be passed upon him, but his spirits rose wonderfully when he found that his life was to be spared, and he became a great favourite with the sailors. Before the steamer left the river he begged hard to be allowed to go home, saying that he was a poor man, and had left some little children who would starve as there was no one to look after them.   This story moved the Rajah, but the difficulty was to protect him from the numerous parties of Dayaks attached to the expedition, who, though they went out under pretence of foraging, were apt to take the heads of lonely fugitives.   The Rajah, however, took such an interest in Saribas Jack that he directed a guard of his Malays to escort him past all danger.

❖   ❖

The boats advanced up the Kanowit to attack the great pirate chief, Buah Ryah, who had established his quarters in the interior of this broad river.   The following account of this part of the expedition is from the pen of Mr. (afterwards Sir) Spenser St. John :

"We advanced rapidly, and were within one day's pull of his forts, while Captain Brooke, with the light division of fast-pulling boats had reconnoitered some miles ahead, and found that the pirates were beginning to show in great numbers, which made us feel assured that we should soon be in touch with the main body.   We landed to inspect a large village house, which was surrounded by a cotton plantation, and found it well built and full of baskets of the skulls of the unfortunates who had been surprised by these marauders.   I counted three hundred heads in one village.   We then fell down the river to join Sir James Brooke and the English force, in great spirits at the prospect of coming in contact with the enemy next day.   We were, therefore, astonished to hear, on our arrival, that it had been decided to give up the object of our expedition and return.   As dinner was over, we removed to a short distance from our chiefs to have our meal in quiet, and to express to each other our indignation at the decision to which our naval commander had come.   Some others joined us, equally disappointed. Towards the end of the meal I could not help raising my

THE ATTACK ON KANOWIT.

[From *Rajah Brooke's Journals*.

glass and saying aloud : ' Oh, for one hour of bonnie Keppel ! ' Captain Farquhar sprang up and came over to us to inquire what I meant. We told him why we considered his determination very detrimental to the cause, as we were approaching Buah Ryah's stronghold. He urged, however, the fatigue of his men, who had been pulling many days in succession against a strong current. We proposed a day's rest, but on a hint from Sir James I gave up the discussion. He thought as I did, that Buah Ryah would, with some reason, proclaim that we were afraid to attack him, and would be thus encouraged to hold out. This actually happened, and thus the pacification of these districts was delayed for many years. There is no doubt that the English sailors were really tired, and possibly also dissatisfied, as all the skirmishing was done by our native contingent, who forged ahead of the slow-pulling men-of-war's boats. How we missed the special boats of the *Maeander* ! The sailors, however, might have been sure that had there been any real fighting ahead, all would have waited for them.

" As we gloomily fell down the river we met thousands of natives who were coming to join our expedition, and who were desperately disappointed that Buah Ryah had not been punished. When near the mouth of the Kanowit we were hailed by the inhabitants of the villages we had destroyed. A conference ensued; they showed their faith in the white man by boldly pulling out to our prahus. They did not attempt to deny their piracies, but promised amendment ; and most of these chiefs kept their word." [1]

Among the prisoners taken during the expedition was a Dayak boy, about nine years old, whose father, as well as a brother, had been in the pirate fleet and had fallen on the night of July 31. This child was brought to the Rajah's prahu. He was an intelligent little fellow,

[1] *Rajah Brooke*, pp. 100-102.

Ranjah by name. After a while he appeared quite at home, smoked a cigarette and chatted away quite unconcerned. When the boats, on their return, approached his late home, now deserted, he stated that he knew where some jars with many valuables had been buried; they were found at the spot pointed out by him. The moment they were put on board, Ranjah thought that he had paid sufficiently for his ransom, and, with tears in his eyes, for the first time begged that he might be put on shore.

"If I let you go," said the Rajah, "how will you find your way to your friends? For three days they have left their houses."

"If you let me go," answered the boy, "I will find my way; I know the jungle well, and my mother will not be far away, as she does not know what has become of me."

The Malays who were present said this was true enough, and that at his age it would be quite safe to trust a Dayak to his own guidance and instinct. So the Rajah told him he should have his liberty, and gave him some clothes. Ranjah soon forgot his tears, and asked for a wineglass and a tin of preserved meat, to show his mother. These, too, were given to him, and also a packet of food, enough to last him three days, and a bottle of water. He embarked in a canoe under the care of a trustworthy Malay and a well-armed escort, and was landed near where his mother's house had stood. He was guarded beyond the reach of any of the scattered bands from the expedition, and then left to find his own way.

From his brother, who subsequently visited Kuching, the Rajah learnt that for two days Ranjah had wandered along the jungle path before he met any of his tribe; but he had been careful of his provisions, and had plenty left when they fell in with him. The treatment of this child had a good effect upon the Sekrang, as was proved by the confidence with which numbers of them afterwards came in to Kuching.

The expedition reached Kuching on August 24, and a few weeks later a great peace conference was held. Many of the pirate chiefs who came to make their submission to the Rajah had never seen a European before. Many others who had dared not take the oath of allegiance to him through fear of the Saribas and the Sekrang, now came in, anxious to accept the blessings that were likely to accrue from peaceful trade and friendly intercourse. Yet although both oppressors and oppressed mingled together at this meeting no untoward incident occurred. Nor did the chiefs whose settlements had received punishment appear to bear any ill-will for injuries inflicted or seek to deny the justice of their punishment.

" Instead of betraying any desire for revenge," wrote Captain Keppel, " all seemed to have merged every other feeling in one of respect for the Rajah of Sarawak. Surely these facts justify the intermeddling, if such it is to be designated, which brought about so happy a resolution." [1]

As an example of the chastened spirit of the Saribas, the following story may be related. Among the followers of the Saribas Chief, Lingir, the Rajah saw a face he recognised : that of Saribas Jack. During the audience with the Rajah he was silent, but appeared to be ill at ease. After the chiefs and their followers had departed he approached the Rajah, and, hanging his head, asked forgiveness for the part he had acted on board the *Nemesis*. For, he confessed, he had deceived the Rajah. He was not the poor man he had represented himself to be, but a chief, both powerful and rich, and the brother-in-law of Lingir himself. He had been on many a cruise with the pirate fleet, but now he was determined to mend his ways and live at peace.

So far as one can tell he kept his word, for neither the Saribas nor the Sekrang ever took to piracy again. The means of breaking their power had been severe, yet it

---

[1] *A Visit to the Indian Archipelago*, i, 298.

R

was justified, for from that day trading ships, both native and European, plied in safety along the Sarawak coast; shipwrecked crews were protected instead of being robbed and enslaved; and the farmers could plant their fields without fear of sudden raids upon their defence-less villages.

Yet the man who had been instrumental in bringing about this change from piracy to peace became the subject of bitter and malignant attacks in England, both in and out of Parliament. Rajah Brooke met those attacks with that trenchant courage which was his out-standing characteristic. In a letter to his friend Mr. John Templer, dated April 1, 1850, he said:

> *If you hear the nonsense advanced about more blood being shed than was necessary, you may mention the fact, that I had it in my power on the morning following the engagement to cut off every soul—some 3,000—landed on the neck of land at the entrance of the Serebas. The ground was known, and the arrangement made and rejected by me, not because the punishment would have been too severe, but because I hoped the lesson received would be sufficient. This is still a matter of doubt, and ren-dered more doubtful by the silly and unworthy clamour raised in England. The time will come in our country, when no gentle-man will serve the public, and your blackguards and your imbeciles may have a monopoly of appointments; though I believe there is not a cosy demagogue amongst the pack, who would lead the life I lead, for double the lucre I receive. It would not suit any of these ranting lovers of peace and popularity, either in its exposure to danger, and climate, or its monotony.*[1]

Yet the clamour against him persisted, and on July 10, 1850, Mr. Hume, the member for Montrose, brought forward in the House of Commons his motion for a Commission of Inquiry into the proceedings of Sir James Brooke on the coast of Borneo, and it was felt that, under the mask of inquiry, Mr. Hume's real object was

---

[1] *Private Letters of Sir James Brooke*, ii, 279.

censure. An elaborate debate of seven hours' duration followed. Every accusation was urged—that Brooke had destroyed the Saribas and Sekrang as pirates, when they were not pirates but merely indulging in harmless inter-tribal wars; that he had exercised undue influence over the officers of the Navy to aid him in his designs; that as a Government servant he had been improperly engaged in trading speculations; and that he had used his powers as Consul-General to the detriment rather than the advancement of British commerce. The decisive majority of 230 to 19 by which Mr. Hume's motion was rejected sufficiently marked the feeling of the House of Commons, and, so far as could be gathered from the tone of the Press of the day, the nation unanimously approved the judgment of the House. The following extract from a letter written from Sarawak by Rajah Brooke's nephew, Captain Brooke, to Captain Keppel, on August, 1852, serves to show that it was right:

I wish you were here to command our expedition about to start for Serebas and Sakarran, though the object this time is peace not war. . . . If you should come out again you will find, I think, considerable changes in Borneo; Sarawak is decidedly steadily advancing. The whole coast, from having been one in-cessant scene of bloodshed is now as safe as the British Channel; as an instance of which, let me tell you that about three weeks ago a schooner from Singapore was capsized at night in a squall, about forty miles to seaward of Tanjong Sirik. Out of ninety-two passengers, only twelve, including five Europeans escaped in a leaky boat, without arms, food, or even decent clothing. They made the shore; the natives received them, gave them clothes and food, and fitted out a large boat to bring them comfortably to Sarawak; I need not tell you what their probable fate would have been had they been thrown on this coast a few years ago. To the Rajah, to yourself, and Farquhar, these poor people owe their freedom, if not their lives.[1]

---

[1] Quoted from *A Visit to the Indian Archipelago*, i, 296.

CHAPTER XX

"MURDERED AT BORNEO" : THE STRANGE HISTORY OF ROBERT BURNS'S GRANDSON

Mr. Robert Burns visits the Kayan country in Borneo—Obtains cession from the Sultan of Brunei to work antimony mines—Rajah Brooke receives complaints about his conduct—Mr. Burns removed from Borneo—His paper on the Kayans—He abuses the Sultan and complains to Lord Palmerston about Rajah Brooke—The dead letter—Mr. Burns sails on a trading expedition in the schooner *Dolphin*—He and Captain Robertson murdered by pirates—Pirates sail the *Dolphin* to the east coast of Borneo—Serip Yassin seizes her and surrenders her to Mr. St. John—The destruction of Tunku—From piracy to peace.

THE first white man to explore the hinterland of north-western Borneo was Mr. Robert Burns, a grandson of the Bard. What first attracted him to the pirate-infested seas of the Malay Archipelago there is nothing to show ; but it must have been the love of adventure and the hope of making his fortune that turned his thoughts to Borneo, for in 1847 the country watered by the Baram and Bintulu rivers was completely unexplored, and its inhabitants were the powerful Kayan tribe, who had the reputation of being ruthless head-hunters.

At that time the Kayan country was not part of the realm of Sarawak, as it is to-day, but was under the nominal sovereignty of the Sultan of Brunei, whose authority, such as it was, extended little farther than the river settlements near the coast. So that whatever Mr. Burns's faults may have been (and that he had faults the ensuing narrative will show) lack of courage was not one of them, for he penetrated the territory of the Kayans un-accompanied by a single European companion and spent

several months trading amongst them and their neighbours. According to his own account he was well
received wherever he went, and became the blood-brother
of one of the chiefs; and while he traded and kept his
eyes open for minerals, he found time to make notes of
native customs and to collect vocabularies of the Kayan
dialects.

During this visit he discovered some rich antimony
deposits in the neighbourhood of the Bintulu River. On
leaving the district he repaired to Brunei and obtained
from the Sultan (in return for a cash advance) a lease to
work the mines. A Mr. Nichol, the Singapore representative of the Glasgow firm of Hamilton, Gray and Co.,
agreed to finance him, and early in 1848 he returned to
Bintulu, with an escort provided by the Sultan himself
and a letter from His Highness to the Bintulu chiefs con-
firming the concession. At that time fortune must have
seemed within his grasp.

Unfortunately for Mr. Burns, however, the concession was subject to the approval of the British Naval
Commander-in-Chief. Mr. Burns had not considered it
necessary to wait for that approval. Indeed he may not
have known it was required, for in justice to him it must
be said that in the Treaty of Friendship and Commerce
which had been signed in 1847 by the Sultan and Rajah
Brooke (acting as British Confidential Agent in Borneo)
there was no clause prohibiting the Sultan from giving
what concessions he chose in his own territories. The
British Government was, however, keeping a paternal
watch over the Sultan's conduct at this time, and when
the antimony concession was referred to Lord Auckland,
he did not prove so amenable as the Sultan (whose good-
will had doubtless been prompted by the prospect of the
royalties he was to receive), and he declined to sanction
it, on the grounds that it would be likely to " give rise to
dangerous misunderstandings and disputes in portions
of the country where the Sultan's rule was hardly recognised." As a result of this decision a letter was

despatched to the Bintulu chiefs asking them to give Mr.
Burns their protection, and at the same time pointing out
that no European had authority to force them to labour
against their inclination.

Rajah Brooke was then in England, but he returned to
the East shortly after the despatch of this letter, and in his
capacity of Governor of the newly-established British
colony of Labuan, and Her Majesty's Commissioner and
Consul-General in Borneo, he lost no time in seeing
Mr. Nichol, who acquiesced in the Government's decision
and agreed to recommend Mr. Burns to be guided by
Rajah Brooke's advice.

Mr. Burns, however, remained in Borneo, and before
long complaints about his conduct began to come in.
It appeared that he had been going about the Kayan
country representing himself as a son of Rajah Brooke,
and had thus induced one of the chiefs to give him his
daughter in marriage. "Heaven bless me if I had such
a son, or such a relative!" wrote the Rajah in his Journal.
Then a letter was received at Labuan from three of the
principal Baram chiefs stating that Mr. Burns had been
causing trouble by interfering with the women :

Mr. Burns does very treacherously (so the translation
of this letter runs), *he wishes to take persons' wives :
whether they like it or not, he takes people's wives. And
also Mr. Burns ordered us to kill people who enter the River
Baram, of whatever description or race they be ; whoever
enters it is good to kill them.*

Rajah Brooke does not seem to have given Mr. Burns
an opportunity of answering these allegations. He
replied to the chiefs' letter personally, requesting :

that in future, whenever an Englishman (sic) *does wrong like
Mr. Burns, my friends will order him out of their country, and
hold no intercourse with him ; and should he refuse obedience or
otherwise commit crime, or conduct himself badly, my friends*

*can act justly and rightly in support of their authority, and for
the protection of their people.*

This letter was taken to Bintulu by the Honourable
East India Company's steamer *Phlegethon*, and left Mr.
Burns very little option but to return in her to
Singapore.

On his arrival he appears to have made no complaints
to the authorities about the treatment he had received;
and this is significant, in view of his behaviour later on.
But so far from being regarded as a " disreputable
adventurer " (which is the expression Captain Keppel
applied to him after his death), he had a paper on the
Kayans published in the *Journal of the Indian Archipelago
and Eastern Asia* (February, 1849) with the following
editorial note:

" We have great pleasure in presenting to our readers
the first authoritative account that has been given of the
greatest aboriginal people of Borneo Proper—the Kayans.
Mr. Burns is the first European who has ventured to
explore the interior of Borneo Proper. . . . All difficulties, real as well as imaginary, in the way of research in
the Archipelago vanish before an indefatigable spirit like
that which has enabled Mr. Burns to explore the country
of the Kayans, without any assistance, or protection from
either the English Colonial Government or the Sultan
of Borneo, for the authority of the latter is, as he found,
totally disowned by the Kayan chiefs."

Mr. Burns's paper contained a detailed account of the
Kayans, their customs and mode of life, and was accompanied by the vocabularies he had collected during his
sojourn amongst them. It was the work of an intelligent
and shrewd observer and was unquestionably a valuable
first-hand contribution to knowledge; and his description of his initiation into blood-brotherhood with
one of the chiefs is worth quoting:

" On the day appointed, a number of the neighbouring chiefs having arrived, several of them commenced

proceedings by haranguing on the greatness and power of their own selves, and of all the wonders they had heard of the white people, and of their satisfaction in being visited by one of them, of whom their fathers had heard so much but had never seen. Next a large pig provided for the occasion was killed, the throat-cutting part of the business being performed by one of the fair sex, seemingly with great satisfaction to the attendant crowd of men. Next was brought three jars full of arrack of three sorts, severally made from rice, sugar-cane, and the fruit *tampui*. In pieces of bambu it was dealt out in profusion to all present, the ladies excepted.

" On the chief taking a bambu filled with arrack, we repaired to the balcony in front of the house, and stood side by side with our faces towards the river. The chief then announced his intention of becoming the friend or brother of a son of the white man, on which one of the attending chiefs gave me a small, sharp, pointed piece of bambu with which I made a slight incision in the right fore-arm of the chief, and the blood drawn was put on a leaf. The chief then with a similar instrument drew blood from my left fore-arm, which was put on the same leaf and mingled with the other. The blood was then mixed with tobacco and made up into a large cigar which we puffed alternately until it was finished, when my friend delivered himself of a long and eloquent speech invoking their god Tanagan, the sun, moon and stars, and rivers, the woods and mountains to witness his sincerity. Three times during this proclamation he sprinkled the arrack on the ground towards the river.

" My speech being delivered, several of the principal chiefs present held forth both long and loud enough. We afterwards returned to the hall and the cheering beverage went round more merrily than before, calling forth their good nature and social disposition. Although no toasts were given, still each successive bumper was accompanied by a merry and noisy chorus. The feast came afterwards, and the whole affair was wound up by music and dancing which lasted until about mid-night."

During the course of his paper Mr. Burns very properly avoided politics, but he made reference to certain " extravagant statements of Sarawak historians " (of whom Rajah Brooke was obviously one), regarding the Kayans' mania for head-hunting, and denounced as slanderous a Dutch missionary's statement that they were a race of prostitutes. His criticisms were answered (rather more warmly than academic discussion demanded) by a correspondent who signed himself " A Friend of the Absent."

Mr. Burns did not reply. He appears to have been prepared to bide his time.

❖ ❖

On leaving Singapore he made his way to Brunei and demanded from the Sultan the amount of the advance he had paid that potentate on account of the concession. This demand would seem to have been reasonable enough, but His Highness disliked the idea of parting with money received, and demurred. It must have been then that Mr. Burns lost his temper and, according to one of the Brunei ministers, " at a crowded audience applied the grossest epithets which the Malayan language affords, accompanied by such insulting gestures, to the Sultan that His Highness was obliged to retire." This same minister subsequently reported to Rajah Brooke that had it not been for the respect in which the English were held at the Court of Brunei Mr. Burns would never have left the audience hall alive.

Here again is an *ex parte* statement made by a native. One need not, however, doubt its essential truth. Mr. Burns was unquestionably a hot-tempered man, and it is easy to understand that the loss of both his concession and his money was more than he could bear in patience. Not only did he lose his temper with the Sultan, but threatened to sue him, until Rajah Brooke, to avoid " a scandalous litigation," prevailed upon the Sultan to pay.

Having obtained his money, Mr. Burns determined to return to Bintulu to trade, but to his chagrin he found that, in consequence of Rajah Brooke's letter to the chiefs, he could not prevail upon the native traders to give him a passage from Labuan. The steamer *Nemesis* was then in harbour and was about to sail with Rajah Brooke to Sarawak, and this encouraged Mr. Burns to request the Rajah to allow him to travel in her and be landed at Bintulu. The letter containing this application was couched in respectful terms, but the Rajah considered it a piece of effrontery, and Mr. Burns received the following reply :

Labuan, June 18, 1849.
Sir,

I am instructed by Sir James Brooke to inform you that after your highly improper letter he declines all further communication.

Your obedient servant,

C. Grant.

Undeterred from his purpose, Mr. Burns chartered a schooner and spent a year trading along the Borneo coast. On his return to Labuan his captain charged him with assault in the local court, stating that Mr. Burns had attacked him with a cutlass and had tried to take the vessel out of his hands. Mr. Burns denied the charge and asserted that he had seized the cutlass in self-defence, having had some high words with the captain. The case was dismissed for lack of evidence, but the Court made some scathing remarks on the conduct of both parties, and deplored the bad example they had shown to the crew.

Mr. Burns continued his trading operations, but all this time his grievances must have been simmering in his mind, and at length, when the conduct of Rajah Brooke became the subject of the violent attacks in the House of

Commons after the destruction of the Saribas fleet, he must have seen his opportunity of having some attention paid to him in high quarters. That the Rajah eventually justified himself against his detractors we have seen, but Mr. Burns chose this moment to join in the attack, and on June 28, 1851, he wrote to Lord Palmerston, the Secretary of State for Foreign Affairs, setting down, for the first time, his complaints: that he had obtained a concession to work the antimony deposits, and had gone to Bintulu; that a month later an armed vessel arrived with a letter informing the chiefs " that they were not to permit any white man either to work the mines or to reside in the country, and that if they disobliged a steamer would be sent from Sarawak to punish them "; that subsequently he had been turned out of the country at the instance of the Rajah; all of which, he claimed, was unjustifiable interference with a peaceful trader.

Lord Palmerston sent a copy of this letter to Rajah Brooke, who was then in London. The Rajah, in a letter written from the United Service Club, dated December 2, 1851, explained the measures he had considered it necessary to take after Lord Auckland had declined to sanction the concession; he spoke of numerous charges made against Mr. Burns by " all classes of natives," referred to his " unruly temper, his abusive language and his violent conduct," and related his outrageous behaviour to the Sultan. A copy of this letter was transmitted to Mr. Burns by Lord Granville in a despatch dated December 31, 1851. The despatch was non-committal, but about this time the Scottish Press began to champion Mr. Burns's cause, and the *North British Mail* demanded:

" Why should not Mr. Robert Burns be as free to explore, to open mines, to establish trading relations in the Archipelago as Sir James Brooke? What was Sir James Brooke but a poor friendless adventurer when he began his career in the Indian Seas? Is Borneo to be less accessible to the enterprise of British subjects

since than it was before ? So long as Mr. Burns
does not poach on Sir James Brooke's manor, we do
not see why the latter should be suffered to interfere
with him, and the country which condemned the
Scottish Bard to a guagership would be utterly in-
excusable if it closed the path of honourable adventure
to his grandson."

It was fated that Mr. Burns should read neither this
loyal outburst nor Rajah Brooke's answers to his charges.
The explanation is to be found in a forgotten file that lies
in the archives of the Public Record Office, where there
is preserved the envelope in which the Foreign Office
letter was enclosed. It is addressed to

> *Robert Burns, Esq.,*
> *Singapore.*

It is dated December 31, 1851, and is franked by Lord
Granville. On one corner is a note " Returned through
the Dead Letter Office " and across it, written in a bold
hand and in ink still very black, is the legend

> *Murdered at Borneo.*

Shortly after writing his letter to Lord Palmerston,
Mr. Burns set off on another trading cruise. This time
he determined to visit the north-east coast of Borneo,
and to ascend the Kinabatangan River, which he had
learnt was rich in camphor and in edible birds'-nests, so
sought after by the Chinese for making soup. He was
warned that this part of the coast was not yet free from
the incursions of the Illanun pirates. But Mr. Burns had
sailed those waters before and no harm had come to him.
His experiences among the wild Kayans had perhaps made
him over-confident of his ability to handle natives in all
emergencies. At all events, he disregarded the warnings
of his friends and left Labuan in the schooner *Dolphin*.

The *Dolphin* sailed under the British flag and was
commanded by a Captain Robertson, with a Portuguese
cook and a crew of thirteen, mostly Javanese. There
was one woman on board, the captain's native girl.

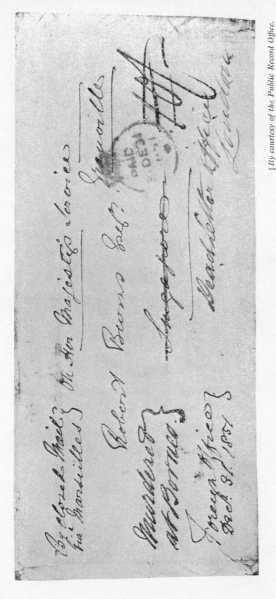

[By courtesy of the Public Record Office.

THE ENVELOPE OF LORD GRANVILLE'S LETTER TO MR. BURNS.

One morning early in September the schooner doubled the most northerly cape of Borneo and came into the waters of Marudu Bay. Mr. Burns went ashore to the principal village in the bay and arranged with its chief, Serip Hassan, that he should pilot the *Dolphin* round the coast to the Kinabatangan.

Before they could start on this expedition the *Dolphin* had the misfortune to run aground. The writer of these chronicles, having sailed Marudu Bay often enough himself and knowing its dangerous shoals, has full sympathy for Captain Robertson. In those uncharted waters it was a mishap that might have occurred to the most experienced navigator. Mr. Burns, however, made no such allowances. He flew into a rage and abused the captain, who, harassed as he must have been with the working of his ship, would have been scarcely human had he not retaliated. The two came to blows, and Mr. Burns seems to have got the worst of the encounter, for one of the crew subsequently deposed that he received a black eye.

The *Dolphin* was eventually got off and was anchored at a little distance from Limau-Limauan, a point on the north-western side of the bay. But the result of the quarrel was that Captain Robertson refused to continue the voyage with Mr. Burns, and it was agreed that they should return to Labuan.

This was on the morning of September 10, and about noon two small boats pulled alongside with eleven natives in them. On being hailed, one of their number, an Illanun named Memadam, called out that they had some tortoiseshell, camphor and pearls they wished to trade. They appeared to be unarmed and harmless enough, so six of them were allowed on board and were given rice and fish, but no business was done that day. In the evening they returned to their boats and held on astern.

The following morning, about seven o'clock, ten of the party went on board the schooner again. Mr. Burns was aft sitting near the wheel. Captain Robertson was pacing the deck on the other side. The crew were forward, getting ready a new jib-boom. A few minutes later one of the Marudu chiefs, Serip Hussein, paddled alongside in his boat and went aboard.

Mr. Burns was bargaining with Memadam over the pearls when the Malay who had remained with the boats handed up some rolled mats. One of Memadam's companions, Ibrahim, a Sulu, stepped to the side to take one of the mats and presented it to Mr. Burns, who put out his hands to receive it. At that instant Ibrahim snatched a naked sword which had been concealed in the mat, and with one blow severed Mr. Burns's head from his shoulders.

Meanwhile Memadam seized a weapon from another mat and attacked Captain Robertson, slashing him on the jaw. The captain ran forward, pursued by Ibrahim and his companions, who by this time were all armed. He succeeded in climbing out on to the bowsprit. He turned to face his assailants, but while he was begging for his life a spear-thrust sent him into the water and he was drowned.

The pirates then turned their attention to the crew. One man was killed on deck. Mr. Burns's servant-boy was cut down near the foremast. The remainder either jumped overboard or took to the rigging.

Going below two of the pirates came upon the captain's native girl cowering terrified in the cabin. One of them seized her by the left arm, shouting that she was his property as he had seen her first. The other swore he should not have her. They were on the point of coming to blows when Memadam entered the cabin. Taking in the situation he stabbed the wretched girl through the back, crying that he would have no quarrelling and that she should belong to neither. That settled the matter, for one blow of his long Illanun sword had done its work, and she was dead.

The pirates, being Mohammedans, respected the holy

character of Serip Hussein, who succeeded in escaping to his boat, although not without receiving a cut or two during the confusion of the attack. Why some of the crew who were in the water did not seek refuge in his boat or take one of the others is not clear, and perhaps the shore was too far off for them to reach by swimming. But after some time Memadam demanded both of them and of those who were up aloft :

" Will ye sail the ship and live, or refuse and die ? "

On their promising to work the ship they were allowed on deck. At first they had their hands tied, but were later released to get the schooner under weigh.

Once outside the bay they headed for Tunku, on the east coast, the notorious pirate settlement to which Memadam and his friends belonged. The bodies of Mr. Burns, the girl and the others were flung overboard. Memadam then mounted the guns and got up the arms, which had hitherto been stowed in the hold—a proof of Mr. Burns's lack of precaution—and a watch was kept night and day.

The passage from Marudu Bay to the east coast of Borneo is one of the most dangerous in the world, and even to-day captains of steamers prefer to make their way through that maze of tiny islands and sunken reefs by daylight. Memadam wisely anchored the *Dolphin* each night, and on the ninth day after leaving Marudu reached the mouth of the Bongaya River in Labuk Bay.

It was then that Memadam made his first mistake. Instead of making straight for Tunku he anchored at Bongaya and saluted the chief, Serip Yassin, with seven guns. The Serip sent a boat off to inquire whose vessel the *Dolphin* was. " It is our vessel," replied Memadam. One of the Serip's men then said he believed her to belong to Mr. Burns, whereupon Memadam swore he had captured her from the Spaniards.

For the time being the Serip took no action, and both pirates and crew went ashore. It was not long, therefore, before he learnt the truth, and on the second

day after the *Dolphin's* arrival he sent twenty-four men
on board with orders to bring the whole of the ship's company before him.   The only one of the pirates to resist
was Memadam, who succeeded in escaping to the jungle,
accompanied by the Portuguese cook and one of the
Javanese crew.   As he fled he turned and shouted that
within forty days he would return from Tunku with a
fleet of war-boats and carry the *Dolphin* off.

When the remainder of the pirates appeared before
Serip Yassin they were ordered to surrender the schooner.

"Never!" cried one of them, an Illanun named
Urau.   "It is our good fortune to have taken her.   We
will never give her up!"

The Serip immediately drew his *kris* and killed Urau
where he stood.   Another man, Krabau, who showed
signs of resistance, was cut down by the Serip's men and
the remainder were seized and bound.

The Serip then ordered one of the *Dolphin's* crew to
cut off the dead pirates' heads, and this was done.   Then
said the Serip, pointing to the corpses :

"These men were murderers.   Preserve their heads
in salt or gin and take them to Labuan as evidence that
Serip Yassin has assisted the Europeans."

A guard was then placed on board the schooner, and
she was taken up the river, in case Memadam should
carry out his threat.   The prisoners were subsequently
claimed by a Sulu chief as being his people, and the
Serip, not caring to offend a neighbour, let them go.

When the news of Mr. Burns's fate reached Labuan
Mr. Spenser St. John was acting Consul-General (in the
absence of Rajah Brooke), and he immediately set off for
the east coast in the East India Company's steamer
Pluto.   He called in at Marudu, where the chiefs confirmed the story, and then went on to Bongaya.   At the
mouth of the river he was met by some of the *Dolphin's*
crew and a messenger from Serip Yassin.   The sailors told

him that the schooner was safe, with her cargo intact, and they themselves had been fed and well-treated by the Serip.

Fifteen miles up the river he found the *Dolphin*. A dozen of the Serip's men were on guard. The hatches were nailed down, and the door of the cabin secured. Inside the cabin the white paint was darkly sprinkled with the bloodstains of the murdered girl.

Yassin's village was still further up the river, and thither Mr. St. John made his way. On entering the Serip's house he was conducted to a seat covered with white cloth, while Yassin himself sat on the end of an enormous bed, his women being concealed by a curtain that fell round it. The Serip was a young man, pale, with a dissipated look (the result of opium-smoking), but with quiet and pleasing manners. On Mr. St. John asking him whether he had ever met a white man before, he smiled and answered that he had seen Europeans on one previous occasion, and Mr. St. John subsequently learnt that, six years before, Yassin had taken part in the Battle of Marudu and had helped to defend Usman's fortress against the attack of the British Navy.

Since then, it appeared, he had mended his ways. Indeed, his action in holding the *Dolphin* might have cost him dear, for he had only seventy fighting-men, and Memadam's threat to return with a fleet had caused him some uneasiness, so that he was unaffectedly relieved when Mr. St. John appeared.

He provided a supper of sliced sweet potatoes, rice and soup, and Mr. St. John slept that night on a raised platform at the end of which three young chiefs, each with a drawn *kris*, kept guard. The following day the Serip handed over a portion of the *Dolphin's* cargo— arms, guns, powder and cloths—which he had stowed away in the house for greater safety. Under his house (which was built on piles) he had made a large aviary in which he kept Argus pheasants, and he graciously presented a pair to Mr. St. John when he said good-bye.

The *Dolphin* must have been towed back into Labuan harbour just about the time that Lord Palmerston's reply to Mr. Burns was being despatched, and the letter must have reached Singapore just as a naval force, consisting of H.M.S. *Cleopatra* and two steamers, under the command of Captain Massie, set out to exact retribution from the Tunku pirates, who had long been a menace to peaceful trade in the Borneo seas.

Having reached the mouth of the Tunku River, Captain Massie decided to give the pirates an opportunity to surrender, and with an armed force he ascended the river in the ships' boats, flying a flag of truce.

As soon as the boats came in sight of the chief's fortified house the pirates opened fire, disregarding the white flag. They must have known they had little to gain by parley, and they preferred to die fighting, if need be, rather than to be taken prisoners. The British force then landed and advanced to the attack, whereupon the pirates betook themselves to the security of the jungle. Their stronghold was burnt, and the sailors returned to the ships with a loss of two men killed and four wounded. The punishment they had inflicted was not so severe as it might have been, for the pirate fleet was away on one of its periodical raiding expeditions, and it was not until 1879 that this nest of sea robbers was finally wiped out, when Captain Edwards, in H.M.S. *Kestrel*, again attacked it and destroyed sixteen war-boats fitted-out for sea.

Then, and not till then, were the murders of Mr. Burns and Captain Robertson finally avenged, for from that day Tunku, the last of the great pirate strongholds, ceased to exist; and with the inception of the British North Borneo Chartered Company, which, by cessions obtained from the Sultans of Brunei and Sulu, took over the government of northern Borneo two years later, these coasts, so long the hunting-grounds of the sea-robbers gradually became safe for peaceful trade.

CHAPTER XXI

THE " LIZZIE WEBBER " SEES IT THROUGH

Captain John Dill Ross builds up a trade between Singapore and
Brunei—His brig, the *Lizzie Webber*—Sights a pirate squadron
off Brunei—Si Rahman, the pirate chief—His invulnerability
—Captain Ross decides to fight his ship—The pirates' re-
peated attempts to carry her—Si Rahman's boat destroyed—
The last shot—Captain Ross's desperate move.

ONE of the pioneers of British trade between Singapore
and the Borneo Coast was Captain John Dill Ross, who
made his appearance in the Archipelago with his brig the
Wild Irish Girl at a time when trade was booming and
tonnage was scarce. He might have chosen the safer
run between Singapore and Bangkok, but, besides being
a capable seaman with a shrewd head for business, he
had a dauntless spirit which cheerfully accepted risks
that would have made other men waver, and a masterful
personality which was accustomed to brush obstacles
aside. It was just these qualities that led him to brave
the perils of the Borneo trade, for although the pirates
were still a menace in those seas, freights were high and
expenses low, and the future seemed to offer a rich
reward to a man of courage and determination.

For several years all went well. In the *Wild Irish
Girl* he built up a regular trade between Singapore,
Labuan and Brunei, and made it pay handsomely. He
had no trouble with the pirates. His fair dealing won
the confidence of the native traders, and he handled the
Brunei Court with such diplomacy that the Sultan came
to trust him as he trusted no other man. Before long
he had run his one competitor, the *Black Diamond*, off the
coast, and had secured a monopoly of the trade.

The *Wild Irish Girl* was succeeded by a larger vessel, the *Lizzie Webber*, a fine brig with a battery of six twelve-pounders, and in 1863 Captain Ross determined to replace her with a barque named the *Don Pedro*.

While the *Don Pedro* was being refitted in Singapore harbour Captain Ross sailed on his last trip in the *Lizzie Webber*, accompanied by his wife and his little son, Johnny, who was then four years old.[1]

The outward voyage was uneventful. While the return cargo was being loaded at Brunei the captain of a native trading boat paid several visits to the ship. There was nothing odd in that, for Captain Ross was popular with the natives and had always encouraged them to come on board to trade. But this man, Si Rahman, although trade was his ostensible object, never came down to actual business in spite of his persistent visits, and so deep was his interest in the *Lizzie Webber's* guns that Kassim, Captain Ross's chief native officer, began to grow suspicious.

Kassim made a few inquiries of his own and discovered that Si Rahman was an Illanun. There was nothing to show that the man was not the peaceful trader he represented himself to be, but even in 1863 Illanun was a synonym for pirate, and Kassim's uneasiness was increased on learning that it was common knowledge in the town that Captain Ross was taking a large sum of money with him to Singapore.

He hastened to his master and warned him to be on his guard, but the friendliness of the natives had made Captain Ross over-confident, so that he paid little heed to Kassim's fears. A day or two later the *Lizzie Webber* dropped down the Brunei River and called at Labuan, where she completed her cargo and took on board a Mr. Meldrum as passenger for Singapore.

On the afternoon the brig sailed from Labuan there

---

[1] Mr. John Dill Ross is alive to-day, and the following narrative is based on the account in his *Sixty Years' Life and Adventures in the Far East*, supplemented by information he has been kind enough to give me personally.

was but a light and fitful breeze, and during the night the current set her over towards the Brunei coast. At dawn on the following morning she was slowly rounding the point of a little bay when the wind died away altogether, leaving her without so much as steerage-way on her. At the same moment Captain Ross saw eight long native vessels lying inside the bay. It needed no more than a single glance to tell him that they were Illanun war-boats.

Instantly he remembered Kassim's warning, and saw his danger. There was only one decision he could make. He had no chance of running from the pirates ; he must fight his ship. There was not a moment to be lost, for already the Illanun squadron was pulling towards the brig. Captain Ross shouted his orders. The native crew beat to quarters. The guns were run out. While rifles and cutlasses were being served to the men, Captain Ross hurried below to find his wife. In a few words he told her of their peril. She knew as well as he the fate that would await her if the pirates carried the ship. He handed her a revolver, telling her to shoot herself and the boy if the worst befell.

❖   ❖

By the time Captain Ross regained the quarter-deck the pirate fleet was sweeping towards the brig, each boat, crowded with warriors, pulling forty oars. The *Lizzie Webber* lay helpless in the dead calm. The pirates pulled right round her, and then the leading boat made towards her until within easy hail. On a raised platform erected amidships stood a figure arrayed in scarlet. It was Si Rahman.

The pirate chief hailed Captain Ross by name. He came as a friend, he said. He was short of tobacco and he desired nothing more than to come on board to purchase a supply.

Captain Ross had been deceived at Brunei, but he could be tricked no longer. He shouted back that he

knew pirates when he saw them, and warned Si Rahman
that if the boats did not sheer off immediately he would
open fire. Whereupon Si Rahman, abandoning his
peaceful pretences, called upon Captain Ross to surrender
the ship without a useless struggle, and boasted that
neither shot nor steel could harm him since he was
rendered invulnerable by a magic charm.

Before Captain Ross could reply to this demand
Kassim, anxiously watching from the main deck, took a
gesture of his master's for a signal to begin the action
and promptly fired his gun at Si Rahman's boat. The
other guns followed—each had been loaded with a
round shot and a canvas bag of bullets rammed home on
top of it—and at the same time a hot fire of musketry
was poured into the pirate boats. The Illanuns, although
disconcerted for a moment, were not daunted, and,
yelling their war-cries, they began to reply vigorously
with their swivel guns.

With their oars they had the advantage of mobility,
and their boats were strengthened with breastworks of
hard ironwood, strong enough to withstand a round
shot. On the other hand, the *Lizzie Webber* carried a
large crew besides her three European officers, and there
was no lack of arms, for a short time previously Captain
Ross had bought a few cases of muskets from an American
captain he had met at sea. There had been just time to
have these weapons loaded before the attack, so that
each sailor had half a dozen ready to his hand, and in
this way a rapid and effective fire was maintained.

Within a few minutes, however, Mr. Simpson, the
first officer, and three of the crew were seriously wounded.
They were carried below, and Mrs. Ross, disregarding
her husband's injunction to remain in her cabin, attended
to their wounds as best she could. Her difficulties were
not made easier by her small son, who, so far from being
frightened by the din of the fight, wanted to get on deck
to see what his father was doing. He frantically resisted
his mother's attempts to stop him, and was finally carried

off, kicking and screaming with rage, and locked up in a spare cabin.

Meanwhile Captain Ross was putting up a desperate fight. Instead of trying to rush the ship immediately, Si Rahman seemed determined to wear down her resistance first, when, doubtless, he expected her to become an easy prey. The resolute fire from the ship had so far kept the pirates at a distance, but Captain Ross knew that the end could be only a matter of time so long as they had their chief to encourage them. He therefore fired repeatedly at Si Rahman—but to no purpose, for the chief, recklessly exposing himself, and prancing upon his platform like a scarlet demon, continued to direct the attack unscathed.

" For goodness sake, do bowl over that ruffian in the scarlet dress," roared Ross to Meldrum at last ; and Meldrum quietly loaded his rifle—a new American weapon of which he was very proud—and took deliberate aim, but without effect. Ross fired again, with the same result. From the main deck and the forecastle scores of shots were now directed at Si Rahman. He remained untouched, brandishing his *kris* and yelling defiance. Kassim turned his gun upon him, but even the combination of round shot and bullets had no effect upon the pirate, although it wrought havoc among his crew. To those anxious defenders of the brig it must have seemed as though he were invulnerable indeed.

Still the fight went on, and when powder for the guns began to run short Mr. Jenkins, the second mate, told off a couple of sailors to fetch up some kegs from the magazine, which was placed aft with an entrance through a scuttle in a storeroom. With the usual thoughtlessness of Malays, the men were on the point of entering the magazine with a naked light when Mrs. Ross saw them and was just in time to seize the flaring lamp and fling it through an open porthole into the sea. After this incident she went into the magazine herself to superintend the powder being handed up. Her presence of mind undoubtedly saved the *Lizzie Webber* from being blown sky-high.

◇   ◇

The action had started at dawn, and after three hours' continuous fighting Captain Ross saw Si Rahman give a signal to his fleet. The boats ceased firing and drew away. To those in the brig it seemed that the pirates had had enough, but Captain Ross was taking no chances, and he went round his decks, saw that the heated twelve-pounders were sponged out and made ready for further service, and ordered all the small-arms to be reloaded.

It was well he did so, for barely had he completed his round when he saw those Illanun war-boats sweeping once more towards the starboard side of the brig. There could be no doubt of Si Rahman's intention. He meant to get alongside at all costs and carry the ship by force of numbers.

It must have been the darkest moment of Captain Ross's life when he saw the pirate fleet dashing towards him with Si Rahman in the van. None knew better than he that there would be no mercy shown once those warriors had gained his deck. Yet to stop them seemed impossible. The starboard guns were firing, but the Illanun craft were now so close, and lay so low in the water, that the shots went flying harmlessly over them. For one despairing moment Captain Ross was tempted to rush below, despatch his wife and child, and blow up the magazine. Then his dogged spirit reasserted itself, and he swore that he would fight the *Lizzie Webber* to the end.

By this time Si Rahman's boat, ahead of the rest, was almost alongside. Ross saw Kassim about to fire his twelve-pounder, but knew that the muzzle of the gun was not sufficiently depressed and that the shot could not tell. Leaping to the main deck, he restrained Kassim's hand, telling him to train the gun down on to the boat's platform where Si Rahman was making ready to leap on board. Kassim showed him that he had driven the

wedge beneath the gun's breech as far as it would go, and
that he could depress the muzzle no farther.

That must have seemed the end. But suddenly, as
he looked round in his extremity, Captain Ross saw a
spare spar lying on the deck, and the sight of it gave him
fresh hope. He was immensely strong, and without a
moment's hesitation he bent down and lifted the gun
carriage, calling upon Kassim and another sailor to roll
the spar beneath it. Then, taking a hasty look along the
sights, he fired the gun himself.

Before the smoke had cleared away a burst of cheering
ran along the *Lizzie Webber's* decks, mingled with
screams of pain from the sea. As he looked over the
bulwarks Captain Ross beheld a mass of wreckage where,
but a moment before, had been the pirate boat. A
scarlet patch, lying on the swirling water like a great
hibiscus blossom, showed that Si Rahman had not been
invulnerable after all.

The death of Si Rahman must have had a profound
effect upon the minds of his followers, for they had
believed in the power of his magic charm as implicitly as
he. Bereft of their leader, they did not attempt to continue the attack, but having rescued as many of their
comrades as they could from the sinking boat they
sheered off. At the same time a light breeze sprang up
and the *Lizzie Webber* began to get way on her. It
seemed that the ship was saved. Even so, the guns and
small-arms were reloaded once more, and then, for the
first time that day, the worn-out crew found time to eat.

By this time it was late afternoon, and although the
pirates had drawn off they still followed the ship, as
persistent as a swarm of mosquitoes. There was little
strength in the breeze, so that their boats could pull
faster than the brig could sail, and it became clear that
they were only waiting for the darkness to renew their
attempt to carry her. Then, as the sun began to sink,

the wind freshened; the *Lizzie Webber* started to slip faster through the water, and the pirates, fearing that they would lose her if they waited, closed on her once more.

While the fight was raging afresh, Mrs. Ross rushed on to the quarter-deck to tell her husband that there were only six kegs of gunpowder left in the magazine. Knowing that this was barely enough for the guns to fire one round more she had not dared to entrust the message to other lips.

Captain Ross told her to send up the kegs and then go to her cabin. The guns received their last charges as the pirates bore down upon the brig.

The situation was now more desperate than ever, yet Captain Ross had one thing in his favour: his ship no longer lay helpless and becalmed in the water, but given life by the wind could answer to her helm. He saw his last chance and took it. Instead of flight, he determined on attack.

Down went his helm, he spilled his sails, and before the pirates could recover from their surprise he was in the midst of their fleet, firing his last broadside. One of the boats was caught at a disadvantage. Springing to the wheel, Captain Ross altered the brig's course by a few points. A moment later there was a rending crash as the *Lizzie Webber's* keel ground over the wreck of the pirate craft. Some of the Illanuns were shot as they swam in the water. Others managed to seize the ship's chains, but were cut down as they tried to reach the deck.

Then came the sudden darkness of the tropics. Captain Ross put the *Lizzie Webber* about once more; her sails filled and she slipped away into safety before the wind.

AUTHORITIES

THE leading authorities for the historical events recorded in the foregoing pages are given below. The names or initials in brackets are used for convenience in the detailed references.

The Journal of the Indian Archipelago and Eastern Asia, vols. I–VI (1845–1850). [J. I. A.]

Captain the Honourable Henry Keppel's *Expedition to Borneo of H.M.S. " Dido,"* 2 vols, 1847. [Dido.]

The same author's *Visit to the Indian Archipelago in H.M.S. " Maeander,"* 2 vols, 1853. [Maeander.]

Captain Sir Edward Belcher's *Voyage of H.M.S. " Samarang,"* 2 vols, 1848. [Belcher.]

F. S. Marryat's *Borneo and the Indian Archipelago*, 1848. [Marryat.]

Captain Rodney Mundy's *Narrative of Events in Borneo and Celebes*, 2 vols, 1848. [Mundy.]

The Private Letters of Sir James Brooke, Edited by John Templer, 3 vols, 1853. [P. L.]

Spenser St. John's *Life in the Forests of the Far East*, 2 vols, second edition, 1863. [St. John.]

John Dill Ross's *Sixty Years' Life and Adventure in the Far East*, 2 vols, 1912. [Ross.]

Reference to other works will be found in the chapter notes.

CHAPTER NOTES

Chapter I.—*The Pirate Wind.*

Details of the Dutch and American ships attacked are taken from J. I. A., vols. iv and v ; St. John also refers to the story of the *Maria Frederika* (ii, 193, 197–8). The case of the *Regina* is mentioned by Ross (i, 7). Sulu is described by Belcher (i, 217–18, 272, 277) and Marryat 41–2. Mundy mentions the Pirate Wind (ii, 17). For further details of European responsibility, destruction of native trade, etc., see Dido i, 387–8, 411 ; Belcher i, 16–17 ; St. John ii, 212–13 ; and also *Sarawak under Its Two White Rajahs* by C. A. Bamfylde and S. Baring-Gould (1909), which may be recommended to the student as a general modern authority for this period.

Chapter II.—*The Illanun Pirates.*

General characteristics : Dido i, 194, 200 ; Belcher i, 263 ; St. John ii, 194, 196, 231. Strongholds : Belcher i, 264, 266. War-boats and cruises ; Dido i, 194–7 ; Belcher i, 265–8 ; Marryat 63, 119–20 ; St. John ii, 196, 211. The story of Mr. Wyndham's escape is given by St. John ii, 196–7. Details of the *Diana's* action etc., are to be found in J. I .A. vol. iv, 620 *et seq*, 738.

Chapter III.—*The Balanini.*

General characteristics : Belcher i, 209, 268 ; Mundy ii, 16 ; St. John ii, 211. Strongholds : Belcher i, 260, 269 ; St. John ii, 225–6, 231. War-boats and cruises : Belcher i, 269–70 ; Mundy ii, 16–17 ; St. John ii, 194, 211–12. Details of the fate of the *Sarah and Elizabeth* are taken from St. John ii, 194–5, J. I. A. iv, 741.

Chapter IV.—*Slaves.*

Details relating to the treatment of slaves are to be found in Belcher i, 208 ; St. John 199–200 ; J. A. I. iv, 410 ; *Sarawak under its Two white Rajahs*, 271. Details of the status of *anak mas* and the prices paid for slaves are taken from W. H. Treacher's *British Borneo*, 132–3. The story of the Dayak pirate and the slave girl is based on Marryat 101–2.

Chapter V.—*The Raiding of Balambangan.*

The Early Relations of England with Borneo, by Johannes Willi of Gais (1922),gives a detailed account of the two settlements of Balambangan and the events which led up to them. Belcher also gives an account of the raid (i, 285–92), and further information is to be found in Captain T. Forrest's *Voyage to New Guinea* (1779) 332, 336–7. The letters quoted are in the Records Department of the India Office, Home Misc. 771.

Chapter VI.—*The Loss of the " Sultana."*

The main authorities for the loss of the ship and the subsequent fate of her officers and crew are Dido, i, 235–50 (Rajah Brooke's Journal) ; J. I. A. iv, 734, and despatches in the Public Record Office, from which the lascar's statement is taken. The search for the European woman at Ambong is related by Belcher, i, 163–96.

Chapter VII.—*The Pirates of Sarawak.*

Details of the general activities of the Saribas and Sekrang are taken from Dido i, 225–6, 256, 264–5, 275–6. ii, 144–5 ; Maeander i, 126–9, 131–2 ; P. L. 62–3. The account of the attack on the Saribas strongholds is taken partly from Dido ii, 27–68 and from Keppel's official despatch, in the P. R. O. (Admiralty I., 5546).

Chapter VIII.—*The Attack on the Sekrang Strongholds.*

Here the authorities are Dido ii, 79–121, and Keppel's despatch in P. R. O. (Admiralty I., 5547).

Chapter IX.—*The Pirates of Pedir.*

The papers relating to the fate of the *Futtal Khair* and the *Robert Spankie* and the despatches describing the expedition to Achin are taken from the P. R. O., (Admiralty I., 5547.)

Chapter X.—*The Pirates of Jilolo.*

Sir Edward Belcher's published narrative of the actions (in i, 125–45) is supplemented by his official despatch (P. R. O. Admiralty I.) and Marryat 46–55. St. John's evidence is to be found in i, 198–9, and Brooke's meeting with the pirates is described in his Journal (Dido i, 194).

Chapter XI.—*The Strange Case of the " Premier."*

The narrative is from Belcher i, 201–57 and Marryat 128–36.

Chapter XII.—*The Sultan of Brunei.*

For description of Brunei and the Sultan see Dido i, 328 ; Belcher i, 58–9 ; Marryat 106–7, 112–13. For the Sultan's pedigree see Mundy ii, 20, 267. For the political situation at Brunei see Marryat 104–5. Details of the activities of Pangeran Usop and Serip Usman are to be found in Belcher i, 194 ; Dido ii, 146 ; Mundy ii, 17–18. The account of the negotiations for the treaty is taken from Belcher i, 53–8, 174–85 ; Marryat 108–15.

Chapter XIII.—*The Downfall of Pangeran Usop.*

For Brooke's instructions to visit Brunei see Dido ii, 163–4. The Sultan's letter is quoted from P. L. ii, 55. For Rajah Brooke's visit to Singapore. see Mundy ii, 31–3. The narrative of the attack on Usop is based on Mundy ii, 35–6 ; Dido 170–1, 180–2,

289–91 ; P. L. i, 80–83 ; Admiral Cochrane's official despatch, in P.R.O., Admiralty I., 5548. Details of the death of Usop appear in Mundy ii, 183–4 and St. John i, 296–7.

Chapter XIV.—*The Battle of Marudu.*

The following authorities have been drawn upon for this account of the battle : Dido ii, 173–9 ; St. John ii, 192 ; an article in the *Illustrated London News* of November 29, 1845 (on which the sketch is also based) ; a letter from Captain Pascoe in the *British North Borneo Herald* of April, 1886, and the Admiral's official despatch, forwarding Captain Talbot's report of the action, with details of the force employed. (P. R. O., Admiralty I., 5548.)

Chapter XV.—*The Murder of Rajah Muda Hassim.*

For Muda Hassim's appointment, see Mundy ii, 87. The account of the massacre of the royal family is based mainly on Mundy ii, 129–134 and P. L. ii, 136–9.

Chapter XVI.—*The Capture of Brunei.*

The narrative follows Mundy ii, 104–177.

Chapter XVII.—*How Labuan Became British.*

The narrative is based on Mundy ii, 187–308.

Chapter XVIII.—*The Destruction of a Pirate Fleet.*

The narrative follows Mundy ii, 359–66 and St. John ii, 195, 208–11.

Chapter XIX.—*The Last of the Saribas.*

Except where noted in text, the account of the battle and subsequent expedition is based on Maeander i, 138–79, and papers in the P. R. O. (F.O. 9–12) whence details of the prize money are also taken. The letter from Captain Brooke is quoted from Maeander i, 296–7.

Chapter XX.—" *Murdered at Borneo.*"

Mr. Burns's papers and vocabularies on the Kayan are in the J. I. A., 1849. The account of his trading activities up to the taking of the *Dolphin* are based on Maeander ii, 89–98 ; and his letters to the Foreign Office, and complaints against Rajah Brooke are to be found in *Correspondence respecting Mr. Burns,* presented to the House of Commons, March 23, 1851, and *Further papers respecting Mr. Burns,* presented to the House of Commons, March 23, 1851. These papers, and the original of the envelope reproduced, may be seen in the P. R. O., F.O. 10. The recovery of the *Dolphin* and H.M.S. *Cleopatra's* action is described by St. John ii, 215–24.

Chapter XXI.—*The " Lizzie Webber " Sees it Through.*

By permission of the author, the account of the *Lizzie Webber's* action is based on Ross i, 25–32.

INDEX

ABBAS, Tuanku, 128-9, 137, 140-1
Abdullah, Haji, 132-6, 144-6
Achin, Rajah of, 127-8, 130-1, 137, 139
Agincourt, H.M.S., 186, 194, 213-4, 221
Albatross, H.M.S., 247
Ali, Datu Patinggi, 121, 123-5
Ambong, pirate settlement at, 32; story of European woman at, 85-9
Auckland, Lord, 261

BAJAUS, the, 32
Bakar, Said Abu, 127-32, 138, 140
Balambangan, buried treasure on, 71-2; cession of, 56-7; description of, 56; directions to Chief, 62-3; etymology, 56; objects of occupation 57-8; raid on, 69-71; settlements on, 65, 74
Balanini pirates, action with *Nemesis*, 236-41; with Spaniards, 241-2; alliance with S. Usman, 173; capture the *Sarah and Elizabeth*, 45-8; cruises, 45, 237; immunity from attack, 24; methods of attack, 44; strongholds, 43; war-boats, 44, 236
Banggi Island, 68, 74
Baugh, Lt., 147
Bedrudin, Pangeran, character, 209; on Sekrang expedition, 115, 121, 126; withdraws to Sarawak, 172; returns to Brunei, 175-6; at audience with Sultan, 177-81; defeats P. Usop, 190; death, 207-8
Belcher, Capt. Sir E., search for European female slave, 87-91; action against Jilolo pirates, 147-58; releases lascars from *Premier*, 159-68
——————— quoted, 31, 34, 163, 165, 168, 175-6
Bellinghurst, Capt., 45
Black Diamond, the, 275
Britannia, H.E.I.C's., 62, 65
British Government, apathy of, 29, 183-4, 211
Brooke, Capt., quoted, 259

Brooke, James, becomes first white Rajah of Sarawak, 76-8; assists Capt. Page, 80-4; saves *Sultana's* lascars, 85; meeting with pirate fleet, 95-6; first regulations, 97; expeditions against Saribas, 102-12, 246-57; against Sekrang, 115-26, 246; against Pedir, 138, 144; visits Brunei, 176-81, 183-5, 187-90, 224-5, 236; on occupation of Labuan, 181-2, 212, 229; appointed H.M. Confidential Adviser in Borneo, 183; meets Admiral Cochrane, 185; at Marudu, 202; on expedition against Brunei, 213, 215, 218-19; against Tempasuk, 221-2; against H. Saman, 223-4; in engagement with Balanini, 236-40; appointed Governor of Labuan, 244; political attacks on, 258, 267; dealings with Mr. Burns, 262-3, 265-8
——————— quoted, 74, 76-7, 96, 144, 181-2, 186-7, 210-12, 224-5, 258
Brownrigg, Capt., 159-62, 164-5, 167
Brunei, description of, 28, 169-70; population enslaved, 28, 45, 237
——————— Sultan of, descent, 171; appearance and character, 172; confirms grant of Sarawak to James Brooke, 78; his treatment of *Sultana's* crew, 80-5; receives Capt. Belcher, 176-81; professes anxiety to suppress piracy, 185; receives Admiral Cochrane, 187; signs P. Usop's death-warrant, 191; massacre of his relatives, 207-9; attacked by Admiral Cochrane, 213-20; receives Capt. Mundy, 225-7; cedes Labuan, 230-3; orders execution of Balanini prisoners, 241; dealings with Mr. Burns, 261-2, 265-6
Bulongan, Sultan of, 166-7
Burns, Mr. Robert, 260-70
Buting Maru, Battle of, 248-52
Butterworth, Colonel J. W., 87, 136-8

CAMBODIA

GEORGE COEDES
Angkor

CENTRAL ASIA

PETER FLEMING
Bayonets to Lhasa

LADY MACARTNEY
An English Lady in Chinese
Turkestan

ALBERT VON LE COQ
Buried Treasures of Chinese
Turkestan

AITCHEN K. WU
Turkistan Tumult

CHINA

All About Shanghai:
A Standard Guide

HAROLD ACTON
Peonies and Ponies

ERNEST BRAMAH
Kai Lung's Golden Hours*

ERNEST BRAMAH
The Wallet of Kai Lung*

ANN BRIDGE
The Ginger Griffin

CARL CROW
Handbook for China

PETER FLEMING
The Siege at Peking

CORRINNE LAMB
The Chinese Festive Board

W. SOMERSET MAUGHAM
On a Chinese Screen*

G. E. MORRISON
An Australian in China

PETER QUENNELL
Superficial Journey Through
Tokyo and Peking

OSBERT SITWELL
Escape with Me! An Oriental
Sketch-book

J. A. TURNER
Kwang Tung or Five Years in
South China

HONG KONG

The Hong Kong Guide 1893

INDONESIA

S. TAKDIR ALISJAHBANA
Indonesia: Social and Cultural Revolution

DAVID ATTENBOROUGH
Zoo Quest for a Dragon*

VICKI BAUM
A Tale from Bali*

MIGUEL COVARRUBIAS
Island of Bali*

BERYL DE ZOETE AND
WALTER SPIES
Dance and Drama in Bali

AUGUSTA DE WIT
Java: Facts and Fancies

JACQUES DUMARÇAY
Borobudur

JACQUES DUMARÇAY
The Temples of Java

GEOFFREY GORER
Bali and Angkor

JENNIFER LINDSAY
Javanese Gamelan

EDWIN M. LOEB
Sumatra: Its History and People

MOCHTAR LUBIS
Twilight in Djakarta

MADELON H. LULOFS
Coolie*

COLIN McPHEE
A House in Bali*

HICKMAN POWELL
The Last Paradise

E. R. SCIDMORE
Java, Garden of the East

MICHAEL SMITHIES
Yogyakarta: Cultural Heart
of Indonesia

LADISLAO SZEKELY
Tropic Fever: The Adventures of
a Planter in Sumatra

EDWARD C. VAN NESS AND
SHITA PRAWIROHARDJO
Javanese Wayang Kulit

MALAYSIA

ABDULLAH ABDUL KADIR
The Hikayat Abdullah

ISABELLA L. BIRD
The Golden Chersonese: Travels
in Malaya in 1879

PIERRE BOULLE
Sacrilege in Malaya

MARGARET BROOKE
RANEE OF SARAWAK
My Life in Sarawak

C. C. BROWN (Editor)
Sejarah Melayu or Malay Annals

K. M. ENDICOTT
An Analysis of Malay Magic

HENRI FAUCONNIER
The Soul of Malaya

W. R. GEDDES
Nine Dayak Nights

JOHN D. GIMLETTE
Malay Poisons and Charm Cures

JOHN D. GIMLETTE AND
H. W. THOMSON
A Dictionary of Malayan Medicine

A. G. GLENISTER
The Birds of the Malay Peninsula,
Singapote and Penang

C. W. HARRISON
Illustrated Guide to the Federated
Malay States (1923)

TOM HARRISSON
World Within: A Borneo Story

DENNIS HOLMAN
Noone of the Ulu

CHARLES HOSE
The Field-Book of a Jungle-Wallah

SYBIL KATHIGASU
No Dram of Mercy

MALCOLM MacDONALD
Borneo People

W. SOMERSET MAUGHAM
Ah King and Other Stories*

W. SOMERSET MAUGHAM
The Casuarina Tree*

MARY McMINNIES
The Flying Fox*

ROBERT PAYNE
The White Rajahs of Sarawak

OWEN RUTTER
The Pirate Wind

ROBERT W. C. SHELFORD
A Naturalist in Borneo

J. T. THOMSON
Glimpses into Life in Malayan Lands

RICHARD WINSTEDT
The Malay Magician

PHILIPPINES

AUSTIN COATES
Rizal

SINGAPORE

PATRICK ANDERSON
Snake Wine: A Singapore Episode

ROLAND BRADDELL
The Lights of Singapore

R. W. E. HARPER AND
HARRY MILLER
Singapore Mutiny

JANET LIM
Sold for Silver

G. M. REITH
Handbook to Singapore (1907)

J. D. VAUGHAN
The Manners and Customs of the
Chinese of the Straits Settlements

C. E. WURTZBURG
Raffles of the Eastern Isles

THAILAND

CARL BOCK
Temples and Elephants

REGINALD CAMPBELL
Teak-Wallah

MALCOLM SMITH
A Physician at the Court of Siam

ERNEST YOUNG
The Kingdom of the Yellow Robe

* Titles marked with an asterisk have restricted rights